Fodor's

VENICE

WELCOME TO VENICE

Venice is a city unlike any other. No matter how often you've seen it in photos and films, the real thing is more dreamlike than you could imagine. With canals where streets should be, water shimmers everywhere. The fabulous palaces and churches reflect centuries of history in what was a wealthy trading center between Europe and the Orient. Getting lost in the narrow alleyways is a quintessential part of exploring Venice, but at some point you'll almost surely end up in Piazza San Marco, where tourists and locals congregate for a coffee or an aperitif.

TOP REASONS TO GO

★ **Landmarks:** The Rialto bridge and Palazzo Ducale are simply unforgettable.

★ **Festivals:** Carnevale and the Biennale are celebrations of art, film, music, and dance.

★ **Art:** Titian, Tintoretto, and Tiepolo, as well as contemporary artists, are represented.

★ **Seafood:** Fish so fresh many restaurants boast they don't even own a refrigerator.

★ **Churches:** The Basilica di San Marco and Santa Maria della Salute are two of many.

★ **Shopping:** Spectacular masks, candy-colored glass, paper goods, lace, and linens.

Fodor's VENICE

Publisher: Amanda D'Acierno, *Senior Vice President*

Editorial: Arabella Bowen, *Editor in Chief;* Linda Cabasin, *Editorial Director*

Design: Fabrizio La Rocca, *Vice President, Creative Director;* Tina Malaney, *Associate Art Director;* Chie Ushio, *Senior Designer;* Ann McBride, *Production Designer*

Photography: Melanie Marin, *Associate Director of Photography;* Jessica Parkhill and Jennifer Romains, *Researchers*

Maps: Rebecca Baer, *Senior Map Editor;* David Lindroth, Mark Stroud (Moon Street Cartography), *Cartographers*

Production: Linda Schmidt, *Managing Editor;* Evangelos Vasilakis, *Associate Managing Editor;* Angela L. McLean, *Senior Production Manager*

Sales: Jacqueline Lebow, *Sales Director*

Marketing & Publicity: Heather Dalton, *Marketing Director;* Katherine Fleming, *Senior Publicist*

Business & Operations: Susan Livingston, *Vice President, Strategic Business Planning;* Sue Daulton, *Vice President, Operations*

Fodors.com: Megan Bell, *Executive Director, Revenue & Business Development;* Yasmin Marinaro, *Senior Director, Marketing & Partnerships*

Writers: Bruce Leimsidor, Nan McElroy

Lead Editor: Caroline Trefler
Editors: Stephen Brewer, Heidi Johansen
Production Editor: Elyse Rozelle

1st edition

ISBN 978-0-8041-4207-6

ISSN 2330-0620

All details in this book are based on information supplied to us at press time. Always confirm information when it matters, especially if you're making a detour to visit a specific place. Fodor's expressly disclaims any liability, loss, or risk, personal or otherwise, that is incurred as a consequence of the use of any of the contents of this book.

SPECIAL SALES

This book is available at special discounts for bulk purchases for sales promotions or premiums. For more information, e-mail specialmarkets@randomhouse.com

PRINTED IN THE UNITED STATES OF AMERICA

10 9 8 7 6 5 4 3 2

CONTENTS

Fodor's Features

CONTENTS

ABOUT
THIS GUIDE

Fodor's Recommendations

Everything in this guide is worth doing—we don't cover what isn't—but exceptional sights, hotels, and restaurants are recognized with additional accolades. Fodor's Choice★ indicates our top recommendations; and **Best Bets** call attention to notable hotels and restaurants in various categories. Care to nominate a new place? Visit Fodors.com/contact-us.

Trip Costs

We list prices wherever possible to help you budget well. Hotel and restaurant price categories from **$** to **$$$$** are noted alongside each recommendation. For hotels, we include the lowest cost of a standard double room in high season. For restaurants, we cite the average price of a main course at dinner or, if dinner isn't served, at lunch. For attractions, we always list adult admission fees; discounts are usually available for children, students, and senior citizens.

Hotels

Our local writers vet every hotel to recommend the best overnights in each price category, from budget to expensive. Unless otherwise specified, you can expect private bath, phone, and TV in your room. For expanded hotel reviews, facilities, and deals visit Fodors.com.

Restaurants

Unless we state otherwise, restaurants are open for lunch and dinner daily. We mention dress code only when there's a specific requirement and reservations only when they're essential or not accepted. To make restaurant reservations, visit Fodors.com.

Credit Cards

The hotels and restaurants in this guide typically accept credit cards. If not, we'll say so.

Top Picks
★ Fodor's Choice

Listings
- ✉ Address
- ✉ Branch address
- ☎ Telephone
- 🖷 Fax
- ⊕ Website
- ✍ E-mail
- 🎫 Admission fee
- ⊙ Open/closed times
- Ⓜ Subway
- ✛ Directions or Map coordinates

Hotels & Restaurants
- 🏨 Hotel
- ⇥ Number of rooms
- ⑂ Meal plans
- ✕ Restaurant
- ✍ Reservations
- 🏛 Dress code
- ▭ No credit cards
- Ⓢ Price

Other
- ⇨ See also
- ☞ Take note
- 🏌 Golf facilities

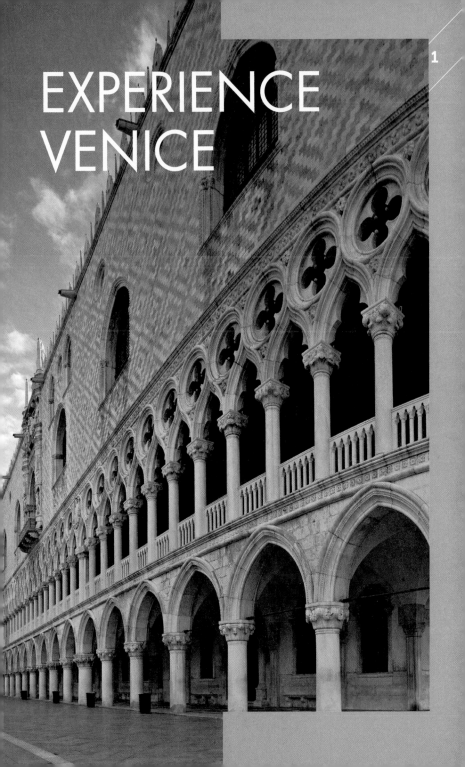

EXPERIENCE
VENICE

VENICE TODAY

While Venice spends a great deal of energy preserving its past, this city is also entrenched in the here and now and modern Venetian life has many fascinating facets. Specifically, Venice . . .

. . . feels the influence of immigration but still retains its cultural integrity

Venice, like the rest of Italy, has recently experienced an influx of foreign immigrants, but unlike other Italians, Venetians are fairly open to these newcomers. The city has a proud cosmopolitan tradition. Renaissance Venice had one of the largest, and richest, Jewish communities in Europe, and the Greek, Turkish, Armenian, German, Albanian, and Slavic communities have given their names to important streets and buildings in Venice. Pressure upon immigrants to assimilate culturally is much less intense here than it is in other Italian cities. They are hired and befriended, and some even learn Venetian dialect, but they are not expected to become Venetians. Local Venetian culture has, overall, maintained itself pretty well. The local dialect is spoken by all levels of society. Venetians still enjoy the 18th-century dialect comedies of Goldoni, and it's not uncommon to hear dialect spoken by elegant operagoers at La Fenice. Local festivals, such as the Redentore, Salute, and la Sensa, are celebrated with enthusiasm.

. . . is a city of piscivores

As is to be expected in a maritime republic, fish plays the starring role on the traditional Venetian table. Certain fish, such as sardines, are plentiful and always fresh, and working class neighborhoods are frequently pungent with the perfume of grilled sardines, which you can frequently also find in inexpensive restaurants. Or you can try the traditional Venetian classic, sarde in saor, fresh fried sardines marinated in olive oil, sautéed onions, vinegar, raisins, and pine nuts, an ancient recipe from Venice's time as part of the Byzantine Empire. Another classic and inexpensive fish dish is seppie in nero, cuttlefish stewed in a sauce made with its own ink, generally served with creamy polenta. The one classic Venetian pasta dish is bigoli in salsa, thick homemade whole wheat spaghetti, with a sauce featuring anchovies, fried onions, and cinnamon; the anchovies are totally transformed by the sweetness and pungency of the onions and cinnamon.

. . . goes crazy for fresh vegetables

Venetians are passionate about vegetables from the islands in the Venetian lagoon, especially from the island of Sant'Erasmo, and those from the adjacent mainland. In the spring Venetians wait anxiously for the castraore, the tiny white artichokes from Sant'Erasmo, with as much zeal as the Piemontesi wait for the white truffles of Alba in the fall. But the castraore are even rarer. Since they grow only one to a plant, their number is very limited, and each year's crop is consumed almost totally in Venice. Springtime also brings the plump, succulent white asparagus from Bassano, in the foothills of the Dolomites north of Venice, and in the fall there is the famous radicchio, a red and white endive, from Treviso, just a stone's throw from Venice on the mainland. Pasta e fagioli, bean soup with pasta, is enjoyed all over Italy, but in Venice it is frequently made with beans from the mainland Veneto town of Lamon, which have a delicate and complex taste and beat out the beans from other places hands down.

...is one with the sea

Venetians historically have taken great pleasure from rowing out into the lagoon to gaze back at their city. They are acutely aware of the beauty of Venice—they, just like the visitors, never tire of it—and there are few views more breathtaking than sunset on the lagoon with the domes and towers of the city in the background. Venetian youth take to the waters for fun. Although soccer, the Italian national passion, is widely followed in Venice, Venetian youths seem to prefer sailing and cruising in motorboats on the lagoon or duck hunting in the salt marshes, and a Venetian swain will take his girlfriend out for a moonlit sail on the lagoon. Many Venetian young men, and now even some women, join rowing clubs and learn how to row "alla veneta," standing up in the stern, like a gondolier.

...does not live by tourism alone

Because of the hordes of tourists, many visitors get the false impression that Venice is simply a tourist attraction and is no longer a real city. While tourism is obviously important for the economy, most visitors are unaware that Venice is also a major educational center, home to three major institutions of higher learning. The largest of the three, Ca' Foscari, has more than 17,000 students; the School of Architecture is one of the most prestigious in Italy; and Venice International University (IUV) attracts students and scholars from all over the world. Venice also has thriving glass, fishing, shipbuilding, and petroleum-refining industries.

...battles rising waters

While Venice may be sinking slightly, it is raising water levels that are the main problem. Industrial land fill in the lagoon and the channels dug to accommodate the oil tankers and cruise ships have increased the frequency and intensity of the floods, as have the rising sea levels caused by worldwide climatic change and an increase in the frequency of the sirocco winds from North Africa that force the waters of the Adriatic up into the Venetian lagoon. The city is pinning hopes on a long-term solution: the construction of movable dikes at the entrances to the lagoon on the Lido is underway, with completion scheduled for 2016.

...strives to combine the new with the old

Most visitors to Venice enter into a world of the past, and the city seems more suited to life in the 18th century than to the exigencies of modern life. Nevertheless, Venice is also a center of contemporary artistic creativity. There is, of course, the Biennale dell'Arte, Venice's biannual international festival of contemporary art, its annual festival of cinema on the Lido, and the Biennale dell'Architettura. Even more significant for everyday life in Venice, however, is one of the first things visitors see when they enter the city: the elegant and graceful bridge crossing the Grand Canal and linking the bus station at Piazzale Roma with the train station, by noted Spanish contemporary architect Santiago di Calatrava. At the other end of the Grand Canal is Tadao Ando's inventive remodeling of the 17th-century customs depot to house contemporary art. But modernity in Venice has its limits: protests prohibited the construction of two concrete obelisks at the entrance to the collection, and Charles Ray's contemporary statue of a nude boy holding a frog, which had become an icon of the collection, had to be removed and replaced with a traditional lantern.

WHAT'S WHERE

1 San Marco. Monument-filled Piazza San Marco famously houses Basilica di San Marco, Doge's Palace, and other museums and architectural treasures.

2 Dorsoduro. Visitors head here for top sights like the Santa Maria della Salute, the Gallerie dell'Accademia, and the Peggy Guggenheim Collection; Venetians relax in the land stroll on the Zattere promenade.

3 San Polo. Two of Venice's great treasure houses, the Frari church and the Scuola di San Rocco, rise above bustling streets near the Rialto fish and produce markets.

4 Santa Croce. The main attractions of this residential district are the baroque church of San Stae and the lovely and peaceful Campo San Giacomo all'Orio.

5 Cannaregio. The sunny Fondamenta della Misericordia is a hub of restaurants and cafés, the Jewish Ghetto reveals a fascinating history.

6 Castello. This workaday district is home to the churches of Santi Giovanni e Paolo, Carpaccio's paintings in the Scuola di San Giorgio, and the Quirini Stampalia gallery.

7 San Giorgio Maggiore. This island across from Piazza San Marco is graced with Palladio's magnificent church.

8 The Giudecca. Palladio's elegant Redentore church is the major landmark on this large island where the main attractions are the wonderful views of Venice.

9 The Lido. This barrier island closes the Venetian lagoon off from the Adriatic and is Venice's beach, with bathing establishments and turn-of-the-20th-century villas.

10 Islands of the Northern Lagoon. Torcello, even older than Venice, has a romantic atmosphere and a mosaic-rich cathedral; Murano is the center of the Venetian glass industry; colorful Burano is the center of lace production; and San Michele is the cemetery island.

11 Side Trips. To the west of Venice are three great art cities: Padua, noted for Giotto's frescoes in the Cappella degli Scrovegni; Vicenza, bearing the signature of the great 16th-century architect Andrea Palladio; and Verona, one of the oldest and most beautiful cities in Italy. The Friuli–Venezia Giulia area bears the mark of the Romans (in Aquileia), the 18th-century painter Gianbattista Tiepolo (in Udine), and Habsburg nobility (in Trieste).

CANNAREGIO
5

Misericordia

Grande

Ca' d'Oro

SAN POLO
3

SAN MARCO
1

Piazza
San Marco

Basilica di
San Marco

Palazzo Ducale

CASTELLO
6

Gallerie dell'
Accademia

Canal   Grande

Peggy
Guggenheim
Collection

Santa Maria
della Salute

DORSODURO
2

Zatterre
Promenade

SAN
GIORGIO
MAGGIORE
7

Canal Della Giudecca

TORCELLO
BURANO

Laguna
Veneta

10

MURANO

←**11**

SAN MICHELE

VENICE

THE
LIDO
9

Adriatic
Sea

VENICE PLANNER

When to Go

Spring: Late April through early June is a good time to visit Venice: the weather is mild, but the volume of tourists is larger than it is in summer.

Summer: Summers are warm and humid. The advantages are fewer tourists (but their numbers are still substantial), it almost never rains, and the beaches of the Lido are just a boat ride away.

Fall: Autumn, like spring, is a good time for visiting Venice. It's usually pleasant and sunny well into October, and it doesn't really begin to get cold until mid-November. *Acqua alta* is most frequent, and severe, in later November.

Winter: Venetian winters are relatively mild, with frequent rainy spells, but also many more sunny days than there are in Northern Europe or much of North America. There are substantial crowds during Carnevale, and prices for hotels and even in some restaurants skyrocket.

Making the Most of Your Time

Most visitors will want to take the *vaporetto* (water bus) down the Grand Canal to Piazza San Marco, see the piazza and the basilica, and walk up to the Rialto and back to the station. You will want to make this circuit, too, but do so in the early morning, before most tourists have finished their breakfast cappuccinos. Also, choose week-days, instead of weekends, to visit the city.

Away from San Marco and the Rialto, the streets and quays of Venice's beautiful medieval and Renaissance residential districts and important artistic monuments receive only a moderate amount of traffic. Even on weekends you probably won't have to queue up to get into the Accademia museum.

Venice proper is quite compact, and you should be able to walk across it in a couple of hours. The water buses will save wear and tear on tired feet but won't always save you much time.

Passes and Discounts

Avoid lines by booking services and venue entry online with **Venice Connected** (⊕ *veniceconnected.com*), a convenient way of booking parking, public transit passes, museum passes, Wi-Fi access, and airport transfers. Sixteen of Venice's most significant churches are part of the **Chorus Foundation** (☎ *041/2750462* ⊕ *www.chorusvenezia.org*) umbrella group, which coordinates their administration, hours, and admission fees. Churches in the group are open to visitors all day except Sunday morning; you have a year to visit all 16 with the Chorus Pass (€10). The **Museum Pass** (€18) from **Musei Civici** (☎ *041/2715911* ⊕ *www.museicivicivenezian.it*) includes onetime entry to 12 Venice museums. The **Museums of San Marco Pass Plus** (€13; April–October) is good for the museums on the piazza, plus another civic museum of your choice. The **Museums of San Marco Pass** (€12; November–March) is good only for the piazza's museums. All these passes are available through ⊕ *www.VeniceConnected.com*.

Getting Here

Venice's Aeroporto Marco Polo serves international destinations. You can get to from the airport to Venice's historic center by bus to Piazzale Roma (€6), from where you can get a vaporetto, or by ferry to San Marco and other landing stages around the city (€15). A motoscafo (water taxi) is another option, but you'll spend about €60 for a short trip in town. However, a water taxi can carry up to 14 passengers, so if you're traveling in a group, it may not be that much more expensive than a bus or ferry. Trains from throughout Italy and the rest of Europe arrive at Venice's Santa Lucia station, on the Grand Canal with a vaporetto stop right in front. If you're arriving by car, Venice is at the end of SR11, just off the east–west A4 autostrada; you'll have to leave your car at one of the garages on the outskirts of the city.

Getting Around

Venice's primary public transportation is the *vaporetto* (water bus). A single ticket costs €7 and is good for 60 minutes one way; a ticket to take the vaporetto one stop across the Grand Canal is €4. A better option is a Travel Pass: €18 for 12 hours, €20 for 24 hours, €35 for 72 hours, and €50 for a week of unlimited travel. Tickets are available at main vaporetto stops and at some tobacconists. Line information is posted at each landing. If you board without a valid ticket, ask immediately to buy one to avoid a €59 fine. (⇨ *see Travel Smart for more information.*)

Hiring a gondola is fun but not a practical way to get around. The price of a 40-minute ride is €80 for up to six passengers, increasing to €100 between 7:30 pm and 8 am. Agree on cost and duration of the ride beforehand.

Traghettos are gondolas that cross the Grand Canal at strategic points along the waterway. A one-stop traghetto crossing takes just a few minutes—it's customary to stand—and can be a lot more convenient than using one of the few bridges over the waterway. A one-stop ride costs **€2 for** tourists (it's cheaper for residents).

Finding your way around Venice by foot is complicated. Figure out which landmark your destination is near and then get directions from that point.

Tourist Offices

The multilingual staff of the **Venice tourism office** (☏ *041/5298711* ⊕ *www.turismovenezia.it*) can provide directions and up-to-the-minute information. Tourist office branches are in Marco Polo Airport; the Venezia Santa Lucia train station; Piazza San Marco near Museo Correr at the southwest corner; the Venice Pavilion (including a Venice-centered bookstore), on the *riva (canal-front street)* between the San Marco vaporetto stop and the Royal Gardens; and on the Lido at the main vaporetto stop. It is open daily 10–6.

Speaking the Language

People who interact regularly with tourists—such as hotel, restaurant, museum, and transportation personnel—generally speak some English. However, often even highly educated Italians speak only Italian. Many are slightly offended if a foreigner assumes they speak English without first asking politely *"Parla lei inglese?"* If you do ask, most Venetians, even those with no English, will try to be helpful. Venetians tend to be very tolerant of foreigners who try to speak their language and do wonders in understanding fractured Italian.

VENICE TOP ATTRACTIONS

Piazza San Marco

(**A**) Perhaps nowhere else in the world gathers together so many of man's noblest artistic creations. The centerpiece of the piazza is the Basilica di San Marco, the most beautiful Byzantine church in the West, with not only its shimmering Byzantine Romanesque facade, but also its jewel-like mosaic-encrusted interior. Right next door is the Venetian Gothic Palazzo Ducale, which was so beloved by the Venetians that when it burnt in the 16th century, they rejected projects by the greatest architects of the Renaissance and had their palace rebuilt *come era, dove era*—exactly how and where it had been. Across from the Palazzo Ducale is Sansovino's elegant Biblioteca Marciana, which master architect Palladio deemed "beyond envy."

Grand Canal

(**B**) No one ever forgets a first trip down the Grand Canal. The sight of its magnificent palaces, with the light reflected from the canal's waters shimmering across their facades, is one of any world traveler's great experiences.

Gallerie dell'Accademia

(**C**) The greatest museum in northern Italy is a treasure trove of Venetian masters: Titian, Veronese, Tintoretto, Tiepollo, Bellini, Giorgione, and Carpaccio are all represented by some of their finest work. After a visit here, you'll understand why art historians are so enamored of the way Venice's great painters used color.

Ca' Rezzonico

(**D**) Designed by Baldassare Longhena in the 17th century, this gigantic palace, the last home of English poet Robert Browning (1812–89), has hosted some of the grandest parties in the city's history, from its 18th-century heyday to balls recreated

for Heath Ledger's 2005 *Casanova* film, and is today home to the especially delightful **Museo del Settecento** (Museum of Venice in the 1700s).

Santa Maria Gloriosa dei Frari

(E) Completed in 1442, this immense Gothic church of russet-color brick—known locally as *I Frari*—is famous worldwide for its array of spectacular Venetian art: Giovanni Bellini's 1488 triptych *Madonna and Child with Saints,* a fine sculpture of Saint John the Baptist by Donatello, Titian's *Assumption,* and many others.

Scuola Grande di San Rocco

(F) Although this elegant example of Venetian Renaissance architecture, built between 1517 and 1560 and including the work of at least four architects, is bold and dramatic outside, its contents are even more stunning—a series of more than 60 paintings by Tintoretto.

Torcello

With its ancient mosaics, green spaces, and picnic opportunities, this atmospheric, almost deserted island is one of the most magical place in Venice.

The Villas and Palazzi of Palladio

(G) The great 16th-century architect Palladio created harmoniously beautiful buildings that were influential in spreading the neoclassical style to Northern Europe, England, and, later, America. He did most of his work in and around his native city of Vicenza.

Giotto's Frescoes in the Scrovegni Chapel, Padua

(H) Dante's contemporary Giotto decorated this chapel with an eloquent and beautiful fresco cycle. Its convincing human dimension helped to change the course of Western art.

QUINTESSENTIAL VENICE

Il Caffè (Coffee)

The Venetian day begins and ends with coffee, and more cups of coffee punctuate the time in between. To live like the Venetians do, drink as they drink, standing at the counter or sitting at an outdoor table of the corner bar. (In Italy a "bar" is a coffee bar.) A primer: *caffè* means coffee, and Italian standard issue is what Americans call espresso—short and strong. *Cappuccino* is a foamy half-and-half of espresso and steamed milk; cocoa powder *(cacao)* on top is acceptable, cinnamon is not. If you're thinking of having a cappuccino for dessert, think again—Venetians drink only caffè or caffè *macchiato* (with a spot of steamed milk) after lunchtime. Confused? Homesick? Order caffè *americano* for a reasonable facsimile of good-old filtered joe.

Il Gelato (Ice Cream)

During warmer months, *gelato*—the Italian equivalent of ice cream—is a national obsession. It's considered a snack rather than a dessert, bought at stands and shops in piazzas and on street corners, and consumed on foot, usually at a leisurely stroll (⇨ *see La Passeggiata, below)*. It is the only food that is socially acceptable to eat on the street and not at a table. Gelato is softer, less creamy, and more intensely flavored than its American counterpart. It comes in simple flavors that capture the essence of the main ingredient. Standard choices include, besides chocolate and vanilla, pistachio, *nocciola* (hazelnut), caffè, and numerous fresh-fruit varieties. Quality varies; there are still some excellent *gelaterie* in Venice, but many who advertise themselves as *artiginale* (homemade) do very little more than mix factory-made flavors into a chemically treated base.

If you want to get a sense of contemporary Venetian culture and indulge in some of its pleasures, start by familiarizing yourself with the rituals of daily life. These are a few highlights—things you can take part in with relative ease.

La Passeggiata (Strolling)

A favorite Italian pastime is the *passeggiata* (literally, the promenade), and in Venice, the favorite place for the ritual is the Zattere, the southern walkway of the city, facing the Giudecca. In the late afternoon and early evening, especially on sunny weekends, couples, families, and groups of teenagers stroll the Zattere. It's a ritual of exchanged news and gossip, flirting, and gelato eating that adds up to a uniquely Venetian experience. You may feel more like an observer than a participant, until you realize that observing is what la passegiata is all about.

L'Aperitivo

A late afternoon or early evening ritual is to meet friends at a bar or café for an aperitif, generally, in Venice, either a *spritz,* a light cocktail made with white wine, aperol (a bright orange herb liquor) or bitters, and soda water, or a glass of prosecco, the Veneto's famous sparkling white wine. The drinks may be supplemented with ciccheti, or traditional Venetian snacks. Venetians are a very social folk, and it is not uncommon for them to get together with friends for an *aperitivo* three or four times a week. Since living space is at a premium in Venice, and many people live in rather cramped quarters, invitations to visit their homes are reserved for very special occasions. For everyday socializing, the aperitivo is the ideal solution.

TOP EXPERIENCES

Churchgoing

Few landmarks are more identifiable with Italy than the country's great churches, amazing works of architecture that often took centuries to build. In Venice, there are more spectacular churches than you can even imagine. During the Middle Ages and Renaissance, Venice was not necessarily more pious than other Italian cities; if fact, Venice was never known for its spirituality. Building or funding a church or convent was a way of demonstrating one's wealth and power; hence, the proliferation of splendid religious buildings.

Il Dolce Far Niente

"The sweetness of doing nothing" has long been an art form in Italy. This is a country in which life's pleasures are warmly celebrated, not guiltily indulged. Of course, doing "nothing" doesn't really mean nothing. It means doing things differently: lingering over a glass of wine for the better part of an evening as you watch the sun slowly set; savoring a slow and flirtatious evening passeggiata; or meeting friends at a bar or café for an aperitivo, and making a commitment—however temporary—to thinking that there is nowhere that you have to be next, and no other time than the magical present.

An opera at La Fenice

Attending an opera at Venice's historic, newly restored XVIII century Opera House not only allows you to hear some of the best music Venice has to offer but also brings you into contact with a good cross section of Venetian society. You'll see everyone there, from your plumber to the family of the countess who lives in a palazzo on the Canale Grande.

A gondola trip through Venice's back canals

Sure, a gondola ride is the quintessential tourist experience, but being rowed through Venice's back canals will allow you to see some of the most beautiful facades in the city: many palazzi that have insignificant street-side entrances have sumptuous and elegant canal side facades, which were, of course, the original main entrances.

Sipping wine at a bacaro

The Venetian hinterland and adjacent provinces comprise one of the major wine growing areas in Europe. A visit to one of the city's friendly *bacari,* or wine bars, will allow you to savor some of the wines that have made the region famous. Your barman will be more than happy to guide you. You'll also be able to sample traditional Venetian ciccheti, the local version of "tapas."

Exploring the Venetian Lagoon

Some of Venice's most important artistic monuments, such as Torcello's spectacular cathedral, are on islands in the lagoon surrounding Venice, and you can, of course, shop for Venetian glass on Murano. Seeing artistic treasures and shopping are, however, not the only reasons for venturing out onto the lagoon. Touring these waters, from its agricultural islands, Sant' Erasmo and la Vignola, to the north, to the fishing centers of Chioggia and Pantelleria to the south, will give you an idea of how the rhythm of Venetian life depends upon the sea.

BEST FESTIVALS IN VENICE

Carnevale and the Biennale are much-acclaimed events that draw crowds from around the world, but throughout the year, other festivals that are distinctly and uniquely Venetian transform this already magical city into an even more wondrous place.

Festa del Redentore. On the third Sunday in July, crowds cross the Canale della Giudecca by means of a pontoon bridge, built every year to commemorate the doge's annual visit to Palladio's Chiesa del Redentore to offer thanks for the end of a 16th-century plague. As evening falls the day before, practically the whole city takes to the streets and tables set alongside the canals, and thousands more take to the water. Half an hour before midnight, fireworks explode over the Bacino, with the colorful bursts reflecting in its waters. Boats decorated with colored lanterns, well provisioned with traditional Redentore meals, jockey for position to watch the grand event; the Riva degli Schiavoni also provides good viewing.

Festa della Madonna della Salute. Every November 21, Venetians make a pilgrimage to the church of Madonna della Salute, where they light candles to thank the Virgin Mary for liberating the city from the plague of 1630–31 and to pray for health in the year to come. It was while the plague was raging that the church was commissioned, but before the saint could intervene, nearly one third of the city's 145,000 inhabitants were dead. To make the pilgrims' progress more expedient, a temporary bridge is erected across the Grand Canal between Campo Santa Maria del Giglio (near the Gritti Palace hotel) and the sestiere of Dorsoduro. Outside and to the back of the church a carnival-like atmosphere prevails, with a plentitude of *frittelle* (fritters), *palloncini* (balloons on strings), clowns, and votive candles.

Festa della Sensa. The oldest Venetian festival, the Festival of the Ascension, was initiated by Doge Pietro Orseolo II in the year 1000, after he led the Venetian fleet to victory over the Slavic pirates (who had invaded the Istrian-Dalamatian coast) on Ascension Day. Today the Ascension is celebrated on the Sunday following Ascension Day, the Thursday that falls 40 days after Easter, and begins at about 9 am with a procession of Venetian-oared boats led by the mayor in the Serenissima, who tosses a ring into the water and pronounces the ritual phrase *"In segno di eterno dominio, noi, Doge di Venezia, ti sposiamo o mare!"* (As a symbol of our eternal dominion, we wed you, o sea!). Masses in the Chiesa di San Nicolò. Boat races follow later in the afternoon.

Festa di San Marco. Legend tells of a soldier enamored of the doge's daughter was mortally wounded in a far-off battle. As his blood spilled, it was transformed into red roses, which he entrusted his companion to bring to the girl. The story doesn't say if the flowers arrived on April 25, the feast day St. Mark, the evangelist who for 1,000 years protected his city, but by tradition Venetians celebrate the miracle on this date by presenting *boccoli* (red roses) for ladies in their lives (wives, mothers, sisters, cousins, friends)—the longer the stem, the deeper the token of love.

CARNEVALE IN VENICE

Ever since its revival in the 18th century, the Venice Carnevale has been aimed at drawing visitors to the city. For the 12 days leading up to *quaresima* (Lent), the city celebrates, with more than half a million people attending masquerade balls, historical processions, concerts, plays, street performances, fashion shows, and all other manner of revelry.

The first record of Carnevale dates back to 1097, but it was in the 18th century that Venice earned its international reputation as the "city of Carnevale." During that era the partying began after Epiphany (January 6) and transformed the city for over a month into one ongoing masquerade. After the Republic's fall in 1797, Carnevale was periodically prohibited by the French and then the Austrian occupiers. After the departure of the Austrians in 1866, Venetians were not particularly avid in reinstating the festivities. Carnevale was not revived until 1979, when the municipality saw a way of converting the unruly antics of throwing water balloons in the days preceding Lent into a more pleasant celebration.

It wasn't long before events became more elaborate, emulating their 18th-century predecessors.

Many of Carnevale's costume balls are open to the public—but they come with an extravagant price tag, and the most popular of them need to be booked well in advance. Balls start at roughly €295 per person, dinner included, and though you can rent a standard costume for €200–€400 (not including shoes or mask), the most elaborate attire can cost much more. (⇨ *See "Costumes and Accessories" in the Shopping chapter for resources.*)

Events to Watch for

Ballo del Doge (☎ *041/5233851, 041/5287543* ⊕ *www.ballodeldoge.com*) is one of the most exclusive (and expensive) events, held at Palazzo Pisani-Moretta the last Saturday of Carnevale. Full participation in the ball, including dinner, costs €1,700 per person, but you can opt for admission after dinner, at only €800 per person.

Those on a tight budget should see ⊕ *www.meetingeurope.com* for the **Ballo Tiepolo** (☎ *041/524668, 041/722285*), which also takes place in the Tiepolo-frescoed ballroom of Pisani-Moretta and costs a mere €550 per person.

You don't have to blow the bank on a masquerade ball in order to take part in Carnevale—many people go simply for the exuberant street life. Be aware, though, that the crowds are enormous, and ball or no ball, prices for everything absolutely skyrocket.

Carnevale events and schedules change from year to year. If you want to attend, first check out these resources:

Consorzio Comitato per il Carnevale di Venezia (☎ *041/717065, 041/2510811 during Carnevale* ⊕ *www.meetingeurope.com*) is one of the primary event organizers.

Venezia Marketing & Eventi (⊕ *www.carnevale.venezia.it*) hosts the official website for Carnevale and other events.

The **tourist office** (☎ *041/5298711* ⊕ *www.turismovenezia.it*) has detailed information about daily events.

A Guest in Venice (⊕ *www.aguestinvenice.com*) gives free advertising to public and private events, and as a result it's one of the most complete—if potentially overwhelming—Carnevale guides.

VENICE'S BIENNALE

The **Biennale dell'Arte** originated in 1894 and, except for World War interruptions, has taken place every two years since. In 1910 Klimt and Renoir had their own exhibition rooms, while Picasso was removed from the Spanish salon over concern his paintings were too shocking. Picasso's work was finally shown in 1948, the same year Peggy Guggenheim brought her collection to Venice at the Biennale's invitation. During the century-plus of its existence it has become one of the world's major interdisciplinary art expositions. "Biennale" now refers to the group that coordinates festivals of art, film, music, dance, theater, and architecture.

Where to Go

The Biennale dell'Arte currently takes place from mid-June to early November in odd-numbered years. The Giardini della Biennale, in the sestiere Castello, was developed specifically for the event. In this parklike setting overlooking the lagoon, 30 countries have permanent pavilions to exhibit works by their sponsored artists. In the neighboring Arsenale's Corderie, a long, beautiful building otherwise off-limits to visitors, has works by artists from smaller nations, as well as some more avant-garde installations. Numerous palaces, warehouses, and churches all over town also hold exhibits, often in buildings not normally open to the public.

Movies

The **Biennale del Cinema** (also known as the Mostra Internazionale d'Arte Cinematografica, or Venice Film Festival) was first held in 1932 and soon became an annual event. Films are shown in several theaters at the **Palazzo del Cinema** (⊠ *Lungomare Guglielmo Marconi 90, Lido* ☎ *041/2726511 Vaporetto: Lido Casinò or S.M. Elizabetta*), which is closed most of the year but comes to life in August with bright lights, movie stars, and thousands of fans.

Ten days of 9 am to 2 am screenings include films vying for awards as well as retrospectives and debuts of mainstream releases. Advance tickets are recommended for the most eagerly awaited films (the tourist office has details). The night after major films play the Palazzo del Cinema, they're shown in Venice proper at Campo San Polo's open-air cinema and at the Giorgione Movie d'Essai. San Polo screens the winner of the Leone d'Oro (Golden Lion) prize the night following the awards ceremony.

Music

Since its launch in 1930, the **Biennale Musica** has attracted world-famous composers and performers. Igor Stravinsky premiered his *Rake's Progress* during the 1951 festival, and four years later it was George Gershwin's turn with *Porgy and Bess*. The annual event stretches over several months, with performances in some of the city's smaller venues.

Theater, Architecture, and More

Biennale Danza and **Biennale Teatro,** both stage performances during the year in the city's *campi* and in other venues. The Teatro Verde, an outdoor amphitheater on the island of San Giorgio, was restored for Biennale use, and you can't beat its lagoon backdrop. The **Biennale of Architecture** began in 1980 and now exhibits in the Corderie in alternate years with the Biennale dell'Arte.

Information

For information on all events, contact **La Biennale di Venezia** (⊠ *Ca' Giustinian, San Marco 1364/A* ☎ *041/5218711* ⊕ *www.labiennale.org*).

A GREAT ITINERARY

Three days are hardly enough to see one of the world's most beautiful cities and one of the cradles of modern Western civilization. But running from museum to museum, church to church would be a mistake, since Venice is a wonderful place to stroll or "hang out," taking in some of the atmosphere that inspired such great art.

Day one

The first things you will probably want to do in Venice are to take a vaporetto ride down the Grand Canal and see the Piazza San Marco. These are best done in the morning; before 8:30 you'll avoid rush hour on the vaporetto, and although there's likely to be a line at San Marco when it opens, you'll be better off then than later in the day. Move on to the adjacent Palazzo Ducale and Sansovino's Biblioteca Marciana.

For lunch, take Vaporetto 1 to the Ca' Rezzonico stop and have a sandwich and a spritz in the Campo Santa Margherita, where you can mingle with university students in one of Venice's most lively squares. From there, make your way to the Galleria dell'Accademia and spend a few hours taking in its wonderful collection of Venetian painting. In the evening, take a walk up the Zattere and have a drink at one of the cafés overlooking the Giudecca Canal.

Day two

If the Accademia has whet your appetite for Venetian painting, visiting churches and institutions where you can see more of it. For Titian, go to Santa Maria Gloriosa dei Frari church and Santa Maria della Salute; for Tintoretto, Scuola Grande di San Rocco; for Bellini, the Frari San Giovanni e Paolo, and San Zaccheria; for Tiepolo, Ca' Rezzonico, Scuola Grande dei Carmini, and the Gesuati; for Carpaccio, Scuola di San Giorgio; and for Veronese, San Sebastiano. If your taste runs to more-modern art, there is the Guggenheim Collection and, down the street from it, the Pinault collection in the impressively refashioned Punta della Dogana.

In the afternoon, head for the Fondamenta Nuova station to catch a vaporetto to one or more of the outer islands: Murano, where you can shop for Venetian glass and visit the glass museum and workshops; Burano, known for lace making and colorful houses; and Torcello, Venice's first inhabited island, home to a beautiful cathedral.

Day three

Venice is more than a museum—it's a lively city, and the best way to see that aspect is to pay a visit to the Rialto Market. Venetians buy their fruits and vegetables and, most important, their fish, at one of Europe's largest and most varied fish markets. Have lunch in one of the excellent restaurants in the market area. There's certainly a good deal more art and architecture to see in the city, and if you can't resist squeezing in another few churches, you may want to see Palladio's masterpiece of ecclesiastical architecture, the Redentore church on the Giudecca, or Tullio Lombardo's lyrical Miracoli, a short walk from the San Marco end of the Rialto Bridge.

TOURS IN VENICE

If you want some expert guidance around Venice, you may opt for private tours or large group tours. Any may include a boat tour as a portion of a longer walking tour. For private tours, make sure to choose an authorized guide.

A Guide in Venice. This popular company offers a wide variety of innovative, entertaining, and informative themed tours for groups of up to 10 people. Tours generally last two to three hours. ☎ *347/7876846 Sabrina Scaglianti ⊕ www.aguideinvenice. com.*

Secret Gardens of Venice. A vine creeping over a wall is often the only hint a visitor gets that this city of stone and water conceals some magnificent gardens. Secret Garden tours, led by companies like Aquaforte, reveal the gardens hidden behind palazzos and within the confines of convents; they are not only luxuriant oases but also full of rich ornamentation and, as your guide explains, have long and colorful histories. Tours start at $30.99. ⊕ *www.getyourguide. com/venice-l35/secret-gardens-of-venice-walking-tour-t33033.*

Venice Art Tours. Half-day guided tours center around the major artistic monuments of the city, but also include residential areas that the casual visitor would probably miss on his own. The tour guide is knowledgeable and willing to adjust his itinerary to suit clients' specific artistic interests. ☎ *041/713793, 348/2699901 ⊕ www.venice-art-tours.com.*

Walks Inside Venice. For a host of particularly creative group and private tours, from historic to artistic to gastronomic, opt for one run by Walks Inside Venice. Tours are for groups up to six people and guides include people with advanced university degrees and published authors.

☎ *041/5241706 Roberta, 041/5202434 Cristina ⊕ www.walksinsidevenice.com.*

Venice Tourism Office. Visit any Venice tourism office to book walking tours of the San Marco area (no Sunday tour in winter). There are also an afternoon walking tour that ends with a gondola ride, and a daily serenaded gondola ride. Check the main branch of the city's tourist office or their website for additional scheduled offerings, meeting places, prices, and times. ✉ *San Marco 2637* ☎ *041/5298711 ⊕ www.turismovenezia.it.*

Walks of Italy. The Walks of Italy company offers a selection of Venice tours, covering the city by foot and by boat, and the guides are almost unfailingly knowledgeable and friendly. Tours start at €49. ⊕ *www.walksofitaly.com.*

CRUISING THE GRAND CANAL

THE BEST INTRODUCTION TO VENICE IS A TRIP DOWN MAIN STREET

Venice's Grand Canal is one of the world's great thoroughfares. It winds its way in the shape of a backward "S" from Ferrovia (the train station) to Piazza San Marco, passing 200 palazzos born of a culture obsessed with opulence and fantasy. There's a theatrical quality to a boat ride on the canal: it's as if each pink- or gold-tinted facade is trying to steal your attention from its rival across the way.

The palaces were built from the 12th to 18th centuries by the city's richest families. A handful are still private residences, but many have been converted to other uses, including museums, hotels, government offices, university buildings, a post office, a casino, and even a television station.

It's romantic to see the canal from a gondola, but the next best thing, at a fraction of the cost, is to take the Line 1 *vaporetto* (water bus) from Ferrovia to San Marco. The ride costs €6 and takes about 35 minutes. Invest in a Travel Card (€15 buys 24 hours of unlimited passage) and you can spend the better part of a day hopping on and off at the vaporetto's 16 stops, visiting the sights along the banks.

Either way, keep your eyes open for the highlights listed here; the major sites also have fuller descriptions later in this chapter.

FROM FERROVIA TO RIALTO

Palazzo Labia
On September 3, 1951, during the Venice Film Festival, the Palazzo Labia hosted what's been dubbed "the party of the century." The Aga Khan, Winston Churchill, Orson Welles, and Salvador Dalì were among those who donned 18th-century costume and danced in the Tiepolo-frescoed ballroom.

Santa Maria di Nazareth

Ponte di Scalzi

R. Di BIASIO

FERROVIA

SANTA CROCE

Stazione Ferrovia Santa Lucia

As you head out from Ferrovia, the baroque church immediately to your left is **Santa Maria di Nazareth**. Its shoeless friars earned it the nickname Chiesa degli Scalzi (Church of the Barefoot).

One of the four bridges over the Grand Canal is the **Ponte di Scalzi**. The original version was built of iron in 1858; the existing stone bridge dates from 1934.

After passing beneath the Ponte di Scalzi, ahead to your left you'll spy **Palazzo Labia**, one of the most imposing buildings in Venice, looming over the bell tower of the church of San Geremia.

A hundred yards or so further along on the left bank, the uncompleted façade of the church of **San Marcuola** gives you an idea of what's behind the marble decorations of similar 18th-century churches in Venice.

Across the canal, flanked by two *torricelle* (side wings in the shape of small towers) and a triangular *merlatura* (crenellation), is the **Fondaco dei Turchi,** one of the oldest Byzantine palaces in Venice; it's now a natural history museum. Next comes the plain brick **Depositi del Megio**, a 15th-century granary—note the lion marking it as Serenissima property—and beyond it the obelisk-topped **Ca' Belloni-Battagia**. Both are upstaged by the **Palazzo Vendramin-Calergi** on the opposite bank: this Renaissance gem was built in the 1480s, at a time when late-Gothic was still the prevailing style. A gilded banner identifies the palazzo as site of Venice's casino.

Palazzo Vendramin-Calergi
The German composer Richard Wagner died in Palazzo Vendramin-Calergi in 1883, soon after the success of his opera Parsifal. His room has been preserved—you can visit it on Saturday mornings by appointment.

CANNAREGGIO

Church of San Marcuola

GHETTO

S. MARCUOLA

Ca' Belloni-Battagia

Ca' d'Oro
Ca' d'Oro means "house of gold." but the gold is long gone—the gilding that once accentuated the marble carvings of the facade has worn away over time.

S. STAE

Ca' Pesaro

Fondaco dei Turchi

Depositi del Megio

San Stae Church

SAN POLO

Ca' Corner della Regina

CA' D'ORO

Pescheria
The pescheria has been in operation for over 1,000 years. Stop by in the morning to see the exotic fish for sale—one of which may wind up on your dinner plate. Produce stalls fill the adjacent fondamenta, and butchers and cheesemongers occupy the surrounding shops.

Rialto Mercato

Fondaco dei Tedeschi

Ca' dei Camerlenghi

RIALTO

SAN MARCO

The white, whimsically baroque church of **San Stae** on the right bank is distinguished by a host of marble saints on its facade. Further along the bank is another baroque showpiece, **Ca' Pesaro**, followed by the tall, balconied **Ca' Corner della Regina**. Next up on the left is the flamboyant pink-and-white **Ca' d'Oro**, arguably the finest example of Venetian Gothic design.

Across from Ca' d'Oro is the loggia-like, neo-Gothic **pescheria**, Venice's fish market, where boats dock in the morning to deliver their catch.

The canal narrows as you approach the impressive Rialto Bridge. To the left, just before the bridge, is the **Fondaco dei Tedeschi**. This was once the busiest trading center of the republic—German, Austrian, and Hungarian merchants kept warehouses and offices here; today it's the city's main post office. Across the canal stands

the curiously angled **Ca' dei Camerlenghi**. Built in 1525 to accommodate the State Treasury, it had a jail for tax evaders on the ground floor.

FROM RIALTO TO THE PONTE DELL' ACCADEMIA

SAN POLO

Ponte di Rialto

▲ RIALTO

Ca' Foscari
Positioned at one of the busiest junctures along the Grand Canal, Ca' Foscari was recently restored after suffering severe foundation damage as a result of the relentless wake from passing boats.

Palazzo Barzizza

Ca' Loredan

S. SILVESTRO ▲

Ca' Farsetti

Palazzo Pisani Moretta

Ca' Grimani

▲ S. ANGELO

Ca' Corner-Spinelli
If Ca' Corner-Spinelli has a familiar look, that's because it became a prototype for later Grand Canal buildings—and because its architect, Mauro Codussi, himself copied the windows from Palazzo Vendramin-Calergi.

TOMA ▲

Ca' Garzoni

Palazzo Grassi

Palazzo Falier
Palazzo Falier is said to have been the home of Doge Martin Fallier, who was beheaded for treason in 1355.

Ca' Rezzonico

SAN MARCO

REZZONICO ▲

ACCADEMIA ▲

Gallerie dell'Accademia

DORSODURO

Until the 19th century, the shop-lined **Ponte di Rialto** was the only bridge across the Grand Canal.

Rialto is the only point along the Grand Canal where buildings don't have their primary entrances directly on the water, a consequence of the two spacious *rive* (waterside paths) once used for unloading two Venetian staples: coal and wine. On your left along Riva del Carbon stand **Ca' Loredan** and **Ca' Farsetti**, 13th-century Byzantine palaces that today make up Venice's city hall. Just past the San Silvestro vaporetto landing on Riva del Vin is the 12th- and 13th-century facade of **Palazzo Barzizza**, an elegant example of Veneto-Byzantine architecture that managed to survive a complete renovation in the 17th century. Across the water, the sternly

Renaissance **Ca' Grimani** has an intimidating presence that seems appropriate for today's Court of Appeals. At the Sant'Angelo landing, the vaporetto passes close to another massive Renaissance palazzo, **Ca' Corner-Spinelli**.

Back on the right bank, in a salmon color that seems to vary with the time of day, is elegant **Palazzo Pisani Moretta**, with twin water entrances. To your left, four-storied **Ca' Garzoni**, part of the Universita di Venezia Ca' Foscari, stands beside the San Toma *traghetto* (gondola ferry), which has operated since 1354. The boat makes a sharp turn and, on the right, passes one of the city's tallest Gothic palaces, **Ca' Foscari**.

The vaporetto passes baroque **Ca' Rezzonico** so closely that

you get to look inside one of the most fabulous entrances along the canal. Opposite stands the Grand Canal's youngest palace, **Palazzo Grassi**, commissioned in 1749. Just beyond Grassi and Campo San Samuele, the first house past the garden was once Titian's studio. It's followed by **Palazzo Falier**, identifiable by its twin loggias (windowed porches).

Approaching the canal's fourth and final bridge, the vaporetto stops at a former church and monastery complex that houses the world-renowned **Gallerie dell'Accademia**.

The wooden pilings on which Venice was built (you can see them at the bases of the buildings along the Grand Canal) have gradually hardened into mineral form.

ARCHITECTURAL STYLES ALONG THE GRAND CANAL

BYZANTINE: 12th and 13th centuries. **Distinguishing characteristics:** high, rounded arches, relief panels, multicolored marble. **Examples:** Fondaco dei Turchi, Ca' Loredan, Ca' Farsetti, Palazzo Barzizza (and, off the canal, Basilica di San Marco).

GOTHIC: 14th and 15th centuries. **Distinguishing characteristics:** Pointed arches, high ceilings, and many windows. **Examples:** Ca' d'Oro, Ca' Foscari, Ca' Franchetti, Palazzo Falier (and, off the canal, Palazzo Ducale).

RENAISSANCE: 16th century. **Distinguishing characteristics:** classically influenced emphasis on order, achieved

through symmetry and balanced proportions. **Examples:** Palazzo Vendramin-Calergi, Ca' Grimani, Ca' Corner-Spinelli, Ca' dei Camerlenghi (and, off the canal, Libreria Sansoviniana on Piazza San Marco and the church of San Giorgio Maggiore).

BAROQUE: 17th century. **Distinguishing characteristics:** Renaissance order wedded with a more dynamic style, achieved through curving lines and complex decoration. **Examples:** churches of Santa Maria di Nazareth and San Stae, Ca' Pesaro, Ca' Rezzonico (and, off the canal, the church of Santa Maria della Salute).

FROM THE PONTE DELL'ACCADEMIA TO SAN ZACCARIA

Ca' Franchetti
Until the late 19th century, Ca' Franchetti was a *squero* (gondola workshop). A few active *squeri* remain, though none are on the Grand Canal. The most easily spotted is Squero di San Trovaso, in Dorsoduro on a small canal near the Zattere boat landing.

Ca' Barbaro
Monet, Henry James, and Cole Porter are among the guests who have stayed at Ca' Barbaro. Porter later lived aboard a boat in Giudecca Canal.

SAN MARCO

Ponte dell' Accademia

Casetta Rossa

Ca' Pisani-Gritti

ACCADEMIA

S. M. DEL GIGLIO

DORSODURO

Ca' Barbarigo

SALUTE

Palazzo Venier dei Leoni
When she was in residence at Palazzo Venier dei Leoni, Peggy Guggenheim kept her private gondola parked at the door and left her dogs standing guard (in place of Venetian lions).

Palazzo Salviati

S. Maria della Salute

Ca' Dario
However tilted Dario might be, it has outlasted its many owners, who seem plagued by misfortune. They include the Italian industrialist Raul Gardini, whose 1992 suicide followed charges of corruption and an unsuccessful bid to win the America's Cup.

The wooden **Ponte dell' Accademia**, like the Eiffel Tower (with which it shares a certain structural grace), wasn't intended to be permanent. Erected in 1933 as a quick replacement for a rusting iron bridge built by the Austrian military in 1854, it was so well liked by Venetians that they kept it. (A perfect replica, with steel bracing, was installed 1986.)

You're only three stops from the end of the Grand Canal, but this last stretch is packed with sights. The lovely **Ca' Franchetti**, with a central balcony made in the style of Palazzo Ducale's loggia, dates from the late Gothic period, but its gardens are no older than the cedar tree standing at their center.

Ca' Barbaro, next door to Ca' Franchetti, was the residence of the illustrious family who rebuilt the church of Santa Maria del Giglio.

Farther along on the left bank, a garden, vibrant with flowers in summer, surrounds **Casetta Rossa** (small red house) as if it were the centerpiece of its bouquet. Across the canal, bright 19th-century mosaics on

Ca' Barbarigo give you some idea how the frescoed facades of many Venetian palaces must have looked in their heyday. A few doors down are the lush gardens within the walls of the unfinished **Palazzo Venier dei Leoni**, which holds the **Peggy Guggenheim Collection** of contemporary art.

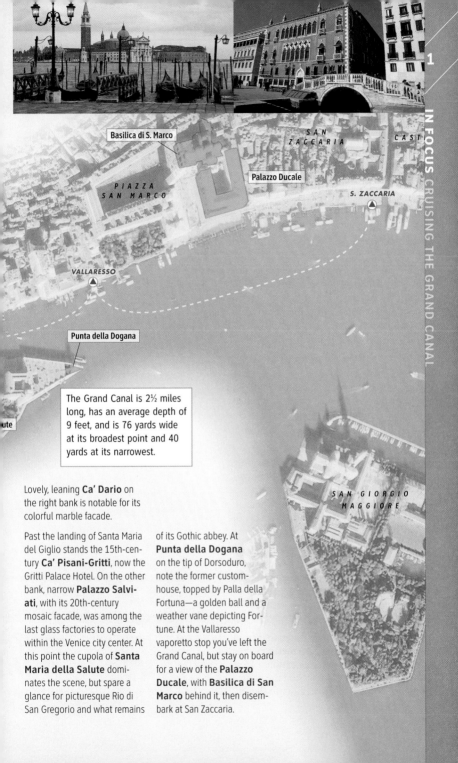

Basilica di S. Marco

SAN ZACCARIA

CAST...

Palazzo Ducale

PIAZZA SAN MARCO

S. ZACCARIA

VALLARESSO

Punta della Dogana

ute

The Grand Canal is 2½ miles long, has an average depth of 9 feet, and is 76 yards wide at its broadest point and 40 yards at its narrowest.

SAN GIORGIO MAGGIORE

Lovely, leaning **Ca' Dario** on the right bank is notable for its colorful marble facade.

Past the landing of Santa Maria del Giglio stands the 15th-century **Ca' Pisani-Gritti**, now the Gritti Palace Hotel. On the other bank, narrow **Palazzo Salviati**, with its 20th-century mosaic facade, was among the last glass factories to operate within the Venice city center. At this point the cupola of **Santa Maria della Salute** dominates the scene, but spare a glance for picturesque Rio di San Gregorio and what remains of its Gothic abbey. At **Punta della Dogana** on the tip of Dorsoduro, note the former custom-house, topped by Palla della Fortuna—a golden ball and a weather vane depicting Fortune. At the Vallaresso vaporetto stop you've left the Grand Canal, but stay on board for a view of the **Palazzo Ducale**, with **Basilica di San Marco** behind it, then disembark at San Zaccaria.

SPEAKING VENETIAN

Venice is one of the few Italian cities where the local dialect is still alive and well. Much of the language you will hear in Venice is not Italian but rather Venetian, or Italian heavily laced with Venetian. Venetian has its own rich and widely respected literature. The Venetian dialect comedies of Goldoni, the great 18th-century playwright, are regularly performed in the city.

Even when speaking Italian, Venetians will use dialect terms to refer to certain common objects. Sometimes the term means something totally different in standard Italian.

Here are a few frequently used words:

sestiere: One of six neighborhoods in central Venice.

rio: A canal. Only the Grand Canal and a few other major waterways are called "canali." Everything else is a "rio."

fondamenta: A quay, a street running along a canal or a "rio."

calle: A street, what is elsewhere in Italy called a "via." "Via" is used in Venice, but it means "boulevard."

campo: A square—what is elsewhere in Italy called a piazza. (The only piazza in Venice is Piazza San Marco.)

bacaro: A traditional wine bar.

ciccheto (pronounced chee-*kay*-toh): An hors d'oeuvre—roughly the Venetian equivalent of tapas—generally served at a bacaro and in many cafés.

ombra: A small glass of wine.

focaccia: A traditional Venetian raised sweet cake, similar to a panettone, but much lighter and without candied fruit or raisins. (Very different from the better-known Genoese focaccia, a dense slightly raised bread sometimes flavored with herbs or cheese.)

Venetians tend to use the informal second person form, *tu,* much more readily than people do in other parts of Italy. Venetians also frequently address each other with the term *amore* (love), as is done sometimes in England. But in Venice it is used even between members of the same sex, without any romantic connotation.

EXPLORING
VENICE

Updated
by Bruce
Leimsidor

It's called La Serenissima, "the most serene," a reference to the majesty, wisdom, and impressive power of this city that was for centuries the leader in trade between Europe and the Orient, and a major source of European culture. Built on and around a cluster of tiny islands in a lagoon by a people who saw the sea as a defense and ally, Venice is unlike any other city.

No matter how often you've seen Venice in photos and films, the city is more dreamlike than you could ever imagine. The key landmarks, the Basilica di San Marco and the Palazzo Ducale, are hardly what we normally think of as Italian: fascinatingly idiosyncratic, they are exotic mixes of Byzantine, Romanesque, Gothic, and Renaissance styles. Shimmering sunlight and silvery mist soften every perspective here; it's easy to understand how the city became renowned in the Renaissance for its artists' use of color. The city is full of secrets, inexpressibly romantic, and, in both art and everyday life, given over to an unabashed celebration of the material world.

You'll see Venetians going about their daily affairs in *vaporetti* (water buses), aboard the *traghetti* (gondola ferries) that carry them across the Grand Canal, in the *campi* (squares), and along the *calli* (narrow streets). They are skilled—and remarkably tolerant—in dealing with the hordes of tourists from all over the world, attracted by the city's fame and splendor.

Venice proper is divided into six *sestieri*, or districts (the word *sestiere* means, appropriately, "sixth"): Cannaregio, Castello, Dorsoduro, San Marco, San Polo, and Santa Croce. More-sedate outer islands float around them—San Giorgio Maggiore and the Giudecca just to the south, beyond them the Lido, the barrier island; to the north, Murano, Burano, and Torcello.

SAN MARCO

Extending from the Piazza San Marco to the Rialto bridge, the Sestiere San Marco comprises the historical and commercial heart of Venice. Aside from the Piazza—San Marco is the only square in Venice given full stature as a piazza and accordingly is often known simply as "the Piazza"—San Marco is graced with some of Venice's finest and most ornate churches and best-endowed museums. San Marco is also the shopping district of Venice, and its mazes of streets are lined with Venetian glass, fine clothing, and elegantly wrought jewelry. Most of the famous Venetian glass producers have boutiques in San Marco, as do most Italian designers.

TIMING

You can easily spend several days seeing the historical and artistic monuments in and around the Piazza San Marco alone, but at a bare minimum plan on at least an hour for the basilica, with its wonderful mosaics. Add on another half hour if you want to see its Pala d'Oro, Galleria, and Museo di San Marco. You'll want at least an hour to appreciate the Palazzo Ducale. Leave another hour for the Museo Correr, through which you also enter the archaeological museum and the Libreria Sansoviniana. If you choose to take in the piazza itself from a café table with an orchestra, keep in mind there will be an additional charge for the music.

TOP ATTRACTIONS

Fodor's Choice ★ **Palazzo Ducale** (*Doge's Palace*). Rising majestically above the Piazzetta San Marco, this Gothic fantasia of pink-and-white marble is a majestic expression of Venetian prosperity and power. Although the site was the doges' residence from the 10th century, the building began to take its present form around 1340; what you seen now is essentially a product of the first half of the 15th century. It served not only as a residence, but also as the central administrative center of the Venetian Republic.

The Palazzo Ducale took so long to finish that by the time it was completed, around 1450, it was already a bit out of fashion. It barely predates the main gate of the Arsenale, built in 1460 in fully conceived Renaissance classical style. The Venetians, however, even later on, were not disturbed by their palazzo's dated look. In the 1570s the upper floors were destroyed by fire and Palladio submitted an up-to-date design for its reconstruction, but the Venetians refused his offer and insisted on reconstruction "*come era, dove era*" (as it was, where it was).

Unlike other medieval seats of authority, the Palazzo Ducale is free of any military defenses—a sign of the Republic's self-confidence. The position of the loggias below instead of above the retaining wall, and the use of pink marble to emphasize the decorative function of that wall, gave the palazzo a light and airy aspect, one that could impress visitors—and even intimidate them, though through opulence and grace rather than fortress-like bulk. Near the basilica you'll see Giovanni and Bartolomeo Bon's Gothic **Porta della Carta** (Gate of the Paper), built between 1438 and 1442, where official decrees were traditionally posted, but you enter the palazzo under the portico facing the water.

Continued on page 45

THE BASILICA DI SAN MARCO
Venice's Cultural Mosaic

Above, 17th century stamp of the winged lion; symbol of Venice.

Below, facade of Basilica di San Marco with Palazzo Ducale in the background.

Standing at the heart of Venice, the spectacular Basilica di San Marco has been, for about a millennium, the city's religious center. Like other great churches—and even more so—it's also an expression of worldly accomplishments and aspirations. As you take in the shimmering mosaics and elaborate ornamentation, you begin to grasp the pivotal role Venice has played for centuries in European culture.

ORIGINS. The basilica began as a political statement. The original church, consecrated in 832, was built to house the body of St. Mark. According to legend, the saint's body had been stolen from Alexandria by two Venetians in 828. The whole enterprise was intended to establish Venice's prominence over neighboring Aquileia, a city with a glorious Roman past that claimed to have been founded by St. Mark.

THE BASILICA'S FACADES

St. Mark and lion, main portal

VENICE'S TROPHY CASE. When the present church was built in the 11th century, Venice was still officially under the rule of the Byzantium, and the basilica was patterned after the Byzantine Church of the Twelve Apostles in Constantinople. The external appearance was initially rather simple, bearing an unadorned brick facade. But the 12th and 13th centuries were a period of intense military and economic expansion, and by the early 13th century the wealth and power of Venice were on display: the facades of the basilica were being adorned with precious marbles and art that were trophies from the military city's triumphs—most notably the conquest and sacking ot its former ruler, Constantinople, in 1204.

Main portal entrance

PORTAL OF SANT ALIPIO. Be sure to take a look at the apse of the portal of Sant Alipio, the farthest north of the five west facade portals. It bears a 13th-century mosaic showing how the church looked at that time. Note how the facade is already decorated with marble columns and the famous gilt bronze ancient Roman horses, taken by the Venetians during the sack of Constantinople.

The portal of Sant Alipio is typical of many parts of the basilica in that it contains elements that far predate the construction of the church. The base of the pointed arch beneath the mosaic, for example, dates from the 5th century, and the Byzantine capitals of the precious marble columns, as well as the window screens, are mostly from the 7th century. The use of these elements, most of them pillaged from raids and conquests, testifies to Venetian daring and power, and they create the illusion of an ancient heritage that Venice itself lacked and looked upon with envy.

Detail of bas-relief

Portal of Sant Alipio with 13th-century mosaic of the basilica

Bronze horses, facade

Detail of lunette in West facade

THE MAIN PORTAL. By the time these ancient trophies were put into place, Venice had both the wealth and the talent to create its own, new decoration. On the inner arches of the main portal, look for the beautiful and fascinating Romanesque and early Gothic allegorical, biblical, and zodiac bas-reliefs.

THE TETRARCHS. The Christian relevance of some of the trophies on the basilica is scant. For a fine example of pride over piety, take a look at the fourth-century group of four soldiers in red porphyry on the corner of the south facade. It's certain that this was taken from Constantinople, because a missing fragment of one of the figures' feet can still be found attached to a building in Istanbul. The current interpretation is that they are the Tetrarchs, colleagues of the Emperor Diocletian, having little if any religious significance.

The incorporation of art from many different cultures into Venice's most important building is a sign of imperial triumph, but it also indicates an embrace of other cultures that's a fundamental part of Venetian character. (Think of Marco Polo, who was on his way to China only a few years after the first phase of decoration of the facade of the basilica began.) Venice remains, even today, arguably the most tolerant and cosmopolitan city in Italy.

Statues of Tetrarchs

TREASURES INSIDE THE BASILICA

The choir

THE MOSAICS. The glory of the basilica is its brilliant, floor-to-ceiling mosaics, especially those dating from the medieval period.

The mosaics of the atrium, or porch, represent the Old Testament, while those of the interior show the stories of the Gospel and saints, ending with the image of Christ in Glory (a Renaissance copy) in the apse. Many of the mosaics of the New Testament scenes are actually somewhat earlier (mid-12th century), or contemporaneous with the 13th-century mosaics of the atrium. You wouldn't know it from the style: the figures of the atrium still bear the late classical character of the early Christian manuscript, brought to Venice after the sack of Constantinople, that inspired them. In the mosaics of the church proper, notice the flowing lines, elongated figures, and stern expressions, all characteristics of high Byzantine art. Look especially for the beautiful 12th-century mosaics in the dome of the Pentecost, the first dome in the nave of the basilica as you enter the main part of the church, and for the 12th-century mosaics in the dome of the Ascension, considered the masterpiece of the Venetian school.

Above, detail of the nave
Below, detail of mosaic

The centerpiece of the basilica is, naturally, ❶ **THE SANTUARIO (SANCTUARY),** the main altar built over the tomb of St. Mark. Its green marble canopy, lifted high on carved alabaster columns, is another trophy dating from the fourth century. Perhaps even more impressive is the ❷ **PALA D'ORO,** a dazzling gilt silver screen encrusted with 1,927 precious gems and 255 enameled panels. Originally commissioned (976–978) in Constantinople, it was enlarged and embellished over four centuries by master craftsmen and wealthy merchants.

❸ **THE TESORO (TREASURY),** entered from the right transept, contains treasures carried home from conquests abroad. Climb the stairway to the Galleria and the Museo di San Marco for the best overview of the basilica's interior. From here you can step out for a sweeping panorama of Piazza San Marco and across the lagoon to San Giorgio. The highlight is a close-up view of the original gilt bronze horses that were once on the outer gallery.

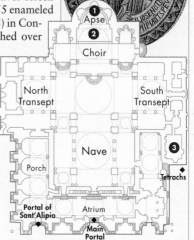

Opposite, detail of ceiling mosaics of the atrium

DID YOU KNOW?

The mosaics of the basilica are illuminated one hour a day, from 11:30 to 12:30. Visit then to see them at their most magnificent.

PLANNING YOUR VISIT

Be aware that guards at the basilica door turn away anyone with bare shoulders, midriff, or knees: no shorts, short skirts, or tank tops are allowed. Volunteers offer free guided tours in English from April to October—look for the calendar to the right of the center entrance, or get more information by calling the phone number below.

■TIP➜ To skip the line at the basilica entrance, reserve your arrival—at no extra cost—on the basilica Web site (choose "Reservations" under "Plan your visit"). You can also skip the line if you check a bag at the nearby bag-check facility (find it on the map at the basilica entrance)—just show your bag-check ticket to the entrance guard and he'll wave you in.

✉ Piazza San Marco

☎ 041/2413817 (10–noon weekdays) tour info

🌐 www.basilicasanmarco.it

🎟 Basilica free, Treasury €3, Sanctuary and Pala d'Oro €2, Museum €5

🕐 May–Sept., Mon.–Sat. 9:45–5, Sun. 2–5.

Above, Piazza San Marco.

Left, Crowds gather around the basilica.

You'll find yourself in an immense courtyard that holds some of the first evidence of Renaissance architecture in Venice, such as Antonio Rizzo's **Scala dei Giganti** (Stairway of the Giants), erected between 1483 and 1491, directly ahead, guarded by Sansovino's huge statues of Mars and Neptune, added in 1567. Though ordinary mortals must use the central interior staircase, its upper flight is the lavishly gilded **Scala d'Oro** (Golden Staircase), also designed by Sansovino in 1555. The palace's sumptuous chambers have walls and ceilings covered with works by Venice's greatest artists. Visit the **Anticollegio,** a waiting room outside the Collegio's chamber, where you can see the *Rape of Europa* by Veronese and Tintoretto's *Bacchus and Ariadne Crowned by Venus.* Veronese also painted the ceiling of the adjacent **Sala del Collegio.** The ceiling of the **Sala del Senato** (Senate Chamber), featuring *The Triumph of Venice* by Tintoretto, is magnificent, but it's dwarfed by his masterpiece *Paradise* in the **Sala del Maggiore Consiglio** (Great Council Hall). A vast work commissioned for a vast hall, this dark, dynamic piece is the world's largest oil painting (23 by 75 feet). The room's carved gilt ceiling is breathtaking, especially with Veronese's majestic *Apotheosis of Venice* filling one of the center panels. Around the upper walls, study the portraits of the first 76 doges, and you'll notice one picture is missing near the left corner of the wall opposite *Paradise.* A black painted curtain, rather than a portrait, marks Doge Marin Falier's fall from grace; he was beheaded for treason in 1355, which the Latin inscription bluntly explains.

A narrow canal separates the palace's east side from the cramped cell blocks of the **Prigioni Nuove** (New Prisons). High above the water arches the enclosed marble **Ponte dei Sospiri** (Bridge of Sighs), which earned its name in the 19th century, from Lord Byron's *Childe Harold's Pilgrimage.* ■TIP➔ Reserve your spot for the palazzo's popular Secret Itineraries tour well in advance: You'll visit the doge's private apartments, through hidden passageways to the interrogation (torture) chambers, and into the rooftop *piombi* (lead) prison, named for its lead roofing. Venetian-born writer and libertine Giacomo Casanova (1725–98), along with an accomplice, managed to escape from the piombi in 1756; they were the only men ever to do so. ✉ *Piazzetta San Marco, Piazza San Marco* ☎ *041/2715911, 041/5209070 Secret Itineraries tour* ⊕ *www.museicivicveneziani.it* ✉ *Museums of San Marco Pass €16, includes entry also to the Museo Correr, the Archeological Museum, and the monumental rooms of the Biblioteca Marciana. Free with MUVE pass. "Secret Itineraries" tour: €20* ☉ *Apr.–Oct., daily 8:30–7; Nov.–Mar., daily 8:30–5:30. Last entry 1 hr before closing. "Secret Itineraries" tour in English 9:55, 10:45, 11:35* Ⓜ *Vaporetto: San Zaccaria, Vallaresso.*

Fodor'sChoice **Piazza San Marco.** One of the world's most beautiful squares, Piazza San
★ Marco (Saint Mark's Square) is the spiritual and artistic heart of Venice, a vast open space bordered by an orderly procession of arcades marching toward the fairy-tale cupolas and marble lacework of the Basilica di San Marco. From midmorning on, it is generally packed with tourists. (If Venetians have business in the piazza, they try to conduct it in the early morning, before the crowds swell.) At night the piazza can be

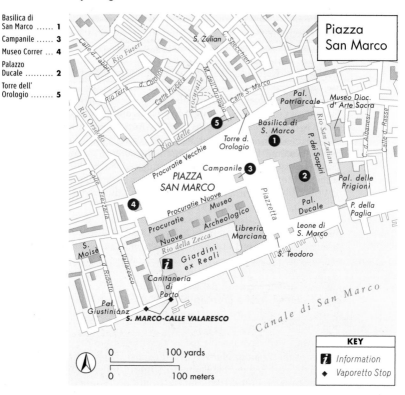

magical, especially in winter, when mists swirl around the lampposts and the campanile.

If you face the basilica from in front of the Correr Museum, you'll notice that rather than being a strict rectangle, the square is wider at the basilica end, creating the illusion that it's even larger than it is. On your left, the long, arcaded building is the **Procuratie Vecchie**, renovated to their present form in 1514 as offices and residences for the powerful procurators (magistrates).

On your right is the **Procuratie Nuove**, built half a century later in a more imposing, classical style. It was originally planned by Venice's great Renaissance architect Jacopo Sansovino (1486–1570), to carry on the look of his Libreria Sansoviniana (Sansovinian Library), but he died before construction on the Nuove had begun. Vincenzo Scamozzi (circa 1552–1616), a pupil of Andrea Palladio (1508–80), completed the design and construction. Still later, the Procuratie Nuove was modified by architect Baldassare Longhena (1598–1682), one of Venice's baroque masters.

When Napoléon (1769–1821) entered Venice with his troops in 1797, he expressed his admiration for the piazza and promptly gave orders to alter it. His architects demolished a church with a Sansovino facade in order to build the Ala Napoleonica (Napoleonic Wing), or Fabbrica

Nuova (New Building), which linked the two 16th-century *procuratie* (procurators' offices) and effectively enclosed the piazza.

Piazzetta San Marco is the "little square" leading from Piazza San Marco to the waters of Bacino San Marco (Saint Mark's Basin); its *molo* (landing) once served as the grand entrance to the Republic. Two imposing columns tower above the waterfront. One is topped by the winged lion, the traditional emblem of Saint Mark that became the symbol of Venice itself; the other supports Saint Theodore, the city's first patron, along with his dragon. (A third column fell off its barge and ended up in the bacino before it could be placed alongside the others.) Though the columns are a glorious vision today, the Republic traditionally executed convicts between them. Even today, some superstitious Venetians avoid walking between the two. ⊠ *San Marco*.

QUICK
BITES

Caffè Florian. Venice's oldest café, continuously in business since 1720, has served coffee to the likes of Wagner, Casanova, Charles Dickens, and Marcel Proust. Counter seating is less expensive than taking a table, but is, of course, less romantic and you don't have the view of the piazza. This is where many upscale Venetians go when they want to meet a friend for a coffee or spritz around Piazza San Marco. ⊠ *Piazza San Marco 56, San Marco* ☎ *041/5205641* ⊕ *www.caffeflorian.com.*

Caffè Quadri. In the Procuratie Vecchie, Caffè Quadri exudes almost as much history as Florian across the way, and is similarly pricey. It was shunned by 19th-century Venetians when the occupying Austrians made it their gathering place. It's closed on Monday. ⊠ *Piazza San Marco 121, San Marco* ☎ *041/5222105* ⊕ *www.caffequadri.it.*

Fodor's Choice
★

Ponte di Rialto (*Rialto Bridge*). The competition to design a stone bridge across the Grand Canal attracted the best architects of the late 16th century, including Michelangelo, Palladio, and Sansovino, but the job went to the less-famous (but appropriately named) Antonio da Ponte (1512–95). His pragmatic design, completed in 1591, featured shop space and was high enough for galleys to pass beneath. Unlike the classical plans proposed by his more famous contemporaries, Da Ponte's bridge essentially followed the design of its wooden predecessor; it kept decoration and cost to a minimum at a time when the Republic's coffers were low due to continual wars against the Turks and the competition brought about by the Spanish and Portuguese opening of oceanic trade routes. Along the railing you'll enjoy one of the city's most famous views: the Grand Canal vibrant with boat traffic. ⊠ *San Marco* Ⓜ *Vaporetto: Rialto.*

WORTH NOTING

Biblioteca Marciana (*Marciana Library*). There's a wondrous collection of centuries-old books and illuminated manuscripts at this library, located across the piazzetta from Palazzo Ducale in two buildings designed by Renaissance architect Sansovino, **Libreria Sansoviniana** and the adjacent **Zecca** (**mint**). The complex was begun in 1537, and the Zecca was finished in 1545. Facing the Bacino, the Zecca forms, along with

The iconic Ponte di Rialto spans the Grand Canal between the sestieri of San Polo and San Marco.

the Palazzo Ducale, across the piazzetta, Venice's front door. It differs from its earlier Gothic pendent not only in style, but also in effect. The Palazzo Ducale, built during a period of Venetian ascendance and self-confident power, is light and decidedly unmenacing. The Zecca, built in a time when the Republic had received some serious defeats and was economically strapped, is purposefully heavy and stresses a fictitious connection with the classical world. The library is, again, much more graceful and was finished according to his design only after Sanso-vino's death. Palladio was so impressed by the Biblioteca that he called it "beyond envy." The books can only be viewed by written request and are primarily the domain of scholars. But the **Gilded Hall** in the Sansoviniana is worth visiting for the works of Veronese, Tintoretto, and Titian that decorate its walls. You reach the Gilded Hall, which often hosts special exhibits relating to Venetian history, through Museo Correr. ⊠ *Piazza San Marco, enter through Museo Correr, Piazza San Marco* ☎ *041/2405211* ⊕ *www.marciana.venezia.sbn.it* 💰 *Museums of San Marco Pass €16, includes entry also to the Museo Correr, the Archeological Museum, and the Palazzo Ducale. Free with MUVE pass.* ⊙ *Apr.–Oct., daily 9–7; Nov.–Mar., daily 9–6. Last tickets sold 1 hr before closing* Ⓜ *Vaporetto: Vallaresso, San Zaccaria.*

Campanile. Construction of Venice's famous brick bell tower (325 feet tall, plus the angel) began in the 9th century, and took on its present form in 1514. During the 15th century, the tower was used as a place of punishment: immoral clerics were suspended in wooden cages from the tower, some forced to subsist on bread and water for as long as a year; others were left to starve. In 1902, the tower unexpectedly collapsed, taking with it Jacopo Sansovino's 16th-century marble loggia at its base. The largest original bell, called the *marangona*, survived. The crushed loggia was promptly reconstructed, and the new tower, rebuilt to the old plan, reopened in 1912. Today, on a clear day the stunning view includes the Lido, the lagoon, and the mainland as far as the Alps, but, strangely enough, none of the myriad canals that snake through the city. Currently, the Campanile is undergoing foundation restoration due to deterioration caused by flooding (*acqua alta*); however, this hasn't affected the visiting hours. ⊠ *Piazza San Marco* ☎ *041/5224064* 💳 *€8* ☉ *Easter–June, Oct., and Nov., daily 9–7; July–Sept., daily 9–9; Nov.–Easter, daily 9–3:45. Last entry 1 hr before closing* Ⓜ *Vaporetto: Vallaresso, San Zaccaria.*

Campo Santo Stefano. In Venice's most prestigious residential neighborhood, you'll find one of the city's busiest crossroads just over the Accademia Bridge; it's hard to believe this square once hosted bullfights, with bulls or oxen tied to a stake and baited by dogs. For centuries the *campo* was all grass except for a stone avenue called the *liston*. It was so popular for strolling that in Venetian dialect *"andare al liston"* still means "to go for a walk." A sunny meeting spot popular with Venetians and visitors alike, the campo also hosts outdoor fairs during Christmas and Carnevale seasons. Check out the 14th-century **Chiesa di Santo Stefano.** The pride of the church is its very fine Gothic portal, created in 1442 by Bartomomeo Bon. Inside, you'll see works by Tintoretto. ⊠ *Campo Santo Stefano, San Marco* ☎ *041/2750462 Chorus Foundation* ⊕ *www.chorusvenezia.org* 💳 *Church of Santo Stefano €3, free with Chorus Pass* ☉ *Church of Santo Stefano: Mon.–Sat. 10–5* Ⓜ *Vaporetto: Accademia.*

Galleria Ravagnan. The exclusive dealer since 1967 of some of the most famous living artists on the Italian scene shows work by Venetian surrealist Ludovico de Luigi, metaphysical painter Andrea Vizzini, and others. You also find glass sculptures by Primo Formenti and collages by Piero Principi. ⊠ *Procuratie Nuove, Piazza San Marco 50/A* ☎ *041/5203021* ⊕ *www.ravagnangallery.com* Ⓜ *Vaporetto: San Marco.*

Holly Snapp Gallery. The focus is on the works by the eclectic English-born artist Geoffrey Humphries, including paintings, drawings, and etchings ranging from landscapes to portraits; he also produces watercolors of Venetian vistas. ⊠ *Calle delle Botteghe, San Marco 3133* ☎ *041/2960824* ⊕ *www.hollysnappgallery.it* Ⓜ *Vaporetto: San Samuele or Sant'Angelo.*

Museo Archeologico. Venice is the only major Italian city without an ancient past, yet it hosts a collection of ancient art second in Italy only to those in Rome and Naples. This museum housing this collection was first established in 1596, when the heirs of Cardinal Domenico Grimani, a noted humanist, who had left his collection of original Greek (5th–1st centuries BC) and Roman marbles to the Republic, inaugurated the Public Statuary in Sansovino's then recently completed library in Piazza San Marco. You can see part of the collection, displayed just as Grimani, or at least his immediate heirs, had conceived it, in the vestibule of the Libreria Sansoviniana, which the museum shares with the Biblioteca Marciana. Highlights in the rest of the museum include the statue of Kore (420 BC), an Attic original known as Abbondanza Grimani; the 1st-century BC *Ara Grimani,* an elaborate Hellenistic altar stone with a bacchanalian scene; and a tiny but refined 1st-century BC crystal woman's head, which some say depicts Cleopatra. The very beautiful original venue of the collection, the family palazzo built and designed by Domenico Grimani's nephew, Giovanni, near Campo Santa Maria Formosa, is open to the public (call ☎ *041/5200345*). Even though it no longer contains the collection, it is still well worth a visit. ✉ *Piazza San Marco, enter through Museo Correr, Piazza San Marco* ☎ *041/5225978* ⊕ *www.polomuseale.venezia.beniculturali.it* ✉ *Museums of San Marco Pass €16, includes entry also to the Museo Correr, the Bliblioteca Marciana, and the Palazzo Ducale. Free with MUVE pass. Contact the museum for information about free guided tours in English* ⊗ *Apr.–Oct., daily 9–7; Nov.–Mar., daily 9–5; last tickets sold 1 hr before closing* Ⓜ *Vaporetto: Vallaresso, San Zaccaria.*

Fodor'sChoice
★

Museo Correr. This museum of Venetian art and history contains an important sculpture collection by Antonio Canova and important paintings by Giovanni Bellini, Vittore Carpaccio (Carpaccio's famous painting of the Venetian courtesans is here), and other major local painters. It's the main repository of Venetian drawings and prints, which, unfortunately, can be seen only by special arrangement. It also houses curiosities such as the absurdly high-sole shoes worn by 16th-century Venetian ladies (who walked with the aid of a servant). The city's proud naval history is evoked in several rooms through highly descriptive paintings and numerous maritime objects, including ships' cannons and some surprisingly large iron mast-top navigation lights. The museum also has a room devoted entirely to antique games. The Correr exhibition rooms lead directly into the **Museo Archeologico,** which houses the Grimani collection—an important 16th- and 17th-century collection of Greek and Roman art—and the **Stanza del Sansovino,** the only part of the **Biblioteca Nazionale Marciana** open to visitors. ✉ *Piazza San Marco, Ala Napoleonica (opposite the basilica), Piazza San Marco* ☎ *041/2405211* ⊕ *www.museiciviciveneziani.it* ✉ *Museums of San Marco Pass €16, includes entry also to the Museo Archeologico, the Bliblioteca Marciana, and the Palazzo Ducale. Free with MUVE pass.* ⊗ *Apr.–Oct., daily 10–7; Nov.–Mar., daily 10–5. Last entry 1 hr before closing* Ⓜ *Vaporetto: Vallaresso, San Zaccaria.*

NEED A BREAK?

Harry's Bar. If you'd like to attend happy hour with the ghosts of Ernest Hemingway, Aristotle Onassis, and Orson Welles, head to Harry's Bar. Despite astronomical prices, undistinguished 1930s–1950s decor, and some rather brash foreign clientele, Harry's is nevertheless a Venetian institution, and is still patronized by those Venetians who want to see and be seen. Many still remember proprietor Arrigo Cipriani's courageous stand—in contrast to the acquiescence and even profiteering of many Venetian hoteliers and bar owners—during the Nazi occupaton; Jewish patrons were still welcome at Harry's. Although you'll have to use your imagination to conjure up images of the bar's former glory, Harry's still boasts Venice's driest martinis, and makes a Bellini according the original recipe (invented at Harry's). The food, while outrageously expensive and conventional, is nevertheless quite good. ✉ *San Marco 3123* ☎ *041/5285777* ⊕ *www. harrysbarvenezia.com.*

Palazzo Contarini del Bovolo. Easy to miss despite its vicinity to Piazza San Marco, this Renaissance-Gothic palace is accessible only through a narrow backstreet that connects Campo Manin with Calle dei Fuseri. Built around 1500 for the renowned Contarini family, it is indefinitely closed for repairs, but its striking six-floor spiral staircase (*bovolo* means "snail" in Venetian dialect), the most interesting aspect of the palazzo, can be seen from the street. ✉ *Corte del Bovolo, San Marco 4299* ☎ *041/924933* Ⓜ *Vaporetto: Rialto.*

Palazzo Grassi. Built between 1748 and 1772 by Giorgio Massari for a Bolognese family, this palace is one of the last of the great noble residences on the Grand Canal. Once owned by auto magnate Giovanni Agnelli, it was bought by French businessman François Pinaut in 2005 to showcase his highly important collection of modern and contemporary art (which has now grown so large that Pinaut rented the Punta della Dogana, at the entryway to the Grand Canal, for his newest acquisitions). Pinaut brought in Japanese architect Tadao Ando to remodel the Grassi's interior. Check online for a schedule of temporary art exhibitions. ✉ *Campo San Samuele, Campo San Samuele* ☎ *041/5231680* ⊕ *www.palazzograssi.it* 🎟 *€15, €20 includes the Punta della Dogana* 🕙 *Daily 10–7, closed Tues.* Ⓜ *Vaporetto: San Samuele.*

Torre dell'Orologio. This enameled clock, completed in 1499, was most likely designed by Venetian Renaissance architect Mauro Codussi. Twin giant figures (now called Moors because of their tarnished bronze bodies) would strike the hour, and three wise men with an angel would walk out and bow to the Virgin Mary on Epiphany (January 6) and during Ascension Week (40 days after Easter). An inscription on the tower reads "*Horas non numero nisi serenas*" ("I only count happy hours"). Originally, the clock tower had a much lighter, more graceful appearance, and was free standing. The four lateral bays were added in the early 16th century, while the upper stories and balustrades were completed in 1755. The clock itself was neglected until the 19th century, but now, after years of painstaking labor, the clockwork has been reassembled and is fully operational. ✉ *Piazza San Marco (north side of the Piazza at the Merceria), Piazza San Marco* ☎ *041/2405211* ⊕ *www. museiciviciveneziani.it* 🎟 *€12* 🕙 *Tours in English, Mon.–Wed. at 10 and 11; Thurs.–Sun. at 2 and 3. Visits must be booked in advance through the Museo Correr or online* Ⓜ *Vaporetto: Vallaresso, San Zaccaria.*

DORSODURO

The sestiere Dorsoduro (named for its "hard back" solid clay foundation) is across the Grand Canal to the south of San Marco. It is a place of meandering canals, the city's finest art museums, monumental churches filled with works by Titian, Veronese, and Tiepolo, and a promenade called the Zattere, where on sunny days you'll swear half the city is out for a *passeggiata,* or stroll. The eastern tip of the peninsula, the Punta della Dogana, is capped by the dome of Santa Maria della Salute and was once the city's customs point; the old customs house is now a museum of contemporary art. At the western end of the sestiere is the Stazione Marittima, where in summer cruise ships line the dock. Midway between these two points, just off the Zattere, is the Squero di San Trovaso, one of the three remaining workshops where gondolas have been built and repaired for centuries. It is not open to the public.

Dorsoduro is home to the Gallerie dell'Accademia, with an unparalleled collection of Venetian painting, and the gloriously restored Ca' Rezzonico, which houses the Museo del Settecento Veneziano. Another of its landmark sites, the Peggy Guggenheim Collection, has a fine selection of 20th-century art.

TIMING

You can easily spend a full day in the neighborhood. You'll want to spend at a couple of hours exploring the streets and squares, stepping into churches, and having a coffee or "spritz" with the students in Campo Santa Margherita or pausing for a coffee and gelato while taking in the water views along the Fondamenta delle Zattere. You will want, at very least, to devote at least a half an hour to admiring the Titians in the imposing and monumental Santa Maria della Salute, and another half hour for the wonderful Veroneses in the peaceful, serene church of San Sebastiano. The Gallerie dell'Accademia demands a few hours, but if time is short an audio guide can help you cover the highlights in about an hour. Ca' Rezzonico deserves at least an hour, as does the Peggy Guggenheim collection. Those interested in contemporary art should spend an hour at the François Pinault Foundation museum at the Punta della Dogana.

TOP ATTRACTIONS

Fodor'sChoice
★

Ca' Rezzonico. Designed by Baldassare Longhena in the 17th century, this gigantic palace was completed nearly 100 years later by Giorgio Massari and became the last home of English poet Robert Browning (1812–89). Stand on the bridge by the Grand Canal entrance to spot the plaque with Browning's poetic excerpt, "*Open my heart and you will see graved inside of it, Italy*" on the left side of the palace. The spectacular centerpiece is the eye-popping Grand Ballroom, which has hosted some of the grandest parties in the city's history, from its 18th-century heyday to the 1969 Bal Fantastica (a Save Venice charity event that attracted every notable of the day, from Elizabeth Taylor to Aristotle Onassis) to its balls recreated for Heath Ledger's 2005 *Casanova* film. Today the upper floors of the Ca' Rezzonico are home to the especially delightful **Museo del Settecento** (Museum of Venice in the 1700s). Its main floor successfully retains the appearance of a magnificent Venetian palazzo, decorated with period furniture and tapestries in gilded salons, as well as Tiepolo ceiling frescoes and oil paintings. Upper floors contain a fine collection of paintings by 18th-century Venetian artists, including the famous genre and Pucinella frescoes by Giabattista Tiepolo's son, Giandomenico, moved here from the Villa di Zianigo. There's even a restored apothecary, complete with powders and potions. ⊠ *Fondamenta Rezzonico, Dorsoduro 3136* ☎ *041/2410100* ⊕ *www.*

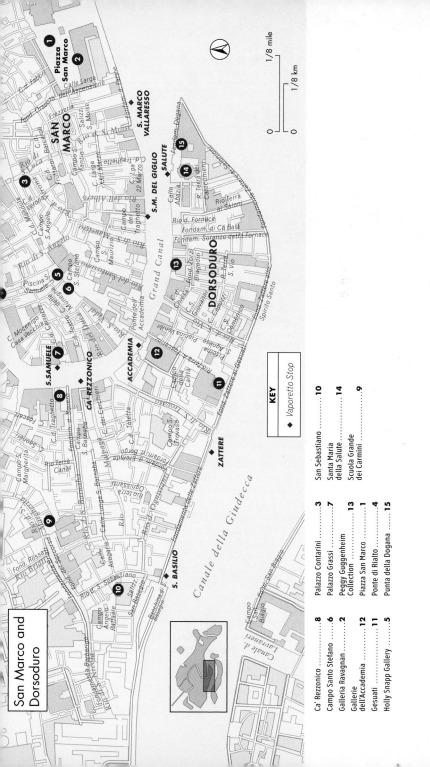

San Marco and Dorsoduro

KEY

◆ *Vaporetto Stop*

Gentile Bellini's *Miracle of the Cross at the Bridge of San Lorenzo* in the Gallerie dell'Accademia presents a view of Venice at the end of the 15th century.

museicivicivaneziani.it €8, *free with MUVE pass* ⊙ *Wed.–Mon. 10–6* Ⓜ *Vaporetto: Ca' Rezzonico.*

Fodor's Choice ★ **Gallerie dell'Accademia.** The greatest collection of Venetian paintings in the world hangs in these galleries founded by Napoléon back in 1807 on the site of a religious complex he had suppressed. They were carefully and subtly restructured between 1945 and 1959 by the renowned architect Carlo Scarpa.

Jacopo Bellini is considered the father of the Venetian Renaissance, and in Room 2 you can compare his *Madonna and Child with Saints* with such later works as *Madonna of the Orange Tree* by Cima da Conegliano (circa 1459–1517) and *Ten Thousand Martyrs of Mt. Ararat* by Vittore Carpaccio (circa 1455–1525). Jacopo's more accomplished son Giovanni (circa 1430–1516) attracts your eye not only with his subject matter but also with his rich color. Rooms 4 and 5 have a good selection of his madonnas. Room 5 contains *Tempest* by Giorgione (1477–1510), a revolutionary work that has intrigued viewers and critics for centuries. It is unified not only by physical design elements, as was usual, but more importantly by a mysterious, somewhat threatening atmosphere. In Room 10, *Feast in the House of Levi*, commissioned as a Last Supper, got Veronese summoned to the Inquisition over its depiction of dogs, jesters, and other extraneous figures. The artist responded with the famous retort, "*Noi pittori ci prendiamo le stesse libertà dei poeti e dei pazzi.*" ("We painters permit ourselves the same liberties that poets and madmen do.") He resolved the problem by simply changing the title, so that the painting represented a different, less solemn biblical feast.

VENICE THROUGH THE AGES

BEGINNINGS

Venice was founded in the 5th century when the Veneti, inhabitants of the mainland region roughly corresponding to today's lower Veneto, fled their homes to escape invading Germanic tribes. The unlikely city, built on islands in the lagoon and atop wooden posts driven into the marshes, would evolve into a maritime republic lasting over a thousand years.

Venice's early fortunes grew as a result of its active role in the Crusades, beginning in 1095 and culminating in the Venetian-led sacking of Constantinople in 1204. The defeat of rival Genoa in the Battle of Chioggia (1380) established Venice as the dominant sea power in Europe.

EARLY GOVERNMENT

As early as the 7th century, Venice was governed by a ruler, the doge, elected by the nobility of the city to a lifetime term. Venice was, therefore, from its beginnings a republic; the common people, however, had little political power, and the city was never a democracy in the modern sense. Beginning in the 12th century, the doge's power was increasingly subsumed by a growing number of councils, commissions, and magistrates. By the late 13th century power rested foremost with the Great Council, which at times numbered as many as 2,000 members.

A LONG DECLINE

Venice reached the height of its wealth and territorial expansion in the early 15th century, during which time its domain included all of the Veneto region and part of Lombardy, but the seeds of its decline were soon to be sown. By the beginning of the 16th century, Pope Julius II, threatened by Venice's mainland expansion, organized the League of Cambrai, allying most of the major powers in Western Europe against Venice, and defeated her in 1505, putting a stop to the Republic's mainland territorial designs. The Ottoman Empire blocked Venice's Mediterranean trade routes, and newly emerging sea powers such as Britain and the Netherlands ended Venice's monopoly by opening oceanic trading routes.

When Napoléon arrived in 1797, he took the city without a fight, gave it briefly to the Austrians, and then got it back in 1805. With his defeat Venice was ceded again to the Austrians at the Council of Vienna in 1815, and they ruled until 1848. In that tumultuous year throughout Europe, the Venetians rebelled, but the rebellion was defeated the following year. Venice remained in Austrian hands until the formation of the Italian Republic in 1866. The period of Austrian rule is still looked upon by most Venetians as an unmitigated misfortune, but although their rule was harsh and humiliating, the Austrians made several changes in Venice that allowed the city to enter the modern world. They built the causeway that connects Venice to the mainland, the now named Ponte della Libertà, and also connected Venice to the rest of Europe by rail. They filled in enough of the canals to make it possible to traverse Venice on foot; previously, parts of the city were accessible only by boat.

2

The dome of Santa Maria della Salute dramatically caps the eastern end of Dorsoduro.

Room 10 also houses several of Tintoretto's finest works, including three paintings from the life of Saint Mark. Titian's *Presentation of the Virgin* (Room 24) is the collection's only work originally created for the building in which it hangs. Don't miss rooms 20 and 21, with views of 15th- and 16th-century Venice by Carpaccio and Gentile Bellini (1429–1507), Giovanni's brother—you'll see how little the city has changed. (Note: The arrangement of the paintings described above may be changed during special exhibitions.)

■ TIP→ **Booking tickets in advance isn't essential but helps during busy seasons and costs only an additional €1.50.** Booking is necessary to see the **Quadreria,** where additional works cover every inch of a wide hallway. A free map notes art and artists, and the bookshop sells a more informative English-language booklet. In the main galleries a €4 audio guide saves reading but adds little to each room's excellent annotation. ⊠ *Dorsoduro 1050, Campo della Carità just off the Accademia Bridge* ☎ *041/5222247 Quadreria reservations, 041/5200345 reservations* ⊕ *www.gallerieaccademia.org* 🎟 *€14, includes admission to Palazzo Grimani and special exhibitions* ⊘ *Galleria: Tues.–Sun. 8:15–7:15, Mon. 8:15–2. Quadreria: Fri. 11–1, Sat. 11–noon* Ⓜ *Vaporetto: Accademia.*

QUICK BITES

Gelateria Nico. Enjoy the Zattere's most scrumptious treat—Nico's famous *gianduiotto,* a slab of chocolate-hazelnut ice cream floating on a cloud of whipped cream—and relax on the big, welcoming deck. Nico's is one of the few places still serving authentic homemade (*artiginale*) ice cream and has been seducing Venetians since 1935. ✉ *Dorsoduro 922* ☎ *041/5225293* ⊕ *www.gelaterianico.com.*

FAMILY **Peggy Guggenheim Collection.** Housed in the surprisingly small and charming Palazzo Venier dei Leoni, this choice selection of 20th-century painting and sculpture represents the taste and extraordinary style of the late heiress Peggy Guggenheim. Through wealth and social connections, Guggenheim (1898–1979) became an important art dealer and collector from the 1930s through the 1950s, and her personal collection here includes works by Picasso, Kandinsky, Pollock, Motherwell, and Ernst (at one time her husband). The museum serves beverages, snacks, and light meals in its refreshingly shady, artistically sophisticated garden. On Sunday at 3 pm the museum offers a free tour and art workshop for children 10 and under; conducted in Italian, anglophone interns are generally on hand to help those who don't *parla italiano.* ✉ *Fondamenta Venier dei Leoni, Dorsoduro 701* ☎ *041/2405411* ⊕ *www.guggenheim-venice.it* 🎫 *€14* ⊘ *Wed.–Mon. 10–6* Ⓜ *Vaporetto: Accademia.*

Fodor's Choice **Santa Maria della Salute.** The most iconic landmark of the Grand Canal,
★ La Salute (as this church is commonly called) is most unforgettably viewed from the Riva degli Schiavoni at sunset, or from the Accademia Bridge by moonlight. En route to becoming Venice's most important Baroque architect, 32-year-old Baldassare Longhena won a competition in 1631 to design a shrine honoring the Virgin Mary for saving Venice from a plague that in the space of two years (1629–30) killed 47,000 residents, or one-third of the city's population. It was not completed, however, until 1687—five years after Longhena's death. Outside, this ornate, white Istrian stone octagon is topped by a colossal cupola with snail-like ornamental buttresses—in truth, piers encircled by finely carved "ropes," an allusion to the sail-making industry of the city (or so say today's art historians). Inside, a white-and-gray color scheme is echoed by a polychrome marble floor and the six chapels. The Byzantine icon above the main altar has been venerated as the *Madonna della Salute* (Madonna of Health) since 1670, when Francesco Morosini brought it here from Crete. Above it is a sculpture showing Venice on her knees before the Madonna as she drives the wretched plague from the city.

Do not leave the church without visiting the **Sacrestia Maggiore,** which contains a dozen works by Titian, including his *San Marco Enthroned with Saints* altarpiece. You'll also see Tintoretto's *The Wedding at Cana.* For the Festa della Salute, held November 21, a votive bridge is constructed across the Grand Canal, and Venetians pilgrimage here to light candles in prayer for another year's health. ✉ *Punta della Dogana* ☎ *041/2411018* 🎫 *Church free, sacristy €2* ⊘ *Daily 9–noon and 3–5:30* Ⓜ *Vaporetto: Salute.*

QUICK BITES

Il Caffè. For more than a portable munch, bask in the sunshine at the popular Il Caffè, commonly called Bar Rosso for its bright red exterior. It dishes up the best *tramezzini* (snack sandwiches) in the campo, is open until midnight, and serves drinks and other light refreshments every day except Sunday. ✉ *Campo Santa Margherita, Dorsoduro 2963* ☎ *041/5287998.*

In warm weather, restaurants and cafés of Campo Santa Margherita spill out onto the square, providing numerous options for alfresco dining.

Pasticceria Tonolo. Venice's premier confectionary has been in operation since 1886. During Carnevale it's still one of the best places in town for *fritelle*, fried doughnuts (traditional raisin or cream-filled), and before Christmas and Easter, Venetians order their *focaccia*, the traditional raised cake eaten especially at holidays, from here well in advance. Closed Monday, and there's no seating any time. ⊠ *Calle Crosera, Dorsoduro 3764* ☎ *041/5237209.*

WORTH NOTING

Campo Santa Margherita. Lined with cafés and restaurants generally filled with students from the nearby university, Campo Santa Margherita also has produce vendors and benches where you can sit and take in the bustling local life of the campo. Also close to the Ca' Rezzonico and the Scuola dei Carmini, and only a 10-minute walk from the Gallerie dell'Accademia, the square is the center of Dorsoduro social life. It takes its name from the church to one side, closed since the early 19th century and now used as an auditorium. ⊠ *Campo Santa Margherita.*

Gesuati. When the Dominicans took over the church of Santa Maria della Visitazione from the suppressed order of Gesuati laymen in 1668, Giorgio Massari was commissioned to build this structure. It has an important Tiepolo illusionistic ceiling and several other works by Giambattista Tiepolo (1696–1770), Giambattista Piazzetta (1683–1754), and Sebastiano Ricci (1659–1734). ⊠ *Zattere* ☎ *041/2750462* ⊕ *www. chorusvenezia.org* ⊠ *€3, free with Chorus Pass* ⊙ *Mon.–Sat. 10–5* Ⓜ *Vaporetto: Zattere.*

Wading Through the Acqua Alta

There are two ways to get anywhere in Venice: walking and by water. Occasionally you walk *through* water, when falling barometers, southeasterly winds, and even a full moon may exacerbate normally higher fall and spring tides. The result is *acqua alta*—flooding in the lowest parts of town, especially Piazza San Marco. It generally occurs in late fall and, to a lesser extent, in spring, and lasts a few hours until the tide recedes.

Contending with *acqua alta*.

Venetians handle the high waters with aplomb, donning waders and erecting temporary walkways, but they're well aware of the damage caused by the flooding and the threat it poses to their city. The Moses Project, underwater gates that will close off the lagoon when high tides threaten, is still in progress and slated to go into operation in 2016. The extensive works threaten to alter the lagoon-scape,

and still represent a much-debated response to an emotionally charged problem. How to protect Venice from high tides—aggravated by the deep channels dug to accommodate oil tankers and cruise ships, as well as the lagoon-altering wave action caused by powerboats—is among the city's most contentious issues.

Fodor's Choice ★ **Punta della Dogana.** Funded by the billionaire who owns Christie's Auction House, the François Pinault Foundation had Japanese architect Tadao Ando redesign this fabled customs house—sitting at the *punta*, or very head, of the Grand Canal—and now home to a changing roster of eye-popping works from Pinault's collection of contemporary art. The streaming light, polished surfaces, and clean lines of Ando's design contrast beautifully with the brick, massive columns, and sturdy beams of the original Dogana. Even if you don't visit the museum, be sure to walk down to the *punta* (point) for a magnificent view of the Venetian basin. Check online for a schedule of temporary exhibitions. ⊠ *Punta della Dogana* ☎ *041/5231680* ⊕ *www.palazzograssi.it* ☜ *€15, €20 includes the Palazzo Grassi* ☉ *Wed.–Mon. 10–7. Last entry 1 hr before closing* Ⓜ *Vaporetto: Salute.*

Fodor's Choice ★ **San Sebastiano.** Paolo Veronese (1528–88), although still in his twenties, was already the official painter of the Republic when he began the oil panels and frescoes at San Sebastiano, his parish church, in 1555. For decades he continued to embellish the church with very beautiful illusionistic scenes. The cycles of panels in San Sebastiano are considered to be his supreme accomplishment. Veronese is buried beneath his bust near the organ. The church itself, remodeled by Antonio Scarpagnino and finished in 1548, offers a rare opportunity to see a monument in Venice where both the architecture and the pictorial decoration all date from the same period. Be sure to check out the portal of the ex-convent, now part of the University of Venice, to the left of the church; it was designed in 1976–78 by Carlo Scarpa, one of the most important Italian architects of the 20th century. ✉ *Campo San Sebastiano* ☎ *041/2750462* ⊕ *www.chorusvenezia.org* 🎫 *€3, free with Chorus Pass* ⊗ *Mon.–Sat. 10–5* Ⓜ *Vaporetto: San Basilio.*

Scuola Grande dei Carmini. When the order of Santa Maria del Carmelo commissioned Baldassare Longhena to finish the work on the Scuola Grande dei Carmini in the 1670s, their brotherhood of 75,000 members was the largest in Venice and one of the wealthiest. Little expense was spared in the decorating of stuccoed ceilings and carved ebony paneling, and the artwork was choice, even before 1739, when Tiepolo began painting the **Sala Capitolare.** In what might consider his best work, Tiepolo's nine great canvases vividly transform some rather conventional religious themes into dynamic displays of color and movement. ✉ *Campo dei Carmini, Dorsoduro 2617* ☎ *041/5289420* 🎫 *€5* ⊗ *Daily 11–4* Ⓜ *Vaporetto: Ca' Rezzonico.*

SAN POLO AND SANTA CROCE

Visitors generally explore San Polo and Santa Croce together, as there is little natural division between them; even Venetians are sometimes unaware of where one ends and the other begins.

SAN POLO

San Polo has two major sites, Santa Maria Gloriosa dei Frari and the Scuola Grande di San Rocco, as well as some worthwhile but lesser-known churches. Food shops abound in the area surrounding the western end of the Rialto Bridge, which connects San Polo with San Marco. You can shop for fruits and vegetables, and buy fish along with the Venetians at the Rialto Market at the San Polo end of the bridge. Visitors to Venice tend to forget that the city is not only a tourist center; it is also a university town: the Università Ca' Foscari is centered in San Polo and has more than 17,000 students. Its administrative center, Ca' Foscari, is located in San Polo on the Grand Canal.

TIMING

To do San Polo justice requires at least the better part of a morning. If you want to take part in the food shopping at the Rialto Market, come early to beat the crowds. It closes at 1 pm. San Polo's Santa Maria Gloriosa dei Frari contains some of the most beautiful and historically important paintings and sculpture in Venice; you'll want to spend an hour there. If you are a Tintoretto fan, an hour will barely suffice to see the two floors of floor-to-ceiling Tintorettos in the Scuola Grande di San Rocco. Also leave a few minutes to see the Scuola de San Giovanni Evangelista, the work of Pietro Lombardi, the most accomplished of Venice's Renaissance architects.

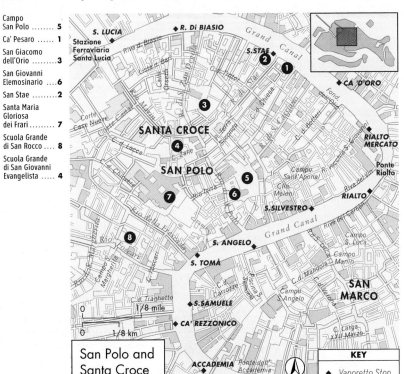

San Polo and
Santa Croce

TOP ATTRACTIONS

Fodor's Choice ★ **Santa Maria Gloriosa dei Frari.** Completed in 1442, this immense Gothic church of russet-color brick—known locally as *I Frari*—is famous worldwide for its array of spectacular Venetian paintings. Visit the sacristy first, to see Giovanni Bellini's 1488 triptych *Madonna and Child with Saints* in all its mellow luminosity, painted for precisely this spot. The Corner Chapel on the other side of the chancel is graced by Bartolomeo Vivarini's (1415–84) 1474 altarpiece *St. Mark Enthroned and Saints John the Baptist, Jerome, Peter, and Nicholas,* which is much more conservative, displaying attention to detail generally associated with late medieval painting. In the first south chapel of the chorus, there is a fine sculpture of Saint John the Baptist by Donatello, dated 1438 (perhaps created before the artist came to Venice), which displays a psychological intensity rare for early Renaissance sculpture. You can see the rapid development of Venetian Renaissance painting by contrasting Bellini with the heroic energy of Titian's *Assumption,* over the main altar, painted only 30 years later. Unveiled in 1518, it was the artist's first public commission and, after causing a bit of controversy, did much to establish his reputation. Upon viewing this painting at the far end of the nave you'll first think it has been specially spotlit: upclose, however, you'll discover this impression is due to the painter's unrivaled use of light and color.

2

Titian's beautiful *Madonna di Ca' Pesaro* is in the left aisle. The painting took seven years to complete (finished in 1526), and in it Titian disregarded the conventions of his time by moving the Virgin out of center and making the saints active participants. The composition, built on diagonals, anticipates structural principals of baroque painting in the following century. The Frari also holds a Sansovino sculpture of St. John the Baptist, and Longhena's impressive baroque tomb designed for Doge Giovanni Pesaro. ⊠ *Campo dei Frari, San Polo* ☏ *041/2728618, 041/2750462 Chorus Foundation* ⊕ *www.chorusvenezia.org* ☒ *€3, free with Chorus Pass* ☾ *Mon.–Sat. 9–6, Sun. 1–6* Ⓜ *Vaporetto: San Tomà.*

Fodor's Choice **Scuola Grande di San Rocco.** Saint Rocco's popularity stemmed from his
★ miraculous recovery from the plague and his care for fellow sufferers. Throughout the plague-filled Middle Ages, followers and donations abounded, and this elegant example of Venetian Renaissance architecture, built between 1517 and 1560 and including the work of at least four architects, built for the essentially secular charitable confraternity bearing the saint's name, was the result. Although San Rocco is bold and dramatic outside, its contents are even more stunning—a series of more than 60 paintings by Tintoretto. In 1564 Tintoretto edged out competition for a commission to decorate a ceiling by submitting not a sketch, but a finished work, which he moreover offered free of charge. *Moses Striking Water from the Rock, The Brazen Serpent,* and *The Fall of Manna* represent three afflictions—thirst, disease, and hunger—that San Rocco and later his brotherhood sought to relieve. ⊠ *Campo San Rocco, San Polo 3052* ☏ *041/5234864* ⊕ *www.scuolagrandesanrocco.it* ☒ *€8 (includes audio guide)* ☾ *Daily 9:30–5:30. Last entry ½ hr before closing* Ⓜ *Vaporetto: San Tomà.*

QUICK BITES

Caffè dei Frari. Just over the bridge in front of the Frari church is this old-fashioned place where you'll find a delightful assortment of sandwiches and snacks. Established in 1870, it's one of the last Venetian tearooms with its original decor. It's frequented more by residents and students than by tourists. Prices are a bit higher (€3.50 for a spritz) than in cafés in nearby Campo Santa Margherita, but the decor and the friendly "retro" atmosphere seem to make the added cost worthwhile. ⊠ *Fondamenta dei Frari, San Polo 2564, San Polo* ☏ *No phone* ☾ *Closed weekends.*

WORTH NOTING

Campo San Polo. Only Piazza San Marco is larger than this square, and the echo of children's voices bouncing off the surrounding palaces makes the space seem even bigger. Campo San Polo once hosted bull races, fairs, military parades, and packed markets, and now comes especially alive on summer nights, when it's home to the city's outdoor cinema. The **Chiesa di San Polo** has been restored so many times that little remains of the original 9th-century church, and sadly, 19th-century alterations were so costly that the friars sold off many great paintings to pay bills. Though Giambattista Tiepolo is represented here, his work is outdone by 16 paintings by his son Giandomenico (1727–1804), including the *Stations of the Cross* in the oratory to the left of the entrance. The younger Tiepolo also created a series of expressive and

Behind its redbrick facade, Santa Maria Gloriosa dei Frari holds some of the most brilliant artwork of any church in Venice.

theatrical renderings of the saints. Look for altarpieces by Tintoretto and Veronese that managed to escape auction. San Polo's bell tower remained unchanged through the centuries—don't miss the two lions playing with a disembodied human head and a serpent that guard it. ☒ *Campo San Polo* ☏ *041/2750462 Chorus Foundation* ⊕ *www.chorusvenezia.org* ▣ *€3, free with Chorus Pass* ☉ *Church: Mon.–Sat. 10–5* Ⓜ *Vaporetto: San Silvestro, San Tomà.*

Scuola Grande di San Giovanni Evangelista. This scuola was founded in the 13th century, but the actual building is the work of various Venetian Renaissance architects and dates from the 15th century. In the 1480s the architect Pietro Lombardo finished the school's most beautiful and important architectural feature, the outdoor atrium and gateway that separate the complex from the campo adjoining it. Shortly after, in 1498, the architect Mauro Codussi finished work on a double staircase connecting the upper and lower halls. It is illuminated by a mullioned window on the landing between the two flights of stairs, an architectural device much used by Codussi. Carpaccio and Gentile Bellini painted their cycle of the miracle of the holy cross, now in the Accademia museum, originally for the Scuola di San Giovanni. ☒ *Campiello della Scuola, San Polo 2454* ☏ *041/718234* ⊕ *www.scuolasangiovanni.it* ☉ *Atrium screen is visible from the street; scuola open to the public frequently, but erratically. Check the website for opening times and entrance fees* Ⓜ *Vaporetto: Ferrovia.*

Venice's Scuola Days

An institution you'll inevitably encounter from Venice's glory days is the *scuola*. These weren't schools, as the word today translates, but important fraternal institutions. The smaller ones (*scuole piccole*) were established by different social groups—enclaves of foreigners, tradesmen, followers of a particular saint, and parishioners. The *scuole grandi*, however, were open to all citizens and included people of different occupations and ethnicities. They formed a more democratic power base than the Venetian governmental Grand Council, which was limited to nobles.

For the most part secular, despite their devotional activities, the scuole concentrated on charitable work, either helping their own membership or assisting the city's neediest citizens. The tradesmen's and servants' scuole formed social-security nets for elderly and disabled members. Wealthier scuole assisted orphans or provided dowries so poor girls could marry. By 1500 there were more than 200 minor scuole in Venice, but only six scuole grandi, some of which contributed substantially to the arts. The Republic encouraged their existence— the scuole kept strict records of the names and professions of contributors to the brotherhood, which helped when it came time to collect taxes.

SANTA CROCE

Santa Croce's two important churches are San Stae on the Grand Canal and San Giovanni Elemosinario, adjacent to the Rialto Market. The quarter's most pleasing architectural assemblage is the Campo San Giacomo dell'Orio, one of Venice's most tranquil squares. Having a spritz or a coffee in the pretty campo is a good alternative to doing the same in one of the packed squares in San Marco or Dorsoduro. Museums in Ca' Pesaro on the Grand Canal fill out Venice's offering of modern art and present the only public collection of Asian art in the city.

TIMING
You will undoubtedly walk through parts of Santa Croce while going to see attractions in San Polo and Dorsoduro. The church of San Stae is well worth a 15- to 20-minute detour, and fans of modern art and/ or Japanese armor will want to spend an hour in the collections in Ca' Pesaro. Any visitor who wants to see the real Venice should plan on idling in the Campo San Giacomo dell'Orio.

WORTH NOTING
Ca' Pesaro. Baldassare Longhena's grand Baroque palace is the beautifully restored home of two impressive collections. The **Galleria Internazionale d'Arte Moderna** has works by 19th- and 20th-century artists such as Klimt, Kandinsky, Matisse, and Miró. It also has a collection of representative works from Venice's Biennale art show that amounts to a panorama of 20th-century art. The pride of the **Museo Orientale** is its collection of Japanese art, and especially armor and weapons, of the Edo period (1603–1868). It also has a small but striking collection of Chinese and Indonesian porcelains and musical instruments. ✉ *San*

Stae, Santa Croce 2076 ☎ *041/721127 Galleria, 041/5241173 Museo Orientale* ⊕ *www.museicivicivenezians.it* 🎫 *€8.50 includes both museums, free with MUVE pass* ⊙ *Open Apr.–Oct., daily 10–6; Nov.–Mar., daily 10–5. Closed Mon.* Ⓜ *Vaporetto: San Stae.*

San Giacomo dell'Orio. This lovely square was named after a laurel tree (*orio*), and today trees lend shade and character. Add benches and a fountain (with a drinking bowl for dogs), and the pleasant, oddly shaped campo becomes a welcoming place for friendly conversation and neighborhood kids at play. Legend has it the **Chiesa di San Giacomo dell'Orio** was founded in the 9th century on an island still populated by wolves. The current church dates from 1225; its short unmatched Byzantine columns survived renovation during the Renaissance, and the church never lost the feel of an ancient temple sheltering beneath its 14th-century ship's-keel roof. In the sanctuary, large marble crosses are surrounded by a group of small medieval Madonnas. The altarpiece is *Madonna with Child and Saints* (1546) by Lorenzo Lotto (1480–1556), and the sacristies contain 12 works by Palma il Giovane (circa 1544–1628). ✉ *Campo San Giacomo dell'Orio, Santa Croce* ☎ *041/2750462 Chorus Foundation* ⊕ *www.chorusvenezia.org* 🎫 *€3, free with Chorus Pass* ⊙ *Mon.–Sat. 10–5* Ⓜ *Vaporetto: San Stae.*

San Giovanni Elemosinario. Storefronts make up the facade, and the altars were built by market guilds—poulterers, messengers, and fodder merchants—at this church intimately bound to the Rialto Market. The original church was completely destroyed by a fire in 1514 and rebuilt in 1531 by Antonio Abbondi, who had also worked on the Scuola di San Rocco. During a recent restoration, workers stumbled upon a frescoed cupola by Pordenone (1484–1539) that had been painted over centuries earlier. Don't miss Titian's *St. John the Almsgiver* and Pordenone's *Sts. Catherine, Sebastian, and Roch*, which in 2002 were returned after 30 years by the Gallerie dell'Accademia. ✉ *Rialto Ruga Vecchia San Giovanni, Santa Croce* ☎ *041/2750462 Chorus Foundation* ⊕ *www.chorusvenezia.org* 🎫 *€3, free with Chorus Pass* ⊙ *Mon.–Sat. 10–5* Ⓜ *Vaporetto: San Silvestro, Rialto.*

San Stae. The church of San Stae—the Venetian name for San Eustacchio (Eustace)—was reconstructed in 1687 by Giovanni Grassi and given a new facade in 1707 by Domenico Rossi. Renowned Venetian painters and sculptors of the early 18th century decorated this church around 1717 with the legacy left by Doge Alvise Mocenigo II, who's buried in the center aisle. San Stae affords a good opportunity to see the early works of Tiepolo, Ricci, and Piazzetta, as well as those of the previous generation of Venetian painters. ✉ *Campo San Stae, Santa Croce* ☎ *041/2750462 Chorus Foundation* ⊕ *www.chorusvenezia.org* 🎫 *€3, free with Chorus Pass* ⊙ *Mon.–Sat. 9–5* Ⓜ *Vaporetto: San Stae.*

CANNAREGIO

Settled primarily in the 15th century, at a time when Renaissance ideas of town planning had some effect, Cannaregio differs from medieval Venice, where the shape of the islands usually defines the course of the

The main entryways to many Venetian homes on side canals are accessible only by water.

canals. The daylight reflected off the bright-green canals (cut through a vast bed of reeds; hence the name Cannaregio, which may mean "Reed Place") and the big sky visible from the *fondamente* (pedestrian walkways) make this a particularly luminous area of town. It's no surprise, perhaps, that Titian and Tintoretto had houses in the sestiere.

The Strada Nova (literally, "New Street," as it was opened in 1871) is Cannaregio's main thoroughfare and the longest street in Venice. Lined with fruit and vegetable stalls, quiet shops, gelaterias, and bakeries, it serves as a pedestrian passage from the train station to the Campo Sant' Apostoli, just a few steps from the Rialto. The Jewish Ghetto, with five historically and artistically important synagogues, is in this quarter, and the churches of Madonna dell'Orto and the Miracoli are among the most beautiful and interesting buildings in the city. Once you leave the Strada Nuova, you'll find the sestiere blessedly free of tourists.

TIMING

Cannaregio's canals are lined with fondamente, or pedestrian walkways, and you can stroll for hours along tranquil waters, taking in the lively residential scene and marveling at some rather impressive architecture. To see its major sites—the churches of San Alvise, Madonna dell'Orto, and the Miracoli, plus the Jewish Ghetto and the Ca' d'Oro— you will need the better part of a day.

TOP ATTRACTIONS

Fodor'sChoice ★ **Ca' d'Oro.** One of the postcard sights of Venice, this exquisite Venetian Gothic palace was once literally a "Golden House," when its marble traceries and ornaments were embellished with gold. It was created by Giovanni and Bartolomeo Bon between 1428 and 1430 for the patrician

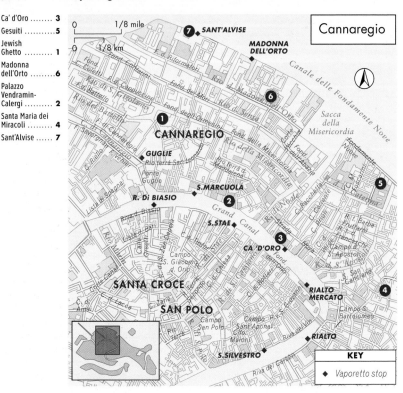

Marino Contarini, who had read about the Roman emperor Nero's golden house in Rome, and wished to imitate it as a present to his wife. Her family owned the land and the Byzantine *fondaco* (palace trading house) previously standing on it; you can still see the round Byzantine arches on the entry porch incorporated into the Gothic building. The last proprietor, Baron Giorgio Franchetti, left Ca' d'Oro to the city, after having had it carefully restored and furnished with antiquities, sculptures, and paintings that today make up the **Galleria Franchetti**. Besides Andrea Mantegna's *St. Sebastian* and other Venetian works, the Galleria Franchetti contains the type of fresco that once adorned the exteriors of Venetian buildings (commissioned by those who could not afford a marble facade). One such detached fresco displayed here was made by the young Titian for the facade of the Fondaco dei Tedeschi near the Rialto. ⊠ *Calle Ca' d'Oro, Cannaregio 3933* ☎ *041/5238790* ⊕ *www.cadoro.org* ⊠*€6, plus €1.50 to reserve; €8 when there is a special exhibition* ⊙ *Tues.–Sun. 8:15–7:15, Mon. 8:15–2. Closed Sun. in Jan.* Ⓜ *Vaporetto: Ca' d'Oro.*

Fodor's Choice
★
Jewish Ghetto. The neighborhood that gave the world the word *ghetto* is today a quiet neighborhood surrounding a large campo. It is home to Jewish institutions, two kosher restaurants, a rabbinical school, and five synagogues. Present-day Venetian Jews live all over the city, and

the contemporary Jewish life of the ghetto, with the exception of the Jewish museum and the synagogues, is an enterprise conducted almost exclusively by American Hassidic Jews of Eastern European descent and tradition.

Though Jews may have arrived earlier, the first synagogues weren't built and a cemetery (on the Lido) wasn't founded until the Askenazim, or Northern European Jews, came in the late 1300s. Dwindling coffers may have prompted the Republic to sell temporary visas to Jews, who were over the centuries alternately tolerated and expelled. The Rialto commercial district, as mentioned in Shakespeare's *The Merchant of Venice*, depended on Jewish moneylenders for trade, and to help cover ever-increasing war expenses.

In 1516 relentless local opposition forced the Senate to confine Jews to an island in Cannaregio, then on the outer reaches of the city, named for its *geto* (foundry). The term "ghetto" also may come from the Hebrew "ghet," meaning separation or divorce. Gates at the entrance were locked at night, and boats patrolled the surrounding canals. Jews were allowed only to lend money at low interest, operate pawnshops controlled by the government, trade in textiles, or practice medicine. Jewish doctors were highly respected and could leave the ghetto at any hour when on duty. Though ostracized, Jews were nonetheless safe in Venice, and in the 16th century the community grew considerably— primarily with refugees from the Inquisition, which persecuted Jews in southern and central Italy, Spain, and Portugal. The ghetto was allowed to expand twice, but it still had the city's densest population and consequently ended up with the city's tallest buildings. Although the gates were pulled down after Napoléon's 1797 arrival, the ghetto was reinstated during the Austrian occupation. The Jews realized full freedom only in 1866 with the founding of the Italian state. Many Jews fled Italy as a result of Mussolini's 1938 racial laws, so that on the eve of World War II, there were about 1,500 Jews left in the ghetto. Jews continued to flee, and the remaining 247 were deported by the Nazis; only eight returned.

The area has Europe's highest density of Renaissance-era synagogues, and visiting them is interesting not only culturally, but also aesthetically. Though each is marked by the tastes of its individual builders, Venetian influence is evident throughout. Women's galleries resemble those of theaters from the same era, and some synagogues were decorated by artists who were simultaneously active in local churches; Longhena, the architect of Santa Maria della Salute, renovated the Spanish synagogue in 1635. ✉ *Campo del Ghetto Nuovo* 🎫*€8.50 Synagogue tour, arranged through the Jewish Museum in the Campo del Ghetto Nuovo.*

Museo Ebraico. The small but well-arranged museum highlights centuries of Venetian Jewish culture with splendid silver Hanukkah lamps and Torahs, and handwritten, beautifully decorated wedding contracts in Hebrew. Hourly tours in Italian and English (on the half hour) of the ghetto and its five synagogues leave from the museum. ✉ *Campo del Ghetto Nuovo, Cannaregio 2902/B* ☎ *041/715359* 🌐 *www.museoebraico.it* 🎫 *Museum €3; guided tour and museum €8.50*

CLOSE UP

Let's Get Lost

Getting around Venice presents some unusual problems: the city's layout has few straight lines; house numbering seems nonsensical; and the six sestieri of San Marco, Cannaregio, Castello, Dorsoduro, Santa Croce, and San Polo all duplicate each other's street names. What's more, addresses in Venice are given by sestiere rather than street, making them of limited help in getting around. Venetians commonly give directions by pinpointing a major landmark, such as a church, and telling you where to go from there.

The numerous vaporetto lines can be bewildering, too, and often the only option for getting where you want to go is to walk. Yellow signs, posted on many busy corners, point toward the major landmarks—San Marco, Rialto, Accademia, and so forth—but don't count on finding such markers once you're deep into residential neighborhoods. Even buying a good map at

a newsstand—the kind showing all street names and vaporetto routes—won't necessarily keep you from getting lost. To make matters worse, map apps on smart phones, for some reason, give frequently erroneous results for Venice.

Fortunately, as long as you maintain your patience, getting lost in Venice can be a pleasure. For one thing, being lost is a sign that you've escaped the tourist throngs. And although you might not find the Titian masterpiece you'd set out to see, you could wind up coming across an ageless *bacaro* (a traditional wine bar) or a quirky shop that turns out to be the highlight of your afternoon. Opportunities for such serendipity abound. Keep in mind that the city is self-contained: sooner or later, perhaps with the help of a patient native, you can rest assured you'll regain your bearings.

☉ *June–Sept., Sun.–Fri. 10–7; Oct.–May, Sun.–Fri. 10–6. Tours hourly starting at 10:30* Ⓜ *Vaporetto: San Marcuola, Guglie* ☉ *Synagogue tours (in English or Italian): June–Sept., Sun.–Fri., hourly 10:30–6:30; Oct.–May, Sun.–Fri., hourly 10:30–5:30.*

Fodor'sChoice ★ **Madonna dell'Orto.** Though built toward the middle of the 14th century, this church takes its character from its beautiful late-Gothic facade, added between 1460 and 1464; it's one of the most beautiful Gothic churches in Venice. Tintoretto lived nearby, and this, his parish church, contains some of his most powerful work. Lining the chancel are two huge (45 feet by 20 feet) canvases, *Adoration of the Golden Calf* and *Last Judgment.* In glowing contrast to this awesome spectacle is Tintoretto's *Presentation of the Virgin at the Temple* and the simple chapel where he and his children, Marietta and Domenico, are buried. Paintings by Domenico, Cima da Conegliano, Palma il Giovane, Palma il Vecchio, and Titian also hang in the church. A chapel displays a photographic reproduction of a precious *Madonna with Child* by Giovanni Bellini. The original was stolen one night in 1993. ■TIP→ **Don't miss the beautifully austere, late-Gothic cloister (1460), which you enter through the small door to the right of the church; it is frequently used for exhibitions but may be open at other times as well.** ⊠ *Campo della*

Madonna dell'Orto, Cannaregio ☎ *041/2750462 Chorus Foundation* ⊕ *www.chorusvenezia.org* ✉ *€3, free with Chorus Pass* ⊙ *Mon.–Sat. 10–5* Ⓜ *Vaporetto: Orto.*

Fodor's Choice
★ **Santa Maria dei Miracoli.** Tiny yet harmoniously proportioned, this Renaissance gem, built between 1481 and 1489, is sheathed in marble and decorated inside with exquisite marble reliefs. Architect Pietro Lombardo (circa 1435–1515) miraculously compressed the building into its confined space, then created the illusion of greater size by varying the color of the exterior, adding extra pilasters on the building's canal side, and offsetting the arcade windows to make the arches appear deeper. The church was built to house *I Miracoli*, an image of the Virgin Mary by Niccolò di Pietro (1394-1440) that is said to have performed miracles—look for it on the high altar. ⊠ *Campo Santa Maria Nova, Cannaregio* ☎ *041/2750462 Chorus Foundation* ⊕ *www.chorusvenezia.org* ✉ *€3, free with Chorus Pass* ⊙ *Mon.–Sat. 10–5* Ⓜ *Vaporetto: Rialto.*

QUICK BITES

Un Mondo di Vino. Conveniently located near the Miracoli church, this is a friendly place to recharge with a *cicchetto* (snack) or two and some wine. It's closed on Monday. ⊠ *Salizzada San Cancian, Cannaregio 5984, Cannaregio* ☎ *041/5211093* ⊙ *Closed Mon.*

WORTH NOTING

Gesuiti. The interior walls of this early-18th-century church resemble brocade drapery, and only touching them will convince skeptics that rather than embroidered cloth, the green-and-white walls are inlaid marble. This tromp l'oeil decor is typical of the late baroque's fascination with optical illusion. Towards the end of his life, Titian tended to paint scenes of suffering and sorrow in a nocturnal ambience. A dramatic example of this is on display above the first altar to the left: Titian's daring *Martyrdom of St. Lawrence* (1578), taken from an earlier church that stood on this site. ⊠ *Campo dei Gesuiti, Cannaregio* ☎ *041/5286579* ⊙ *Apr.–Oct, Thurs.–Sat. 10–noon* Ⓜ *Vaporetto: Fondamente Nove.*

Palazzo Vendramin-Calergi. Hallowed as the place of Richard Wagner's death and today's Venice's most glamorous casino, this magnificent edifice found its fame centuries before: Venetian star architect Mauro Codussi (1440–1504) essentially invented Venetian Renaissance architecture with this design. Built for the Loredan family around 1500, Codussi's palace married the fortress-like design of the Florentine Alberti's Palazzo Ruccelai with the lightness and delicacy of Venetian Gothic. Note how Codussi beautifully exploits the flickering light of Venetian waterways to play across the building's facade and to pour in through the generous windows. Famously, the great German composer Richard Wagner ended his days in an apartment in the rebuilt garden wing of the palazzo. Today, the palazzo itself houses the Casino di Venezia, but even if you are not interested in gambling, you should pay a call to view some of the most sumptuous salons in Venice. ⊠ *Cannaregio 2040* ☎ *041/5297111, 338/4164174 Sala di Wagner tours* ⊕ *www.casinovenezia.it* ✉ *Casino €10, Sala di Wagner tour €5 suggested donation* ⊙ *Casino, Sun.–Thurs. 3:30 pm–2:30 am, Fri. and Sat. 3:30 pm–3* *am; slot machines open daily at 3 pm. Sala di Wagner tours Tues. and Sat. at 10:30, Thurs. at 2:30 (call by noon the day before to reserve)* Ⓜ *Vaporetto: San Marcuola.*

Sant'Alvise. For Tiepolo fans, trekking to the outer reaches of a pleasant residential section of Cannaregio to visit the unassuming Gothic church of Sant'Alvise is well worth the trouble. The little church holds Gianbattista Tiepolo's three panels of the Passion of Christ. He painted these panels, which display a new interest in dramatic intensity, and perhaps the influence of Tintoretto and Titian, for the church during his middle period, between 1737 and 1740. ⊠ *Campo Sant'Alvise, Campo Sant' Alvise* ☎ *041/2750462 Chorus Foundation* 🎟 *€3, free with Chorus Pass* ☽ *Mon.–Sat. 10–5, Sun. 1–5* Ⓜ *Vaporetto: Sant'Alvise.*

CASTELLO

Castello, Venice's largest sestiere, includes all of the land from east of Piazza San Marco to the city's easternmost tip. Its name probably comes from a fortress that once stood on one of the eastern islands.

Not every well-off Venetian family could manage to build a palazzo on the Grand Canal. Many that couldn't instead settled in western Castello, taking advantage of its proximity to the Rialto and San Marco. Most of the men who worked in the sprawling Arsinale, which was the largest industrial complex in medieval and Renaissance Europe, lived in the modest houses of eastern Castello, as have many fishermen over the centuries.

Castello isn't lacking in colorful history. In the early 15th century, large Greek and Dalmatian communities moved into the area along the Riva degli Schiavoni, where many of them sold dried fish and meat; the Confraternity of San Marco, based in what is now the hospital on Campo Santi Giovanni e Paolo, was patronized by Venetian high society in the 16th to 18th century; and nearby Campo Santa Maria Formosa served as a popular open-air theater for shows of various kinds (some including livestock among the cast members).

There is a lot to see here. Carpaccio's paintings at the Scuola di San Giorgio degli Schiavoni are worth a long look. San Francesco della Vigna, with a Palladio facade and Sansovino interior, certainly deserves a stop. The churches of Santi Giovanni e Paolo and San Zaccaria are major attractions, as is the Querini Stampalia museum.

TIMING

It will take at least half a day to do justice to the many worthwhile sights in Castello, since they are scattered throughout the largest sestiere in Venice, and much time will be enjoyably spent walking through colorful neighborhoods to reach them. Schedule at least a half hour to see the Carpaccios at the Scuola di San Giorgio, and an hour for the interior of Santi Giovanni e Paolo and the adjacent campo. The Querini Stampalia museum will take an hour, and the churches of San Zaccaria and San Francesco della Vigna at least a half hour each. You will not want to miss a glance at the beautiful Renaissance entry to the Arsenale. If the Biennale dell'Arte is running while you're in Venice, you'll want to visit

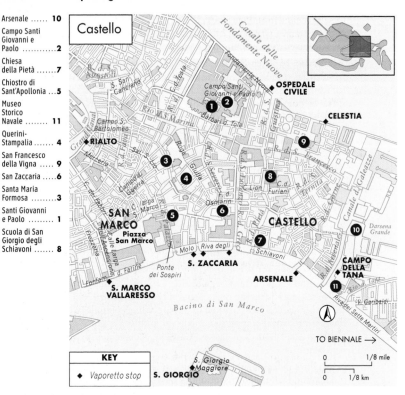

its main exhibition areas, which are in Castello; visiting the Biennale should take the better part of a day itself.

TOP ATTRACTIONS

Arsenale. Visible from the street, the impressive Renaissance gateway, the **Porta Magna** (1460), was the first classical structure to be built in Venice. It is guarded by four lions—war booty of Francesco Morosini, who took the Peloponnese from the Turks in 1687. The 10-foot-tall lion on the left stood sentinel more than 2,000 years ago near Athens, and experts say its mysterious inscription is runic "graffiti" left by Viking mercenaries hired to suppress 11th-century revolts in Piraeus. If you look at the winged lion above the doorway, you'll notice that the Gospel at his paws is open, but lacks the customary *Pax* inscription; praying for peace perhaps seemed inappropriate above a factory that manufactured weapons. The interior is not regularly open to the public, since it belongs to the Italian Navy, but it opens for the Biennale and for Venice's festival of traditional boats, **Mare Maggio** (⊕ *www.maremaggio. it*), held every May. If you're here during those times, don't miss the chance for a look inside; you can enter from the back via a northern-side walkway leading from the Ospedale vaporetto stop.

The Arsenale is said to have been founded in 1104 on twin islands. The immense facility that evolved—it was the largest industrial complex in Europe built prior to the Industrial Revolution—was given the old Venetian dialect name *arzanà,* borrowed from the Arabic *darsina'a,* meaning "workshop." At the height of its activity, in the early 16th century, it employed as many as 16,000 *arsenalotti,* workers who were among the most respected shipbuilders in the world. The Arsenale developed a type of pre–Industrial Revolution assembly line, which allowed it to build ships with astounding speed and efficiency. (This innovation existed even in Dante's time, and he immortalized these toiling workers armed with boiling tar in his *Inferno, Canto 21.*) The Arsenale's efficiency was confirmed time and again—whether building 100 ships in 60 days to battle the Turks in Cyprus (1597) or completing one perfectly armed warship, start to finish, while King Henry III of France attended a banquet. ⊠ *Campo dell'Arsenale* Ⓜ *Vaporetto: Arsenale.*

Campo Santi Giovanni e Paolo. This large, attractive square is the site of two city landmarks: the imposing namesake Gothic church and the Scuola Grande di San Marco, with one of the loveliest Renaissance facades in Italy. The scoula's exterior is the combined work of Venice's most prominent renaissance architects. The facade was begun by Pietro Lombardo in the 1480s, then in 1490 the work was given over to Mauro Codussi, who also added a grand stairway in the interior. In the 16th century, Sansovino designed the facade facing the Rio dei Mendicanti. The campo also contains the only equestrian monument ever erected by La Serenissima. The rider, Bartolomeo Colleoni, served Venice well as a *condottiere,* or mercenary commander—the Venetians preferred to pay others to fight for them on land. When he died in 1475, he left his fortune to the city on the condition that a statue be erected in his honor "in the piazza before San Marco." The Republic's shrewd administrators coveted Colleoni's ducats but had no intention of honoring anyone, no matter how valorous, with a statue in Piazza San Marco. So they collected the money, commissioned a statue by Florentine sculptor Andrea del Verrocchio (1435–88), and put it up before the Scuola Grande di San Marco. ⊠ *Campo Santi Giovanni e Paolo, Campo Santi Giovanni e Paolo.*

Fodor'sChoice
★

Santi Giovanni e Paolo. A venerated jewel, this gorgeous church looms over one of the most picturesque squares in Venice: the Campo Giovanni e Paolo, centered around the magnificent 15th-century equestrian statue of Bartolomeo Colleoni by the Florentine Andrea Verrocchio. Also note the beautiful facade of the Scuola Grande di San Marco (now the municipal hospital), begun by Pietro Lombardo and completed after the turn of the 16th century by Mauro Codussi. The massive Italian Gothic church itself is of the Dominican order and was consecrated in 1430. Bartolomeo Bon's portal, combining Gothic and classical elements, was added between 1458 and 1462, using columns salvaged from Torcello. The 15th-century stained-glass window near the side entrance is breathtaking for its brilliant colors and beautiful figures; it was made in Murano from drawings by Bartolomeo Vivarini and Gerolamo Mocetto (circa 1458–1531). The second official church of the Republic after San Marco, San Zanipolo is the Venetian equivalent of London's Westminster Abbey, with a great number of important people, including 25 doges, buried here. Artistic highlights include an early (1465) polyptych by Giovanni Bellini (right aisle, second altar) where the influence of Mantegna is still very evident, Alvise Vivarini's *Christ Carrying the Cross* (sacristy), and Lorenzo Lotto's *Charity of St. Antonino* (right transept). Don't miss the *Cappella del Rosario* (Rosary Chapel), off the left transept, built in the 16th century to commemorate the 1571 victory of Lepanto, in western Greece, when Venice led a combined European fleet to defeat the Turkish Navy. The chapel was devastated by a fire in 1867 and restored in the early years of the 20th century with works from other churches, among them the sumptuous Veronese ceiling paintings. However quick your visit, don't miss the Pietro Mocenigo tomb to the right of the main entrance, by Pietro Lombardo and his sons. ⊠ *Campo dei Santi Giovanni e Paolo* ☎ *041/5235913* 🖃 *€3* ⏲ *Mon.–Sat. 9:30–6, Sun. 1–6* Ⓜ *Vaporetto: Fondamente Nove, Rialto.*

QUICK
BITES

Didovich Pastry Shop. To satisfy your sweet tooth, head for Campo Santa Marina and the family-owned-and-operated shop. It's a local favorite, especially for Carnevale-time *fritelle* (fried doughnuts). There is limited seating inside, but in the warmer months you can sit outside. ⊠ *Campo Santa Marina, Castello 5909, Castello* ☎ *041/5230017.*

WORTH NOTING

Chiesa della Pietà. Unwanted babies were left on the steps of this religious institute, founded by a Franciscan friar in 1346. The girls were immediately taken in at the adjoining orphanage, which provided the children with a musical education. The quality of the performances here reached Continental fame—the in-house conductor was none other than Antonio Vivaldi (1675–1745), who wrote some of his best compositions here for the hospice. The present church was designed in the 18th century by Giorgio Massari, but the facade was completed only in the early 20th century. The main reason for a visit is to view the magnificent ceiling fresco by Gianbattista Tiepolo. In a room to the left of the entrance is a tiny collection of baroque instruments, including the violin played by Vivaldi. ⊠ *Riva degli Schiavoni, Castello 3701, Castello* ☎ *041/5222171* 🖃 *€3* ⏲ *Thurs.–Sun. 10–5* Ⓜ *Vaporetto: San Zaccaria.*

Chiostro di Sant'Apollonia. Behind the basilica and over a bridge, a short fondamenta leads right toward the unassuming entrance of the **Museo Diocesano** (upstairs), housed in a former Benedictine monastery. Its peacefully shady 12th-century cloister has been modified over the centuries, but it remains the only surviving example of a Romanesque cloister in Venice. The brick pavement is original, and the many inscriptions and fragments on display (some from the 9th century) are all that remain of the first Basilica di San Marco. The museum contains an array of sacred vestments, reliquaries, crucifixes, ex-votos, and paintings from various Venetian churches. ⊠ *Ponte della Canonica, Castello 4312* ☎ *041/5229166* 🖃 *Museum €4, cloister €1* ⏲ *Daily 10–6* Ⓜ *Vaporetto: Vallaresso, San Zaccaria.*

FAMILY **Museo Storico Navale** (*Museum of Naval History*). The boat collection here includes scale models such as the doges' ceremonial *Bucintoro,* and full-size boats such as Peggy Guggenheim's private gondola complete

The Campo Santi Giovanni e Paolo is bordered by its mammoth namesake church and the Scuola Grande di San Marco, which has Venice's finest Renaissance facade.

with romantic *felze* (cabin). There's a range of old galley and military pieces, and also a large collection of seashells. ⊠ *Campo San Biagio, Castello 2148* ☎ *041/2441399* 🖃 *€1.55* ⊘ *Mon.–Fri. 8:45–1:30, Sat. 8:45–1* Ⓜ *Vaporetto: Arsenale.*

Querini-Stampalia. A connoisseur's delight, this art collection at this late-16th-century palace includes Giovanni Bellini's *Presentation in the Temple* and Sebastiano Ricci's triptych *Dawn, Afternoon, and Evening.* Portraits of newlyweds Francesco Querini and Paola Priuli were left unfinished on the death of Giacomo Palma il Vecchio (1480–1528); note the groom's hand and the bride's dress. Original 18th-century furniture and stuccowork are a fitting background for Pietro Longhi's portraits. Nearly 70 works by Gabriele Bella (1730–99) capture scenes of Venetian street life; downstairs is a café. The entrance hall and the beautiful rear garden were designed by Venetian architect Carlo Scarpa during the 1950s. ⊠ *Campo Santa Maria Formosa, Castello 5252* ☎ *041/2711411* ⊕ *www.querinistampalia.it* 🖃 *€10* ⊘ *Tues.–Sun. 10–6* Ⓜ *Vaporetto: San Zaccaria.*

Fodor'sChoice ★ **San Francesco della Vigna.** Although this church contains some interesting and beautiful paintings and sculptures, it's the architecture that makes it worth the hike through a lively, middle-class, residential neighborhood. The Franciscan church was enlarged and rebuilt by Jacopo Sansovino in 1534, giving it the first Renaissance interior in Venice; its proportions are said to reflect the mystic significance of the numbers three and seven dictated by Renaissance neo-Platonic numerology. The soaring, but harmonious facade was added in 1562 by Palladio. The church represents, therefore, a unique combination of the work of the two great stars of

Veneto 16th-century architecture. As you enter, a late Giovanni Bellini *Madonna with Saints* is down some steps to the left, inside the Cappella Santa. In the Giustinian chapel to the left is Veronese's first work in Venice, an altarpiece depicting the Virgin and child with saints. In another, larger chapel, on the left, are bas-reliefs by Pietro and his son Tullio Lombardo. ⊠ *Campo di San Francesco della Vigna* 🕾 *041/5206102* 🕮 *Free* ⊙ *Daily 8–12:30 and 3–7* Ⓜ *Vaporetto: Celestia.*

San Zaccaria. Practically more a museum than a church, San Zaccaria bears a striking Renaissance facade, with central and upper portions representing some of Mauro Codussi's best work. Most of the church was 14th-century Gothic, with its facade completed in 1515, some years after Codussi's death in 1504, and it retains the proportions of the rest of the essentially Gothic structure. Inside is one of the great treasures of Venice, Giovanni Bellini's celebrated altarpiece, *La Sacra Conversazione*, easily recognizable in the left nave. Completed in 1505, when the artist was 75, it shows Bellini's ability to incorporate the esthetics of the High Renaissance into his work. It bears a closer resemblance to the contemporary works of Leonardo (it dates from approximately the same time as the *Mona Lisa*) than it does to much of Bellini's early work. The **Cappella di San Tarasio** displays frescoes by Tuscan Renaissance artists Andrea del Castagno (1423–57) and Francesco da Faenza (circa 1400–51). Castagno's frescoes (1442) are considered the earliest examples of Renaissance painting in Venice. The three outstanding Gothic polyptychs attributed to Antonio Vivarini earned it the nickname "Golden Chapel." ⊠ *Campo San Zaccaria, 4693 Castello* 🕾 *041/5221257* 🕮 *Church free, chapels and crypt €1* ⊙ *Mon.–Sat. 10– noon, Sun. 4–6* Ⓜ *Vaporetto: San Zaccaria.*

Santa Maria Formosa. Guided by his vision of a beautiful Madonna, 7th-century Saint Magno is said to have followed a small white cloud and built a church where it settled. Gracefully white, the marble building you see today dates from 1492, built by Mauro Codussi on an older foundation. Codussi's harmonious Renaissance design is best understood by visiting the interior; the Renaissance facade facing the canal was added later, in 1542, and the baroque facade facing the campo was added in 1604. Of interest are three fine paintings: *Our Lady of Mercy* by Bartolomeo Vivarini, *Santa Barbara* by Palma il Vecchio, and *Madonna with St. Domenic* by Gianbattista Tiepolo. The surrounding square bustles with sidewalk cafés and a produce market on weekday mornings. ⊠ *Campo Santa Maria Formosa, Castello 5267* 🕾 *041/2750462 Chorus Foundation* ⊕ *www.chorusvenezia.org* 🕮 *€3, free with Chorus Pass* ⊙ *Mon.–Sat. 10–5* Ⓜ *Vaporetto: Rialto.*

Scuola di San Giorgio degli Schiavoni. Founded in 1451 by the Dalmatian community, this small scuola was, and still is, a social and cultural center for migrants from what is now Croatia. It contains one of Italy's most beautiful rooms, harmoniously decorated between 1502 and 1507 by Vittore Carpaccio. While Carpaccio generally painted legendary and religious figures against backgrounds of contemporary Venetian architecture, here is perhaps one of the first instances of "Orientalism" in western painting. Note the turbans and exotic dress of those being baptized and converted, and even the imagined, arid Middle

Eastern or North African landscape in the background of several of the paintings. In this scuola for immigrants, Carpaccio focuses on "foreign" saints especially venerated in Dalmatia: Saints George, Tryphone, and Jerome. He combined keen empirical observation with fantasy, a sense of warm color, and late medieval realism. (Look for the

priests fleeing Saint Jerome's lion, or the body parts in the dragon's lair.) ■TIP➜ The opening hours are quite flexible. Since this is a "must see" site, check to confirm opening hours so that you won't be disappointed. ⊠ *Calle dei Furlani, Castello 3259/A* ☎ *041/5228828* ☜ *€5* ⊗ *Tues.– Sun. 9–12, 3–6* Ⓜ *Vaporetto: Arsenale, San Zaccaria.*

SAN GIORGIO MAGGIORE

Beckoning travelers across Saint Mark's Basin, sparkling white through the mist, is the island of San Giorgio Maggiore, separated by a small channel from the Giudecca. A tall brick bell toweron that distant bank perfectly complements the Campanile of San Marco. Beneath it looms the harmonious classical facade of one of Venice's greatest churches, San Giorgio Maggiore, the creation of Andrea Palladio.

You can reach San Giorgio Maggiore via vaporetto Line 2 from San Zaccaria.

TIMING

You will probably want to see San Giorgio together with the adjacent island of the Giudecca. Allow a half hour to see the church of San Giorgio, more if you want to catch the view from the top of the bell tower. Allot an extra hour if you wish to see one of the frequent excellent art exhibits in the space adjacent to the church and to glance into the serenely harmonious Palladian cloister.

TOP ATTRACTIONS

Fodor's Choice ★ **San Giorgio Maggiore.** There's been a church on this island since the 8th century, with a Benedictine monastery added in the 10th century. Today's refreshingly airy and simply decorated church of brick and white marble was begun in 1566 by Palladio and displays his architectural hallmarks of mathematical harmony and classical influence. *The Last Supper* and the *Gathering of Manna,* two of Tintoretto's later works, line the chancel. To the right of the entrance hangs *The Adoration of the Shepherds* by Jacopo Bassano (1517–92); his affection for his home in the foothills, Bassano del Grappa, is evident in the bucolic subjects and terra-firma colors he chooses. The monks are happy to show Carpaccio's *St. George and the Dragon,* hanging in a private room, if they have time. The campanile dates from 1791, the previous structures having collapsed twice.

Adjacent to the church is the complex now housing the **Cini Foundation**, containing a very beautiful cloister designed by Palladio in

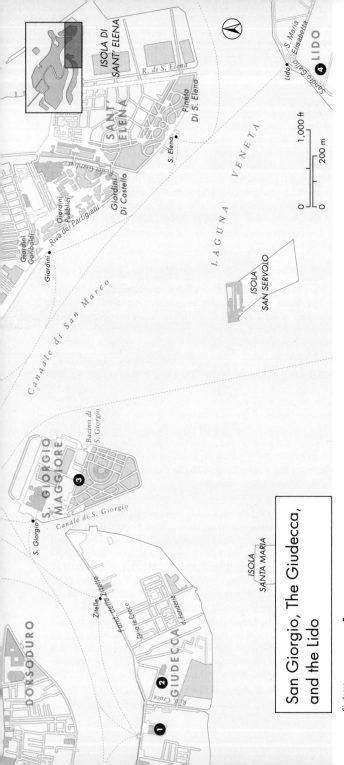

San Giorgio, The Giudecca, and the Lido

San Giorgio Maggiore, as seen from across the Bacino di San Marco.

1560, his refectory, and a library designed by Longhena. Guided tours
are given on weekends (10–4), reservations not required. ⊠ *Isola di
San Giorgio Maggiore* ☎ *041/5227827* ✉ *Church free, campanile
€3* ⊙ *Daily 9:30–12:30 and 2–6, Sun. 2–6 (hrs tend to be flexible)*
Ⓜ *Vaporetto: San Giorgio.*

THE GIUDECCA

The island of Giudecca's name is something of a mystery. It may come
from a possible 14th-century Jewish settlement, or because 9th-cen-
tury nobles condemned to *giudicato* (exile) were sent here. It became a
pleasure garden for wealthy Venetians during the Republic's long and
luxurious decline, but today it's populated by a combination of working-class Venetians and generally expatriate gentrifiers. The Giudecca
provides spectacular views of Venice. Thanks to several bridges, you
can walk the entire length of its promenade, relaxing at one of several
restaurants or just taking in the atmosphere.

You can reach the Giudecca via vaporetto Line 2 from San Zaccaria.
After San Giorgio Maggiore, the next stops on the line take you to
the Giudecca, crossing over to the Zattere in Venice proper between
the Giudecca stops. The island's past may be shrouded in mystery, but
today it's about as down to earth as you can get, and despite substantial
gentrification, it remains one of the city's few essentially working-class
neighborhoods. The view of Venice from the rooftop bar at the Hilton
hotel (Molino Stucky—it used to be a 19th-century flour mill) is perhaps
even more spectacular than the view from San Marco's Campanile.

TIMING

A visit here combines well with seeing San Giorgio Maggiore. The only major site on the Giudecca is Palladio's masterpiece, the church of the Santissimo Redentore, whose major attraction is its architecture itself; so, a visit should not take more than a half hour. Any additional time depends upon how long you want to spend soaking up the local atmosphere and enjoying the spectacular views of Venice proper that the island affords.

TOP ATTRACTIONS

Santissimo Redentore. After a plague in 1576 claimed some 50,000 people—nearly one-third of the city's population (including Titian)—Andrea Palladio was asked to design a commemorative church. Giudecca's Capucin friars offered land and their services, provided the building was in keeping with the simplicity of their hermitage. Consecrated in 1592, after Palladio's death, the Redentore (considered Palladio's supreme achievement in ecclesiastical design) is dominated by a dome and a pair of slim, almost minaret-like bell towers. Its deceptively simple, stately facade leads to a bright, airy interior. There aren't any paintings or sculptures of note, but the harmony and elegance of the interior makes a visit worthwhile.

For hundreds of years, on the third weekend in July the doge would make a pilgrimage here to give thanks to the Redeemer for ending the 16th-century plague. The event has become the Festa del Redentore, a favorite Venetian festival featuring boats, fireworks, and outdoor feasting. It's the one time of year you can walk to Giudecca—across a temporary pontoon bridge connecting Redentore with the Zattere. ⊠ *Fondamenta San Giacomo* ☎ *041/5231415, 041/2750462 Chorus Foundation* ⬚ *€3, free with Chorus Pass* ☾ *Mon.–Sat. 10–5* Ⓜ *Vaporetto: Redentore.*

THE LIDO

The Lido is Venice's barrier island, forming the southern border of the Venetian Lagoon and protecting Venice from the waters of the Adriatic. It forms the beach of Venice, and is home to a series of bathing establishments, both public and private, some luxurious and elegant, some quite simple and catering to Venetian families and their children. Buses run the length of the island. Aside from the Jewish cemetery, the only other attractions are the many villas dating from the early 1900s, which display some interesting modernist architecture, and several art nouveau hotels.

TIMING

Allow an hour and a half from the time you arrive at the Santa Maria Elisabetta vaporetto stop (the main stop on the Lido) to arrive at and see the Jewish cemetery and to return to the vaporetto stop. If you plan on swimming or sunbathing, you may well want to spend the better part of a warm, sunny day on the Lido.

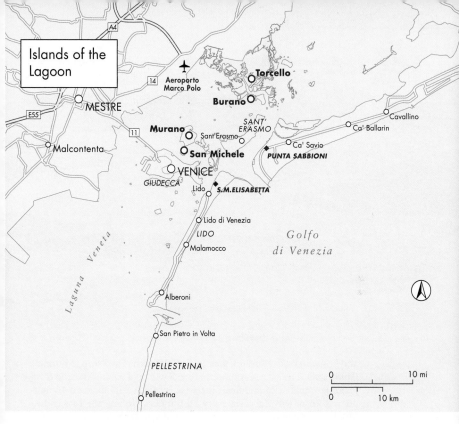

Islands of the
Lagoon

A4

E55

MESTRE

11

14 Aeroporto
Marco Polo

Torcello

Burano

Murano
Sant'Erasmo

SANT'
ERASMO

Cavallino

Ca' Ballarin

Malcontenta

San Michele

Ca' Savio

VENICE

PUNTA SABBIONI

GIUDECCA
Lido

S.M.ELISABETTA

Lido di Venezia

LIDO

Golfo
di Venezia

Malamocco

Laguna Veneta

Alberoni

San Pietro in Volta

PELLESTRINA

0   10 mi
0   10 km

Pellestrina

TOP ATTRACTIONS

Antico Cimitero Ebraico (*Ancient Jewish Cemetery*). You might complete
your circuit of Jewish Venice with a visit to the Antico Cimitero Ebraico,
full of fascinating old tombstones half hidden by ivy and grass. The earliest grave dates from 1389; the cemetery remained in use until the late
18th century. ⊠ *Via Cipro at San Nicolo, Lido* ☎ *041/715359 Jewish
Museum* 🎫 *€8.50* 🕙 *Tours, Apr.–Oct., Sun. at 2:30, by appointment
other days; call to reserve* Ⓜ *Vaporetto: Lido, San Nicolo.*

ISLANDS OF THE NORTHERN LAGOON

The perfect vacation from your Venetian vacation is an escape to
Murano, Burano, and sleepy Torcello, the islands of the northern
lagoon. If you have time to see only one of the islands, your choice
should depend upon your tastes: Torcello is atmospheric and romantic
and contains sights of major historical and artistic importance; Murano
is the place to go to shop for glass and to visit the glass museum; and
Burano is a fishing village awash with local color.

Line 12 goes from Fondamente Nove in Venice direct to Murano and
Burano every 30 minutes (Torcello is a five-minute ferry ride on Line 9
from there); the full trip takes 45 minutes each way. To get to Burano

The view of Burano and the surrounding wetlands from the campanile on Torcello.

and Torcello from Murano, pick up Line 12 at the Faro stop (Murano's lighthouse). The express vaporetto Line 3 will take you to Murano from Piazzale Roma in 25 minutes; otherwise, local Line 4.1 makes a 45-minute trip from San Zaccaria every 20 minutes, circling the east end of Venice, stopping at Fondamente Nove and San Michele island cemetery on the way. To see glassblowing, get off at Colonna; the Museo stop will put you near the Museo del Vetro.

TORCELLO

Torcello offers ancient mosaics, greenery, breathing space, and picnic opportunities. Some people call this tiny island the most magical place in Venice. Nearly deserted today (except for the posh Locanda Cipriani, an inn and restaurant), the island still casts a spell, perhaps because, in the 10th century, this was Venice. In their flight from barbarians 1,500 years ago, the first Venetians landed here, prospering even after many left to found the city of Venice. By the 10th century, Torcello had a population of 10,000 and was more powerful than Venice itself. From the 12th century on, the lagoon around the island began silting up, and a malarial swamp developed. As malaria took its toll, Torcello was gradually abandoned and its palaces and houses were dismantled, their stones used for building materials in Venice. All that's left now is the hauntingly beautiful cathedral (1008), containing exquisite Byzantine mosaics. The Virgin and the Apostles in the apse, as well as the spectacular *Last Judgment,* date from the 12th century, predating most of the mosaics in the Basilica di San Marco. There's also the graceful 11th- and 12th-century church of Santa Fosca.

TIMING

You can see Torcello's cathedral and the church of Santa Fosca easily in a half hour, but to avoid the hordes of tourists, come early in the day during the week or on a bright, mild day in winter. You will want to spend an hour or so appreciating the serene tranquility of the all-but-abandoned island and admiring the sights.

TOP ATTRACTIONS

Fodor's Choice
★

Santa Maria Assunta. The hallowed centerpiece of Torcello, Santa Maria Assunta was built in the 11th century, and the island's wealth at the time is evident in the church's high-quality mosaics. The mosaics show the gradually increasing cultural independence of Venice from Byzantium. The magnificent late-12th-century mosaic of the Last Judgment shows the transition from the stiffer Byzantine style on the left to the more-fluid Venetian style on the right. The virgin in the main apse dates possibly from about 1185, and is of a distinctly Byzantine type, with her right hand pointing to the Christ child held with her left arm. The depictions of the 12 apostles below her are possibly the oldest mosaics in the church and date from the early 12th century. The adjacent Santa Fosca church, built when the body of the saint arrived in 1011, is still used for religious services. ⊠ *Torcello, Isola di Torcello* ☎ *041/730119* 🖻 *Santa Maria Assunta €5, audio guide €1* ⊗ *Mar.–Oct., daily 10:30–6; Nov.–Feb., daily 10–5* Ⓜ *Vaporetto: Torcello.*

MURANO

In the 13th century the Republic, concerned about fire hazard and anxious to maintain control of its artisans' expertise, moved its glassworks to Murano, still renowned for its glass. As in Venice, bridges here link a number of small islands, which are dotted with houses that once were, and still largely are, workmen's cottages. Many of them line the Fondamenta dei Vetrai, the canalside walkway leading from the Colonna vaporetto landing. To avoid being pressured to buy glass, take the regular vaporetto from Piazzale Roma or the Fondamente Nuove to Murano instead of succumbing to the hawkers offering you a "free" trip to Murano. They will take you to inferior glassmakers and will abandon you if you don't buy. If you do buy, rest assured that your taxi driver's commission will be added into the price you pay. Once on the island "guides" herd new arrivals to factories, but you can avoid the hustle by just walking away.

Be aware that some of the glass sold as "Murano" is made in China or Eastern Europe. Even if a piece is, in fact, made on Murano, its origin does not ensure either its quality or status as a good investment. If you are concerned with these issues, stick to pieces by those glassmakers with established reputations, most of whom have pieces displayed in the Murano Glass Museum or quality boutiques in and around Piazza San Marco.

Burano is famous for its colorfully painted houses.

TIMING

Murano has a few interesting churches, which can be seen without much investment of time, but its main sight is the glass museum. You will need about an hour to do the museum justice. But since Murano's main attractions are the glass shops and factories, your time commitment will depend essentially on how much you enjoy shopping and the size of your wallet.

TOP ATTRACTIONS

Basilica dei Santi Maria e Donato. Just past the glass museum, this is among the first churches founded by the lagoon's original inhabitants. The elaborate mosaic pavement includes the date 1140; its ship's-keel roof and Veneto-Byzantine columns add to the semblance of an ancient temple. ⊠ *Fondamenta Giustinian, Murano* ☎ *041/739056* ☉ *Mon.–Sat. 8–6, Sun. 2–6* Ⓜ *Vaporetto: Museo.*

Chiesa di San Pietro Martire. You'll pass this church just before you reach Murano's Grand Canal (a little more than 800 feet from the landing). Reconstructed in 1511, it houses Giovanni Bellini's very beautiful and spectacular *Madonna and Child with Doge Augostino Barbarigo* and Veronese's *St. Jerome.* ⊠ *Fondamenta dei Vetrai, Murano* ☎ *041/739704* ☉ *Weekdays 9–noon and 3–6, Sun. 3–6* Ⓜ *Vaporetto: Colonna, Faro.*

Museo del Vetro (*Glass Museum*). Although the collection leaves out some important periods, glassmakers, and styles, it is still the best way to get an overview of Venetian glassmaking through the ages. You can see an exhibition on the history of glass, along with a chance to review authentic Venetian styles, patterns, and works by some famous glassmakers. Don't miss the famous Barovier wedding cup from around

1470. ✉ *Fondamenta Giustinian 8, Murano* ☎ *041/739586* ⊕ *www. museiciviciveneziani.it* 🎫 *€8, free with MUVE pass; admission with guided tour €13* ⊘ *Apr.–Oct., daily 10–6; Nov.–Mar., daily 10–5. Last entry 1 hr before closing. Guided tours available in English daily at 2:30* Ⓜ *Vaporetto: Museo.*

BURANO

Cheerfully painted houses in a riot of colors—blue, yellow, pink, ocher, and dark red—line the canals of this quiet village where lace making rescued a faltering fishing-based economy centuries ago. Visitors still love to shop here for "Venetian" lace, even though the vast majority of it is machine-made in Asia; visit the island's Museo del Merletto (Lace Museum) to discover the undeniable difference between the two. As you walk the 100 yards from the dock to Piazza Galuppi, the main square, you pass stall after stall of lace vendors. These good-natured ladies won't press you with a hard sell, but don't expect precise product information or great bargains—authentic, handmade Burano lace costs $1,000 to $2,000 for a 10-inch doily.

TIMING
The only official sight on Burano is the Lace Museum, which you should be able to see in a half hour. But the main reason for coming to Burano is simply to visit the charming, colorful fishing. An hour meandering through the streets should suffice.

TOP ATTRACTIONS
Museo del Merletto. Here's the place to marvel at the intricacies of Burano's lace making. The lace-making museum will likely continue to host a "sewing circle" of sorts, where on most weekdays you can watch local women carrying on the tradition. They may have authentic pieces for sale privately. ✉ *Piazza Galuppi 187* ☎ *041/730034* 🎫 *€5, or free with MUVE pass* ⊘ *Apr.–Oct., daily 10–6; Nov.–Mar., daily 10–5* Ⓜ *Vaporetto: Burano.*

SAN MICHELE

San Michele is the cemetery island of Venice, but unless you're interested in paying your respects to notables such as Ezra Pound and Igor Stravinsky, the main reason to make the crossing is to see the very beautiful church of San Michele in Isola by Renaissance architect Mauro Codussi. The cemetery itself, despite the illustrious people buried there, is really quite simple and indistinguishable from most other cemeteries in Italy. Vaporetto line 4.1 from Fondamente Nove stops at San Michele during hours it is open.

TIMING
A half hour should suffice to see Codussi's church; how long you spend in the cemetery depends upon your degree of devotion to the memory of those buried there.

San Michele in Isola. Tiny, cypress-lined San Michele is home to the first church designed by Mauro Codussi and the first example of Renaissance architecture in Venice; the gracefully elegant structure shows the profound influence of Florentine architects Alberti and Rossellino that would come to full fruition in Codussi's palaces on the Canale Grande. The church's dedication to Saint Michael is singularly appropriate, since traditionally he holds the scales of the Last Judgment.

Next to the church is the somewhat later hexagonal Capella Emiliani (1528–1543), whose strangely shaped dome recalls those of Etruscan tombs. ⊠ *Isola San Michele* ☎ *041/7292811* ☉ *Daily 7:30–12:15 and 3–4* Ⓜ *Vaporetto: Cimitero.*

WHERE TO EAT

EATING AND DRINKING WELL IN VENICE

The catchword in Venetian restaurants is fish, often at its tastiest. Even if you're not normally a fish fan, it's worth trying here—there's nothing quite like an expertly prepared fish that was, as the vendors like to say, swimming with its brothers only a few hours before. The best restaurants will proudly assure you they don't even have a freezer on the premises.

You can sample regional wines and scrumptious *cicchetti* (bite-size snacks) in *bacari* (traditional wine bars), a great Venetian tradition. For centuries, locals have gathered at these neighborhood spots to chat over a glass of *sfuso* (wine on tap) or the ubiquitous spritz: an iridescent red cocktail of white wine and seltzer (or Prosecco) and either Aperol, Select, or bitters. *Crostini* (toast with toppings) and *polpette* (meat, fish, or vegetable croquettes) are popular cicchetti, as are small sandwiches, seafood salads, baccalà mantecato, and toothpick-speared items such as roasted peppers, marinated artichokes, and mozzarella balls.

WINES TO LOOK FOR

Tre Venezie regional wines (from the Veneto, Trentino–Alto Adige, and Friuli–Venezia Giulia) go far beyond the famous Amarone and include some spectacular white varieties like the crisp Malvasia and hearty Friulano, the smooth Garganega (Soave) and Ribolla Gialla, along with the versatile, just-dry-enough bubbly Prosecco.

Reds are dry and flavorful and relatively low in alcohol, the ideal accompaniment to regional cuisine: look for Cabernet Franc, Corvina, and Corvinone (Valpolicella, Bardolino), Groppello, Marzemino, Lagrein, Raboso, Refosco, and Teroldego Rotaliano.

SEAFOOD

Granseola (crab), *moeche* (soft-shell crab), sweet *canoce* (mantis shrimp), *capelunghe* (razor clams), calamari, and *seppie* or *seppioline* (cuttlefish) are all prominently featured, as well as *rombo* (turbot), *branzino* (sea bass), *San Pietro* (John Dory), *sogliola* (sole), *orate* (gilthead), *triglia* (mullet)—to name but a few of the options. Trademark dishes include *sarde in saor* (panfried sardines with olive oil, vinegar, onions, pine nuts, and raisins), *la frittura mista* (tempuralike fried fish and vegetables), and *baccalà mantecato* (creamed cod with olive oil). When prepared whole, fish is usually priced by the *etto* (100 grams, about 4 ounces) and can be expensive; but once you try it that way, you'll never want filleted fish again.

RISOTTO, PASTA, POLENTA

As a first course, Venetians favor the creamy rice dish risotto *al onda* ("undulating," as opposed to firm), prepared with vegetables or shellfish. Pasta is accompanied by seafood sauces, too: *pasticcio di pesce* is lasagna-type pasta baked with fish, usually *baccalà* (salt cod), and *bigoli* is a strictly local pasta shaped like short, thick spaghetti, usually served *in salsa* (an anchovy sauce), or with *nero di seppia* (squid-ink sauce). A classic first course is pasta *e fagioli* (creamed bean soup with pasta). Polenta (creamy cornmeal) is another staple; it's often served with *fegato alla veneziana*

(calf's liver and onions) or *schie* (lagoon shrimp).

VEGETABLES

The larger islands of the lagoon are legendary for fine vegetables, such as the tiny Sant'Erasmo *castraure* violet artichokes that herald spring. Many stalls at the Rialto Market sell high-quality produce from the surrounding regions. Spring treats are fat white asparagus and round artichoke bottoms (*fondi*), usually sautéed with olive oil, parsley, and garlic. From December to March, the prized *radicchio di Treviso* is grilled and used in salads and risotto. Fall brings small wild mushrooms like finferli and *chiodini*, as well as *zucca barucca,* a bumpy squash used in soups and to stuff ravioli.

SWEETS

Tiramisu, a creamy concoction made from ladyfingers soaked in espresso and covered with sweetened mascarpone cheese, was invented in the Veneto. In addition to sorbets and *semifreddi* (ice cream and cake desserts), other sweets frequently seen on Venetian menus are almond cakes and strudels, as well as dry cookies served with dessert wine. Gelato (ice cream) is sold all over; the best is homemade, labeled *produzione propria* or *fatto in casa.*

Our favorite pasticcerie (pastry shops) and gelaterie (ice-cream shops) are listed at the end of the Where to Eat chapter.

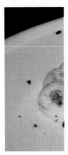

Updated by
Nan McElroy

Dining options in Venice range from the ultra-high end, where jackets and ties are a must, to the very casual. Once staunchly traditional, many restaurants have renovated their menus along with their dining rooms, creating dishes that blend classic Venetian elements with ingredients less common to the lagoon environs.

Mid-range restaurants are often more willing to make the break, offering innovative options while keeping traditional dishes available as mainstays. Restaurants are often quite small with limited seating, so make sure to reserve ahead. It's not uncommon for restaurants to have two seatings per evening, one at 7 and one at 9.

There's no getting around the fact that Venice has more than its share of overpriced, mediocre eateries that prey on tourists. Avoid places with cajoling waiters standing outside, and beware of restaurants that don't display their prices. At the other end of the spectrum, showy *menu turistico* (tourist menu) boards make offerings clear in a dozen languages, but for the same €15–€20 you'd spend at such places you could do better at a *bacaro* making a meal of cicchetti (savory snacks).

Budget-conscious travelers might want to take their main meal at lunch, when restaurant prices tend to be lower. Also keep an eye out for cafés and trattorias that offer meals prepared for *operai* (workers); they'll have daily specials designed for those who have to eat and run, which anyone is welcome to partake in. Bacari offer lighter fare, usually eaten at the bar (prices are higher if you sit at a table) and wine lists that offer myriad choices by the glass.

Although pizzerias are not hard to find, Venice is not much of a pizza town—standards aren't what they are elsewhere in Italy, and local laws impede the use of wood-burning ovens. Seek out recommended pizzerias, or opt for a bacaro snack instead of a soggy slice of pizza *al volo*, which is too commonly precooked and reheated. *Tramezzini*, the triangular white-bread sandwiches served in bars all over Italy, however, are almost an art form in Venice. The bread is white but doesn't at all

BEST BETS FOR VENICE DINING

Fodor's writers and editors have selected their favorite restaurants by price and experience in the Best Bets lists below. Fodor's Choice properties represent the "best of the best."

3

Fodor'sChoice ★

Al Gatto Nero da Ruggero, $$$ p. 118

Alle Testiere, $$$ p. 114

Al Paradiso, $$$ p. 107

Antiche Carampane, $$$ p. 107

Bentigodi di Chef Domenico, $$ p. 110

Caffè Florian, $$$ p. 97

Enoteca ai Artisti, $ p. 104

Harry's Bar, $$$$ p. 98

Il Ridotto, $$$ p. 116

Impronta Cafe, $ p. 104

Osteria alla Bifora, $$ p. 105

Osteria al Squero, $ p. 105

Osteria Da Fiore, $$$ p. 108

Osteria di Santa Marina, $$$ p. 116

Ristorante Quadri, $$$$ p. 99

Vini da Gigio, $$$ p. 113

By Price

$

Enoteca ai Artisti, p. 104

Impronta Cafe, p. 104

Osteria al Squero, p. 105

$$

Bentigodi di Chef Domenico, p. 110

Osteria alla Bifora, p. 105

$$$

Al Gatto Nero da Ruggero, p. 118

Alle Testiere, p. 114

Al Paradiso, p. 107

Antiche Carampane, p. 107

Il Ridotto, p. 116

Osteria Da Fiore, p. 108

Osteria di Santa Marina, p. 116

Vini da Gigio, p. 113

$$$$

Harry's Bar, p. 98

Ristorante Quadri, p. 99

Best by Experience

CASALINGA (HOME COOKING)

La Perla—Ai Bisatei, $, p. 117

La Trattoria ai Tosi, $, p. 116

Osteria Ca' d'Oro (alla Vedova), $, p. 113

CUCINA ALTA (SOPHISTICATED CUISINE)

Il Ridotto, $$$, p. 116

Osteria di Santa Marina, $$$, p. 116

Ristorante Quadri, $$$$, p. 99

EXCEPTIONAL WINE LIST

Antiche Carampane, $$$, p. 107

La Cantina, $$$, p. 112

Osteria Orto dei Mori, $$, p. 113

Osteria di Santa Marina, $$$, p. 116

Vini da Gigio, $$$, p. 113

GOOD FOR FAMILIES

All'Anfora, $, p. 108

Al Nono Risorto, $, p. 106

Casin dei Nobili, $, p. 104

La Perla—Ai Bisatei, $, p. 117

La Trattoria ai Tosi, $, p. 116

GOOD FOR LUNCH

Al Prosecco, $$, p. 109

El Rèfolo, $, p. 115

La Cantina, $$$, p. 112

La Perla—Ai Bisatei, $, p. 117

La Zucca, $$, p. 109

Muro Pizzeria con Cucina, $$$, p. 110

GREAT VIEWS

Busa alla Torre da Lele, $, p. 117

Ristorante Riviera, $$$$, p. 105

OUTDOOR DINING

Anice Stellato, $$, p. 110

Osteria Boccadoro, $$, p. 112

Osteria Orto dei Mori, $$, p. 113

ROMANTIC

Al Paradiso, $$$, p. 107

Anice Stellato, $$, p. 110

Osteria alla Frasca, $, p. 112

Osteria Orto dei Mori, $$, p. 113

resemble the "Wonder" of your youth; many bars here still make their own mayonnaise, and few skimp on the fillings.

Use the coordinate (✦ 1:B2) at the end of each listing to locate a restaurant on the Where to Eat in Venice maps.

PLANNING

The handiest places for a snack between sights are bars, cafés, and the quintessentially Venetian bacari. Bars are small cafés that can serve any sort of drink from coffee to grappa, along with a quick *panino* (sandwich, often warmed on a griddle) or a tasty *tramezzino* (sandwich on untoasted white bread, usually with a mayonnaise-based filling). A café is like a bar but usually with more seating, and it may serve a few additional food items. If you place your order at the counter, ask if you can sit down: many places charge considerably more for table service. In train stations and along the highway, you'll pay a cashier first, then give your *scontrino* (receipt) to the person at the counter who fills your order.

MEALTIMES AND CLOSURES

Breakfast (*la colazione*) is usually served from 7 to 10:30, and it usually consists of little more than coffee and a roll; the only place you may find meat or eggs is at your hotel. Lunch (*il pranzo*) is served from 12:30 to 2, dinner (*la cena*) from 7:30 to 10. Many bacari open as early as 8 am, but they do not serve typical breakfast items or coffee; some Venetians partake of cicchetti for their morning meal.

PRICES AND TIPPING

The standard procedures of a restaurant meal in Venice and throughout Italy are different from those in the United States (and most other places). When you sit down in a *ristorante,* you're expected to order two courses at a minimum, such as a *primo* (first course) and a *secondo* (second course), or an antipasto (starter) followed by a primo or secondo, or a secondo with dessert. Traditionally, a secondo is not a "main course" that would serve as a full meal; and in a country where food comes first, it may behoove you to sample as much as you can. Eateries are quite used to diners who order courses to split; but, if you're not so hungry, you might head for a pizzeria or bacaro to sample some quick bites.

All prices include tax. Prices include service (*servizio*) unless indicated otherwise on the menu. It's customary to leave a small tip in cash (from a euro to 10% of the bill) in appreciation of good service. Do not leave a tip on your credit card. Most restaurants have a "cover" charge, usually listed on the menu as *pane e coperto*. It should be modest (€1–€2.50 per person) except at the most expensive restaurants. Some instead charge for bread, which should be brought to you (and paid for) only if you order it. When in doubt, ask about the policy upon ordering.

The price of fish dishes is often given by weight (before cooking); the price on the menu will be for 100 grams (4 ounces); a typical fish portion will come to 350 grams (14 ounces). Keep some cash on hand because many osterie, bacari, and pizzerias don't take credit cards.

Prices in the dining reviews are the average cost of a main course at dinner, or, if dinner is not served, at lunch.

RESERVATIONS AND DRESS

Reservations are always recommended (and often essential) in restaurants for dinner, especially Friday through Sunday and especially for the first seating. We mention them in reviews only when they are essential or not accepted. We mention dress only when men are required to wear a jacket or a jacket and tie. Keep in mind that Italians never wear shorts or running shoes in a restaurant or bacaro, no matter how humble. Shorts are acceptable in pizzerias and cafés.

SAN MARCO

$
CAFÉ
✕ **Bar all'Angolo.** This corner of Campo Santo Stefano is one of the most pleasing locations to sit and watch the Venetian world go by. The constant motion of the café staff assures you'll receive your coffee, spritz, panino, or *tramezzino* (sandwich on untoasted white bread, usually with a mayonnaise-based filling) in short order; consume it at your leisure either at one of the outdoor tables, at the bar, or take refuge at the tables in the back. They'll whip you up a fresh salad or a hot primo, and they offer a delectable tiramisu for dessert—homemade, just like the sandwiches. Closing time is 9 pm, making the Angolo a good alternative to a more-elaborate evening meal. $ *Average main: €8* ⊠ *Campo Santo Stefano (just in front of the Santo Stefano church), San Marco 3464* ☎ *041/5220710* ⊘ *Closed Sun. and Jan.* Ⓜ *Vaporetto: Sant'Angelo* ✛ *2:D5.*

$$$
INTERNATIONAL
✕ **Caffè Centrale.** Sleek and elegant in the glowing, brick-lined ground floor of a 16th-century palazzo, the Caffè Centrale has vastly improved since it came under new management two years ago. It is a rarity in Venice: a restaurant that serves until 12:45 am. The Centrale is around the corner from the Fenice, so it makes a great place for a post-performance nosh. The menu, while giving a nod to Venetian cuisine (they serve an excellent baccalà mantecato), features mostly creatively prepared Continental dishes, such as sautéed fois gras with Sauternes or a spectacular beef fillet with Amarone. There's also a broad selection of very fresh raw fish specialties. For dessert there's a sinful list of sweet temptations, including three variations on the classic Venetian *sgroppino* (an alcohol-laced sorbet). $ *Average main: €26* ⊠ *Piscina Frezzaria, San Marco 1569B* ☎ *041/2960664* ⊕ *www.caffecentralevenezia. com* ⌕ *Reservations essential* ✛ *2:E4.*

$$$
CAFÉ
Fodor's Choice
★
✕ **Caffè Florian.** Because of the prices and the tourist mobs, Venetians tend to avoid caffè in the Piazza San Marco. But when they want to indulge and regain control of their city, they go to Florian. Founded in 1720, it's not only Italy's first caffè, but with its glittering neo-baroque decor and attractive 19th-century wall panels (depicting Venetian heroes), it's undisputedly the most beautiful. Florian is steeped in local history: favored by Venetians during the long Austrian occupation, it was the only caffè to serve women during the 18th century (hence Casanova's patronage), and it was the caffè of choice for artistic notables such as Wagner, Goethe, Goldoni, Lord Byron, Marcel Proust, and

Charles Dickens. It was also the birthplace of the international art exhibition, which later blossomed into the Venice Biennale. The coffee, drinks, and snacks are quite good (think chocolate, hot or otherwise), but you really come here for the atmosphere and to be part of Venetian history. There's a surcharge for music; so savvy Venetians and travelers in a hurry opt for lower prices at the comfortable bar in the back. $ *Average main: €27* ✉ *Piazza San Marco, San Marco 56* ☎ *041/5205641* ⊕ *www.caffeflorian.com* ☉ *Daily 9 am–midnight* ✛ *2:G4.*

$

WINE BAR

✕ **Enoteca al Volto.** A short walk from the Rialto Bridge, this bar has been around since 1936; the satisfying cicchetti and primi have a lot to do with its staying power. Grab one of the tables out front, or take refuge in two small, dark rooms with a ceiling plastered with wine labels that provide a classic backdrop for simple fare, including a delicious risotto that is served daily at noon. The place prides itself on its solid wine list of both Italian and foreign vintages. If you stick to a panino or some cicchetti at the bar, you'll eat well for relatively little. If you take a table and opt for one of the day's exceptional primi, the price category goes up a notch; however, this is still a good bargain for San Marco. There are, of course, traditional secondi, such as a very good seppie in nero. Al Volto is open every day of the year but Christmas (and closes a bit early on Christmas Eve). $ *Average main: €12* ✉ *Calle Cavalli, San Marco 4081* ☎ *041/5228945* ⊕ *www.alvoltoenoteca.it* ▭ *No credit cards* Ⓜ *Vaporetto: Rialto* ✛ *2:E4.*

$$$$

VENETIAN

Fodor'sChoice

★

✕ **Harry's Bar.** For those who can afford it, and despite its recently having become the watering place of Russian oligarchs and their female spike-heeled retinues, lunch or dinner at Harry's Bar is as indispensable to a visit to Venice as a walk across the Piazza San Marco or a vaporetto ride down the Grand Canal. Harry's is not just a fine restaurant; it's a cultural institution. When founder Giuseppe Cipriani opened the doors in 1931, the place became a favorite of almost every famous name to visit Venice (including Charlie Chaplin, Orson Welles, and Ernest Hemingway) and still attracts much of Venetian high society as regulars. Today, many still remember Harry's as one of the few restaurants in town that continued to serve Jewish patrons during the period of the fascist racial laws. Inside, the suave, subdued beige-on-white decor is unchanged from the 1930s, and the classic Venetian fare is carefully and excellently prepared. Try the delicate baked sea bass with artichokes, and don't miss the Harry's signature crepes flambés or his famous Cipriani chocolate cake for dessert. Since a meal at Harry's is as much about being seen, book one of the cramped tables on the ground floor—the upper floor of the restaurant, despite its spectacular view, is the Venetian equivalent of "Siberia" (but take heart: the second floor has windows with views that look like framed paintings). And be sure to order a Bellini cocktail—a refreshing mix of white peach purée and sparking prosecco—this is its birthplace, after all. On the other hand, true to its "retro" atmosphere, Harry's makes one of the best Martini cocktails in town. $ *Average main: €38* ✉ *Calle Vallaresso, San Marco 1323* ☎ *041/5285777* ⊕ *www.harrysbarvenezia.com* ⚖ *Reservations essential* 🏛 *Jacket required* ☉ *Daily 10:30 am–11 pm* Ⓜ *Vaporetto: San Marco (Calle Vallaresso)* ✛ *2:F5.*

$$$$
VENETIAN
Fodor'sChoice
★
✕**Ristorante Quadri.** Located above the famed café of the same name sits one of the most legendary restaurants in Italy: Quadri, a name steeped in history (as a café, it was the first to introduce Turkish Coffee to an already over-caffeinated city in the 1700s), beauty—the period dark-wood furnishings, lush burgundy damask walls, and sparkling chandeliers epitomize Venetian *ambiente* like few other places—and mise-en-scene, thanks to its extraordinary perch on, and over, the Piazza San Marco. The Alajmo family (of the celebrated Le Calandre restaurant near Padua) has taken over the restaurant and put their accomplished sous-chef from Padua in charge of the kitchen. The menu, while still bearing the creative mark of the Alajmos, offers more traditional dishes than in previous years. For tasting menus that range from €180 to €220 (exclusive of wine), you can savor such delights of creative cuisine as dill-flavored *tagliolini* with spider crab in a sauce of sea urchins and Venetian clams, but you can also be more conservative and enjoy *burrata* ravioli with a seafood- tomato sauce spiked with oregano. Downstairs, the simpler **abcQuadri** (located next to the café)—with impeccably restored neo-Rococo wall paintings—serves more traditional Venetian fare and some of the best Martinis in town; however, a three-course dinner will still set you back €100, without wine. As for Quadri itself: the prices, cuisine, and decor are all *alta*, so beware: some food critics find the fare not up to these high prices. $ *Average main: €65* ✉ *Piazza San Marco 121* ☎ *041/5222105* ⊕ *www.caffequadri.it* ⚐ *Reservations essential* ⊗ *Closed Mon.* ✛ *2:G4.*

DORSODURO

$
CAFÉ
✕**Caffè Bar Ai Artisti.** Sitting on a campo made famous in film by Katharine Hepburn and Indiana Jones, Caffè Ai Artisti gives locals, students, and travelers alike good reason to pause and refuel. The location is central, pleasant, and sunny—perfect for people-watching and taking a break before the next destination—and the hours are long: you can come here for a morning cappuccino, or drop by as late as midnight for an after-dinner spritz. The panini are composed on-site from fresh, seasonal ingredients, their names scribbled in front of each on the glass case; ask about the day's pasta and other primi. There's a varied selection of wines by the glass, as well as herbal teas, and even caffè with ginseng. $ *Average main: €8* ✉ *Campo San Barnaba, Dorsoduro 2771* ☎ *041/5238994* ⊟ *No credit cards* Ⓜ *Vaporetto: Ca' Rezzonico* ✛ *2:B5.*

$
WINE BAR
✕**Cantinone già Schiavi.** A mainstay for anyone living or working in the area, this beautiful, famly-run 19th-century bacaro across from the *squero* (gondola repair shop) of San Trovaso has original furnishings and one of the best wine cellars in town—the walls are covered floor to ceiling by bottles for purchase. Cicchetti here are some of the most inventive—and freshest—in Venice (feel free to compliment the Signora, who makes them up to twice a day). Try the crostini-style layers of bread, smoked swordfish, and slivers of raw zucchini, or pungent slices of *parmigiano,* fig, pistachio, and toast. They also have a creamy version of baccalà mantecato spiced with herbs, and there are nearly a dozen open bottles of wine for experimenting at the bar. You'll have no trouble spotting the Cantinone as you approach: it's the one with throngs of

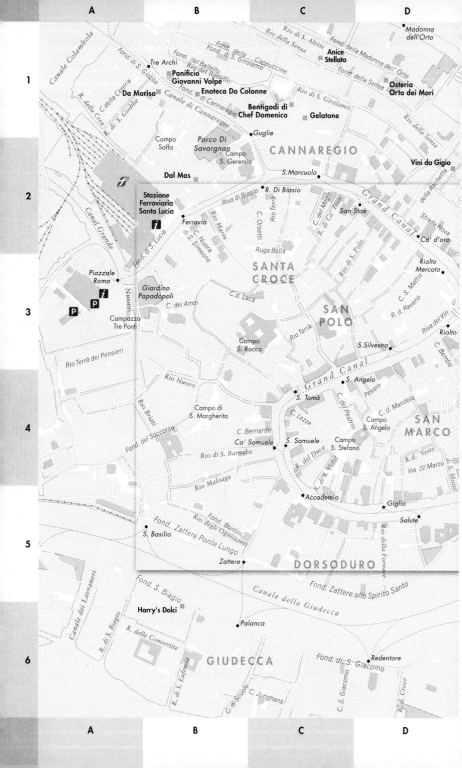

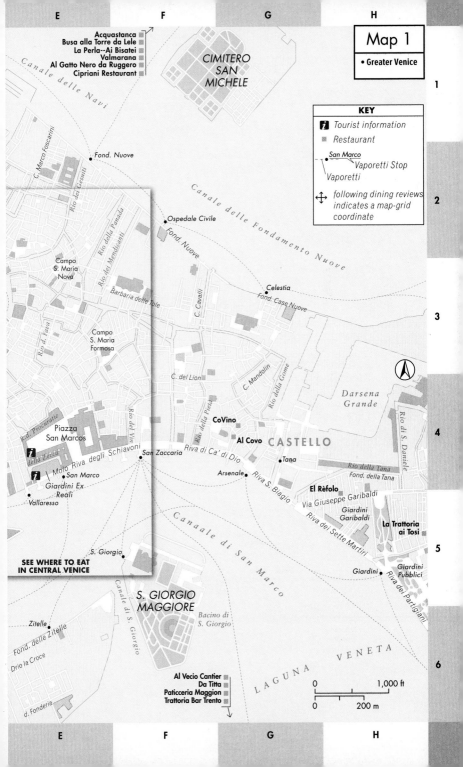

Acquastanca
Busa alla Torre da Lele
La Perla--Ai Bisatei
Valmarana
Al Gatto Nero da Ruggero
Cipriani Restaurant

CIMITERO SAN MICHELE

Map 1
• Greater Venice

Canale delle Navi

C. Marco Foscarini

Fond. Nuove

KEY
- 🛈 Tourist information
- ▪ Restaurant
- San Marco — Vaporetti Stop
- Vaporetti
- ↔ following dining reviews indicates a map-grid coordinate

Canale delle Fondamento Nuove

C. dei Gesuiti

Rio della Panada

Rio dei Mendicanti

Ospedale Civile

Fond. Nuove

Celestia

Fond. Case Nuove

Campo S. Maria Nova

Barbaria delle Tole

C. Cavalli

Campo S. Maria Formosa

Rio d. Fava

C. del Lion

C. della Pietà

C. Mandolin

Rio della Gorne

Darsena Grande

Rio di S. Daniele

R. d. Procuratie

Piazza San Marcos

Rio del Vin

CoVino

Al Covo

CASTELLO

Molo Riva degli Schiavoni

San Zaccaria

Riva di Ca' di Dio

Tana

Rio della Tana

Fond. della Tana

della Zecca

🛈

🛈 San Marco

Giardini Ex Reali

Vallaresso

Arsenale

Riva S. Biagio

El Rèfolo

Via Giuseppe Garibaldi

Giardini Garibaldi

La Trattoria ai Tosi

Riva dei Sette Martiri

Canale di San Marco

S. Giorgio

SEE WHERE TO EAT IN CENTRAL VENICE

Giardini

Giardini Pubblici

Riva dei Partigiani

S. GIORGIO MAGGIORE

Canale di S. Giorgio

Bacino di S. Giorgio

Zitelle

Fond. delle Zitelle

Drio la Croce

LAGUNA VENETA

Al Vecio Cantier
Da Titta
Paticceria Maggion
Trattoria Bar Trento

d. Fonderia

0   1,000 ft
0   200 m

1
2
3
4
5
6

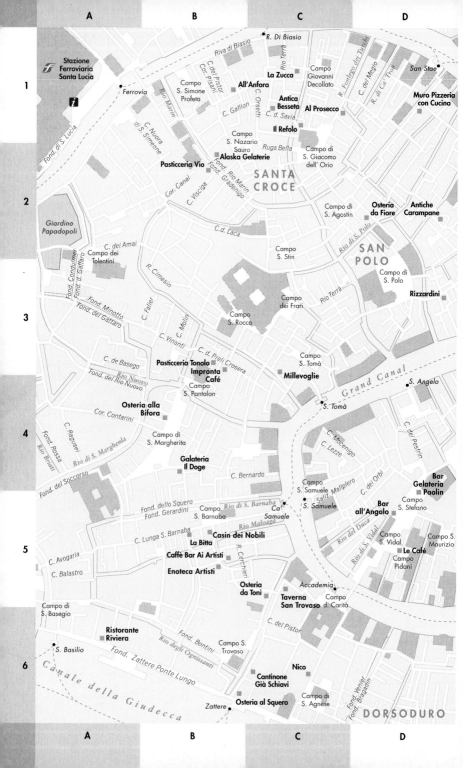

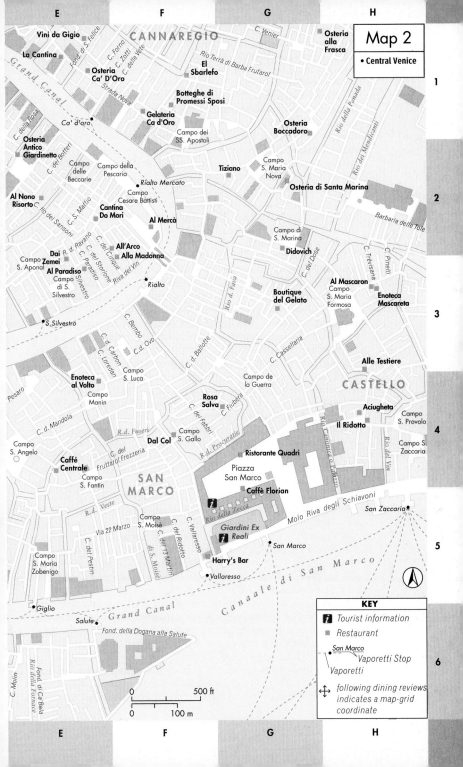

chatty patrons enjoying themselves. ⑤ *Average main: €2* ⊠ *Fondamenta Nani, Dorsoduro 992* ☎ *041/5230034* ▭ *No credit cards* ⊙ *Closed Sundays and 2 wks in Aug.* Ⓜ *Vaporetto: Zattere, Accademia* ✛ *2:C6.*

$

PIZZA

FAMILY

✕ **Casin dei Nobili.** When a Venetian living on the Dorsoduro side of the Grand Canal says, "*Mangiamo una pizza insieme*" (Let's go out for pizza), there's a good chance what he or she means is: "Let's go to the Casin dei Nobili," a pleasant trattoria/pizzeria just off the popular Campo San Barnaba. Pizza is not a Venetian specialty, and matters are made worse by the citywide prohibition of open, wood-fire ovens—the only way to bake a pizza, according to the Neapolitans, who invented the dish. But you can enjoy a pretty good facsimile of a Neapolitan pizza here, along with very good pasta and other fare. The relaxed, informal atmosphere makes this a good bet for families. Reservations are strongly recommended. ⑤ *Average main: €12* ⊠ *Off of Campo San Barnaba, Dorsoduro 2756* ☎ *041/2411841* ⌖ *Reservations essential* ⊙ *Closed Mon.* ✛ *2:B5.*

$

VENETIAN

Fodor's Choice

★

✕ **Enoteca ai Artisti.** Pop into this canalside restaurant at lunch for a satisfying primo or come for dinner to sample fine and fresh (including the pasta) offerings. The posted menu—with choices like tagliatelle with porcini mushrooms and tiger prawns, or a filleted John Dory with tomatoes and pine nuts—changes daily (spot the date at the top) and seasonally. You'll find beef tartare and *tagliata* selections as well. The candlelighted tables that line the fondamenta couldn't be more romantic, and proprietors Enzo and Francesca's welcoming attitude is manifested by a Prosecco on arrival. Each bottle from the lovely wine selection is available by the glass—an oenophile's dream. ⑤ *Average main: €14* ⊠ *Fondamenta della Toletta, Dorsoduro 1169a* ☎ *041/5238944* ⊕ *www.enotecaartisti.com* ⊙ *Closed Sun.* ✛ *2:B5.*

$

VENETIAN

Fodor's Choice

★

✕ **Impronta Cafe.** This sleek café is a favorite lunchtime haunt for professors from the nearby university and local businesspeople. Unlike in more traditional places, it's quite acceptable to order only pasta or a secondo, without an antipasto or dessert. Although the restaurant is also open for dinner—and you can dine well and economically in the evening—the real bargain is lunch, where you can easily have a beautifully prepared primo or secondo, plus a glass of wine, for around €12–€18. There's also a good selection of sandwiches and salads. The attentive staff speaks English, although you may be the only non-Venetian in the place. Unlike most local eateries, this spot is open from breakfast through late dinner (with tea and chocolate served late afternoon). ⑤ *Average main: €12* ⊠ *Crosera–San Pantalon, Dorsoduro 3815–3817, Dorsoduro* ☎ *041/2750386* ⊕ *www.improntacafevenice. com* ⊙ *Closed Sun.* ✛ *2:B3.*

$$$$

NORTHERN

ITALIAN

✕ **La Bitta.** The decor is more discreet, the dining hours longer, and the service friendlier and more efficient here than in many small restaurants in Venice—and the non-fish menu (inspired by the cuisine of the Venetian terra firma) is a temptation at every course. Market availability keeps the menu changing almost every day, although typically you can start with a savory barley soup or gnocchi with winter squash and aged ricotta cheese. Then choose a secondo such as lamb chops with thyme, *anatra in pevarada* (duck in a pepper sauce), or guinea hen in cream.

The homemade desserts are all luscious, and it's been said that La Bitta serves the best *panna cotta* (flavored custard) in town. Trust owner Deborah Civiero's selection from her excellent wine and grappa lists. $ *Average main: €40* ⊠ *Calle Lunga San Barnaba, Dorsoduro 2753/A* ☏ *041/5230531* ⌂ *Reservations essential* ⊟ *No credit cards* ☉ *Dinner only. Closed Sun. and July* Ⓜ *Vaporetto: Ca' Rezzonico* ✢ *2:B5.*

$$
VENETIAN
Fodor's Choice
★

✕ **Osteria alla Bifora.** A beautiful and atmospheric bacaro, alla Bifora has such ample and satisfying food and wine selections that most Venetians consider it a full-fledged restaurant. Most of the offerings consist of overflowing trays of cold, sliced meats and cheeses, various preparations of baccalà, or Venetian classics such as polpette, sarde in saor, or marinated anchovies; there's a good selection of regional wines by the glass as well. La Bifora also serves up a couple of excellent hot dishes; the *seppie in nero* (squid in its ink) is among the best in the city. Owner and barman Franco Bernardi and his sister Mirella are warm and friendly—after a few visits, you'll be greeted like a member of the family. Always open for dinner, you may also find this place open for lunch, if you're lucky. $ *Average main: €18* ⊠ *Campo Santa Margherita, Dorsoduro 2930* ☏ *041/5236119* ⌂ *Reservations essential* ⊟ *No credit cards* ☉ *Closed Sun.* ✢ *2:B4.*

$
WINE BAR
Fodor's Choice
★

✕ **Osteria al Squero.** It wasn't long after this lovely little locale appeared across from the Squero San Trovaso that it became a neighborhood— and citywide—favorite. The Venetian owner of this reimagined bacaro has created a personal vision of what a good one should offer: a variety of sumptuous cicchetti, panini, and cheeses to be accompanied by just the right regional wines (ask for his recommendation). You can linger along the fondamenta outdoors, and there are places to perch and even sit inside, in front of a sunny picture window that brings the outside view in. $ *Average main: €12* ⊠ *Fondamenta Nani, Dorsoduro 943/944* ☏ *335/6007513* ⊕ *osteriaalsquero.wordpress.com* ☉ *Closed Mon.* Ⓜ *Vaporetto: Accademia, Zattere* ✢ *2:B6.*

$
WINE BAR

✕ **Osteria da Toni.** This unpretentious bar-bacaro sits near the western edge of the Zattere promenade on a pretty, breezy side canal. It caters mainly to workers from the harbor over the bridge; there's a raw and real atmosphere full of dialect, rounds on the house, and jokes from the young owners Matteo and Silvano. The classic cicchetti are available, and lunch features a good-value set menu, with dishes such as pasta with shrimp and zucchini. $ *Average main: €10* ⊠ *Fondamenta San Basilio, Dorsoduro 1642* ☏ *041/5238272* ⊟ *No credit cards* ☉ *Closed Mon. and 3 wks in Aug.* Ⓜ *Vaporetto: San Basilio* ✢ *2:C5.*

$$$$
NORTHERN
ITALIAN

✕ **Ristorante Riviera.** The impressive panorama from their Zattare terrace attracts travelers yearning for a view, and the Riviera certainly offers that. Choose from contemporary takes on a variety of traditional Venetian dishes, including calf's liver with figs; "guitar string" pasta with shrimp, tiny green beans, and mint; and venison with blueberry sauce. A regional wine list is well matched to the cuisine; don't be surprised if the owner stops by to be sure you're enjoying your meal. Perhaps suited more to travelers than locals (who never worry about a view), while pleasing, the Riviera is definitely a splurge (note the €6 cover). $ *Average main: €50* ⊠ *Zattere, Dorsoduro 1473* ☏ *041/5227621* ⊕ *www.*

ristoranteriviera.it ⌂ *Reservations essential* ⊘ *Closed Mon. and 4 wks in Jan. and Feb.* Ⓜ *Vaporetto: San Basilio* ✛ *2:A6.*

$ ✕ **Taverna San Trovaso.** A wide choice of Venetian dishes served in robust
ITALIAN   portions, economical fixed-price menus, pizzas, and house wine by the
FAMILY   glass or pitcher keep this two-floor, no-nonsense, reliable tavern abuzz
with young locals and budget-conscious visitors. It's always packed, and
table turnover is fast, so it's not for lingering. Not far from the Gallerie dell'Accademia, this is a good place to slip into while sightseeing
in Dorsoduro. ⑤ *Average main: €12* ⊠ *Fondamenta Priuli, Dorsoduro
1016* ☎ *041/5203703* ⊕ *www.tavernasantrovaso.it* ⊘ *Closed Mon. and
1 wk Dec.–Jan.* Ⓜ *Vaporetto: Accademia, Zattere* ✛ *2:C5.*

SAN POLO

$$$$ ✕ **Alla Madonna.** "The Madonna" used to be world famous as "the"
VENETIAN   classic Venetian trattoria but in the past decades has settled down
to middle-age. Owned and run by the Rado family since 1954, this
Venetian institution looks like one, with its wood beams, stained-glass
windows, and panoply of paintings on white walls. It is frequented
more by regular Italian visitors to Venice and people from the provinces than by Venetians themselves. Folks still head here to savor the
classic Venetian repertoire and, as most dishes are properly prepared
(for the stiff prices, they should be), the rooms here are usually bustling, so get ready to enjoy a festive and lively meal. ⑤ *Average main:
€60* ⊠ *Calle della Madonna, San Polo 594* ☎ *041/5223824* ⊕ *www.
ristoranteallamadonna.com* ⌂ *Reservations essential* ⊘ *Closed Wed.,
Jan., and 2 wks in Aug.* Ⓜ *Vaporetto: San Silvestro* ✛ *2:F3.*

$ ✕ **All'Arco.** Just because it's noon and you only have time between
VENETIAN   sights for a sandwich doesn't mean that it can't be a satisfying, even
awe-inspiring one. There's no menu at All'Arco, but a scan of what's
behind the glass counter is all you need. Order what entices you, or
have Roberto or Matteo (father and son) suggest a cicchetto or panino.
Options here are broad enough to satisfy both conservative and adventurous eaters. Wine choices are well suited to the food. Arrive early or at
the tail end of lunchtime to snag one of the few tables in the calle. ⑤ *Average main: €6* ⊠ *Calle Arco, San Polo 436* ☎ *041/5220619* ⊘ *Closed
Sun.* Ⓜ *Vaporetto: San Silvestro* ✛ *2:E2.*

$ ✕ **Al Mercà.** It's easy to spot this tiny bacaro shoved into corner of
WINE BAR   the campo just beyond the Rialto Market: it's the one mobbed with
chatty patrons—dressed in suits, jeans, or travel wear, shouldering mes-
senger bags or backpacks, with strollers or carts loaded with market
acquisitions—each with a glowing spritz or glass of wine in hand. Step
up to the banco, scan the chalkboards for the lists of wines (whites on
the left, reds are on the right), then choose from the myriad cicchetti
(meat, tuna, or eggplant croquettes; crostini and panini with imaginative combos of radicchio, artichokes, fish, *soppressa, ossocollo,* and
more) in the glass case. ⑤ *Average main: €5* ⊠ *Campo Cesare Battista,
San Polo 213* ☎ *347/1002583* Ⓜ *Vaporetto: Rialto Mercato* ✛ *2:F2.*

$ ✕ **Al Nono Risorto.** Although in the Santa Croce neighborhood, this
VENETIAN   friendly and popular trattoria is really only a short walk from the Rialto
FAMILY   Market. You may not be the only tourist here, but you'll certainly be

outnumbered by the locals (and if just a couple or a trio, the friendly staff may ask you to share a table). There's no English menu, but a server can usually help you out. Although pizza is not a Venetian specialty, it's pretty good here, but the star attractions are the generous appetizers and excellent shellfish pastas. The house wine is quite drinkable, and in good weather, you can enjoy your meal in the pergola-covered courtyard (do reserve if you want to snag a table there). $ *Average main: €9* ⊠ *Ramo de l'Arsenal, Santa Croce 2337, Santa Croce* ☎ *041/5241169* ⌕ *Reservations essential* ▭ *No credit cards* ☉ *Closed Wed. No lunch Thurs.* Ⓜ *Vaporetto: Rialto Mercato* ⊕ *2:E2.*

$$$
MODERN ITALIAN
Fodor's Choice
★

✕ **Al Paradiso.** In a small dining room made warm and cozy by its pleasing and unpretentious decor, proprietor Giordano makes all diners feel like honored guests. Pappardelle "al Paradiso" takes pasta with seafood sauce to new heights, while risotto with shrimp, champagne, and grapefruit puts a delectable twist on a traditional dish. The inspired and original array of entrées includes meat and fish selections such as a salmon with honey and balsamic vinegar in a stunning presentation. Unlike many elegant restaurants, Al Paradiso serves generous portions and many of the delicious antipasti and primi are quite satisfying; you may want to follow the traditional Italian way of ordering and wait until you've finished your antipasto or your primo before you order your secondo. $ *Average main: €26* ⊠ *Calle del Paradiso, San Polo 767* ☎ *041/5234910* ⌕ *Reservations essential* ☉ *Closed Mon. and 3 wks in Jan. and Feb.* Ⓜ *Vaporetto: San Silvestro* ⊕ *2:E3.*

$$$
VENETIAN
Fodor's Choice
★

✕ **Antiche Carampane.** Judging from its rather modest and unremarkable appearance, you wouldn't guess that Piera Bortoluzzi Librai's trattoria is among the finest fish restaurants in the city both because of the quality of the ingredients and because of the chef's creative magic. Like other upscale seafood restaurants in Venice, this trattoria offers a selection of modern dishes such as turbot in citrus sauce; however, Antiche Carampane's kitchen goes a step further: it explores the more complex and interesting, but lesser known, dishes from the traditional Venetian repertoire. Embark on a culinary journey with St. Peter's fish with radicchio di Treviso; mullet in red wine; or an unusual spaghetti with spicy shellfish sauce from the town of Chioggia, the major fishing port on the Venetian lagoon. If you prefer simpler fare, the perfectly grilled fish is always sea caught and fresh, and in spring, try the local, fried soft-shell crabs. $ *Average main: €26* ⊠ *Rio Terà della Carampane, San Polo 1911* ☎ *041/5240165* ⊕ *www.antichecarampane.com* ⌕ *Reservations essential* ☉ *Closed Sun. and Mon., 10 days in Jan., and 3 wks in July and Aug.* Ⓜ *Vaporetto: San Silvestro* ⊕ *2:D2.*

$
WINE BAR

✕ **Cantina Do Mori.** This is the original bacaro—in business continually since 1462. Cramped but warm and cozy under hanging antique copper pots, it has been catering to the workers of the Rialto Market for generations. In addition to young, local whites and reds, the well-stocked cellar offers more-refined labels, many available by the glass. Between sips you can choose to munch the myriad cicchetti crostini on offer, or a few well-stuffed, tiny tramezzini, appropriately called *francobolli* (postage stamps). Don't leave without tasting the delicious baccalà mantecato, with or without garlic and parsley. If you choose to create a light lunch, snag one of the stools at the bar that lines the wall across from the banco. ⑤ *Average main: €2* ⊠ *Calle dei Do Mori, San Polo 429* ☎ *041/5225401* ⊟ *No credit cards* ⊘ *Closed Sun., 3 wks in Aug., and 1 wk in Jan.* Ⓜ *Vaporetto: Rialto Mercato* ✛ *2:E2.*

$ ✕**Dai Zemei.** Loads of travelers happily "discover" this relatively new
WINE BAR   arrival on the bacaro scene traversing west from the Rialto, and a fortunate find it is. It's easy to make a light meal of the inspired bites offered here; the difficult part is choosing among crostini and panini of *lardo e rucola*, radicchio and *alici* (fresh anchovy), spicy Neapolitan sausage, and duck breast with truffle oil. It's an optimum locale for Tre-Venezie wine tasting, too: from regional reds like Teroldego and Refosco to the aromatics of Trentino-Alto Adige; if you're lucky you can grab one of the outdoor tables. See if you can spot the *zemei* (*gemelli*, or twins, in Venetian), Giovanni and Franco, for whom this spot is named. ⑤ *Average main: €2* ⊠ *Ruga Ravana, San Polo 1045/B* ☎ *041/5208596* ⊟ *No credit cards* ⊘ *Closed Tues.* Ⓜ *Vaporetto: San Silvestro* ✛ *2:E3.*

$$$ ✕**Osteria Da Fiore.** The understated atmosphere, simple decor, and quiet
VENETIAN   elegance featured alongside Da Fiore's modern take on traditional Vene-
Fodor'sChoice   tian cuisine certainly merit its international reputation. With such beau-
★   tifully prepared cuisine, you would expect the kitchen to be manned by a chef with a household name; however the kitchen is headed by none other than owner Maurizio Martin's wife, Mara, who learned to cook from her grandmother. The other surprise is that while this restaurant is in an upper price category, it is hardly among the priciest in Venice. It offers several moderately priced (€50), three-course, prix-fixe luncheon menus, and the prix-fixe dinner menu is €80, which brings it very much into line with most of the more elegant choices in town. The menu is constantly changing, but generally frito misto or Da Fiore's tender, aromatic version of *seppie in nero,* cuttlefish in black sauce, is almost always available. Reservations, perhaps made a few days in advance in high season, are essential for dinner, but you can try just dropping in for lunch. ⑤ *Average main: €34* ⊠ *Calle del Scaleter, San Polo 2002* ☎ *041/721308* ⊕ *www.dafiore.net* ⊜ *Reservations essential* ⊘ *Closed Sun. and Mon., plus 3 wks in Jan.* Ⓜ *Vaporetto: San Tomà* ✛ *2:D2.*

SANTA CROCE

$ ✕**All'Anfora.** Expect *allegria.* This lively, informal trattoria-pizzeria
PIZZA   offers more than 50 different pizzas, described by owners Claudio and
FAMILY   Mariano as *buone e gigante* (good and gigantic). The pizza is indeed a main attraction, but you'll also find fresh salads (which are good and gigantic as well), and a full menu of trattoria fare: *baccalà* with polenta, risotto *con rucola e* scampi (with arugula and scampi), and *branzino al forno* (baked sea bass) with roast potatoes. There are two ample indoor dining rooms, but when the weather's fine try for a table

in the garden courtyard, or if it's full, on the calle out front. $ *Average main: €8* ⊠ *Lista dei Bari, Santa Croce 1223* ☎ *041/5240325* ⊕ *www.pizzeriaallanfora.com* ⊘ *Closed Wed.* Ⓜ *Vaporetto: Riva de Biasio* ✛ *2:B1.*

$$ ✕ **Al Prosecco.** Locals stream into this friendly wine bar (*bacaro*) to
WINE BAR explore wines from the region—or from anywhere in the county for that matter. They accompany a carefully chosen selection of meats, cheeses, and other food from small, artisanal producers, used in tasty panini like the *porchetta romane verdure* (roast pork with greens). Proprietors Davide and Stefano preside over a young, friendly staff who reel off the day's specials with ease. There are a few tables in the intimate back room, and when the weather cooperates you can sit outdoors on the lively campo, watching the Venetian world go by. It's open 9 to 9, and later if the mood strikes. Mostly a favorite for lunch, it's also a special place for an early light dinner. $ *Average main: €20* ⊠ *Campo San Giacomo dell'Orio, Santa Croce 1503* ☎ *041/5240222* ⊕ *www.alprosecco. com* ▭ *No credit cards* ⊘ *Closed Sun.* Ⓜ *Vaporetto: San Stae* ✛ *2:C1.*

$$ ✕ **Antica Besseta.** Tucked away in a quiet corner of Santa Croce, with a
SEAFOOD few tables under an ivy shelter, the Antica Besseta dates from the 18th century, and it retains some of its old feel. The menu focuses on vegetables and fish, according to what's at the market: spaghetti with *caparozzoli* or cuttlefish ink, *schie* (tiny shrimp) with polenta, and plenty of grilled fish. $ *Average main: €15* ⊠ *Salizzada de Ca' Zusto, Santa Croce 1395* ☎ *041/5240428* ⊕ *www.anticabesseta.it* ⊘ *Closed Mon. and Tues. No lunch Wed.* Ⓜ *Vaporetto: Rive di Biasio* ✛ *2:C1.*

$$ ✕ **Il Refolo.** This elegant pizzeria is run by the same family who own "Da
PIZZA Fiore." Besides serving excellent versions of classic pizzas, this elegant pizzeria (run by the same family who own the noted Da Fiore) will also tempt you with innovations such as pizza with *castraore,* the delicious and sinfully expensive tiny, white artichokes from the islands in the Venetian lagoon. Excellent pasta dishes and savory, simple mains, such as a wonderful roast chicken and potatoes dish, are also on offer. A pizza, with an appetizer and dessert, or a standard three-course meal should cost about €30, exclusive of wine. $ *Average main: €16* ⊠ *Campo San Giacomo all'Orio, Santa Croce 1459* ☎ *041/5240016* ⊘ *Closed Mon. and Tues. lunch and Nov.–Mar.* Ⓜ *Vaporetto: San Stae* ✛ *2:C1.*

$$ ✕ **La Zucca.** The simple place settings, lattice-wood walls, and mélange
NORTHERN of languages make La Zucca (the pumpkin) feel much like a typical,
ITALIAN somewhat sophisticated vegetarian restaurant that you could find in any European city. What makes La Zucca special is the use of fresh, local ingredients (many of which, like the particularly sweet *zucca* itself, aren't normally found outside northern Italy), and simply great cooking. Though the menu does have superb meat dishes such as the *piccata di pollo ai caperi e limone con riso* (sliced chicken with capers and lemon served with rice), more attention is paid to dishes from the garden: try the radicchio *di Treviso con funghi e scaglie di Montasio* (with mushrooms and shavings of Montasio cheese), the *finocchi piccanti con olive* (fennel in a spicy tomato-olive sauce), or the house's signature dish—the *flan di zucca,* a luscious, naturally sweet, pumpkin pudding topped with slivered, aged ricotta cheese. $ *Average main: €18* ⊠ *Calle del Tintor (at*

Ponte de Megio), Santa Croce 1762 ☎ *041/5241570* ⊕ *www.lazucca.it* ⏃ *Reservations essential* ⊘ *Closed Sun. and 1 wk in Dec.* Ⓜ *Vaporetto: San Stae* ⌖ *2:C1.*

$$$
ITALIAN
✕ **Muro Pizzeria con Cucina.** Don't let the name *pizzeria con cucina* fool you: Muro offers its mostly youthful clientele a varied menu and uses high-quality ingredients, taking its cue from its more refined sister restaurant, Muro Rialto. Select from excellent Venetian fare and pizza in classic and innovative forms—try the *arrotolata amoretesoro* (a rolled pizza) with *bresaola* (thinly sliced air-cured beef), *scamorza* (a delicately flavored melting cheese made from cow's milk), and radicchio. Chef Francesco adds dimension to the menu with classic Italian selections, along with the *piatti unici*, a single course fancifully combining elements of first and second courses. A wide selection of beer is on tap. Ⓢ *Average main: €30* ✉ *Campiello dello Spezier, Santa Croce 2048* ☎ *041/5241628* ⊕ *www.murovenezia.com* ⏃ *Reservations essential* ⊘ *Closed Tues.* Ⓜ *Vaporetto: San Stae* ⌖ *2:D1.*

$
ITALIAN
✕ **Osteria Antico Giardinetto.** The name refers to the intimate garden where co-owner Larisa will welcome you warmly, once you've wound your way from the Rialto or San Stae down the narrow calle to this romantic locale. (There's an indoor dining room as well, but the garden is covered and heated in winter.) Larisa's husband, Virgilio, mans the kitchen, where he prepares such dishes as sea bass in salt crust and a grilled fish platter. Be sure to try the homemade gnocchi or pasta—perhaps the *tagliolini* (thin spaghetti) with scallops and artichokes. You'll also find some fine meat options here. Desserts, like the chocolate mousse or crème caramel, are homemade as well. The wine list features some excellent regional selections. Ⓢ *Average main: €14* ✉ *Calle dei Morti, Santa Croce 2253* ☎ *041/5240325* ⊕ *www.anticogiardinetto. it* ⊘ *Closed Mon. and Jan. 4–31* Ⓜ *Vaporetto: San Stae* ⌖ *2:E2.*

CANNAREGIO

$$
VENETIAN
✕ **Anice Stellato.** Off the main concourse, on one of the most romantic *fondamente* (canalside streets) of Cannaregio, this family-run bacarotrattoria is the place to stop for fairly priced, satisfying fare, though service can feel indifferent and, occasionally but not often, the kitchen is a bit inconsistent. Narrow columns rise from the colorful tile floor, dividing the room into cozy sections. There are also a few outdoor canalside tables. Classics like *seppie in nero* (squid in its ink) are enriched with such offerings as *sarde in beccafico* (sardines rolled and stuffed with breadcrumbs, herbs, and cheese) and tagliatelle with prawns and zucchini flowers. They also serve several meat dishes, including a tender beef fillet stewed in Barolo wine. Ⓢ *Average main: €18* ✉ *Fondamenta de la Sensa, Cannaregio 3272* ☎ *041/720744* ⊘ *Closed Mon. and Tues., 1 wk in Feb., and 3 wks in Aug.* Ⓜ *Vaporetto: San Alvise or San Marcuola* ⌖ *1:C1.*

$$
VENETIAN
Fodor'sChoice
★
✕ **Bentigodi di Chef Domenico.** Many claim that owner Domenico Iacuzio is one of Venice's best chefs, even though he hails from Italy's deep south. In May 2012, he moved from La Colombina, revitalizing the more expansive Bentigodi, just a three-minute walk away. The chef marries delicious Venetian culinary traditions with southern accents;

try sarde in saor, which perfectly balances sweet and savory, and the diced raw tuna *cipolata*, enlivened by sautéed onions and oranges. His seafood risottos are always made to order, and his preparations of freshly caught—never farmed—fish are magical. For the Venetian traditionalist, Domenico prepares a first-class fritto misto (deep-fried seafood) dish. If you've missed his southern accent up to now, you'll find it at dessert with homemade southern specialties such as cannoli or *cassata* (candied Sicilian cake). Portions are ample, the atmosphere is informal, and the service is helpful. $ *Average main: €22* ⊠ *Calesele, Cannargio 1423* ☎ *041/8223714* ⊕ *www.bentigodi.com* ⌂ *Reservations essential* ✢ *1:C1.*

$ ✕ **Botteghe di Promessi Sposi.** The former Promessi Sposi eatery was reju-
VENETIAN   venated when three *fioi* (guys) with considerable restaurant experience joined forces. Join locals at the *banco* (counter) premeal for an *ombra* (small glass of wine) and cicchetto like polpette croquettes or violet eggplant rounds, or reserve a sit-down meal in the dining room or the intimate courtyard. A varied, season-centered menu includes local standards like calf's liver or grilled *canestrelli* (tiny Venetian scallops), along with creative variations on classic Venetian fare, like homemade ravioli stuffed with *radicchio di Treviso* (red chicory leaves) or *orecchiette* ("small ear"–shaped pasta) with a scrumptious sauce of minced duck. The service is friendly and helpful, but it's very popular among locals, so be sure to make a reservation (later is better for a more relaxed environment). $ *Average main: €13* ⊠ *Calle de l'Oca (just off Campo Santi Apostoli), Cannaregio 4367* ☎ *041/2412747* ⌂ *Reservations essential* ⊗ *Closed Mon. No lunch Wed.* Ⓜ *Vaporetto: Ca' d'Oro* ✢ *2:F1.*

$ ✕ **Da Marisa.** It doesn't get any more Venetian than this. At Marisa, a
VENETIAN   beloved Cannaregio institution, don't expect a menu, tourist or otherwise: what Marisa cooks—whether meat, wild game, or fish—you eat. Expect an abundant, five-course, prix-fixe meal of expertly prepared Venetian comfort food. The pasta and gnocchi are always *fatto in casa* (homemade). Primi might include tagliatelle with *sugo del masaro* (duck sauce), risotto *di caroman* (with mutton), or perhaps a *zuppa di funghi,* soup made with fresh mushrooms. *Salmì di cervo* (stewed venison) and *fagiano ripieno arrosto* (stuffed roast pheasant) are possibilities for *secondi di carne,* and on fish nights, *frittura mista.* In temperate weather ask to eat canalside—but be on time or lose your table. $ *Average main: €14* ⊠ *Calle de la Canne (near the Tre Archi bridge, Fondamenta San Giobbe), Cannaregio 652/B* ☎ *041/720211* ⌂ *Reservations essential* ⊟ *No credit cards* ⊗ *No dinner Mon. and Tues. (lunch daily)* Ⓜ *Vaporetto: Crea or Tre Archi* ✢ *1:B1.*

$ ✕ **El Sbarlefo.** This odd name is Venetian for "smirk," although you'd
WINE BAR   be hard pressed to find one of those around this cheery, familiar wine bar with a wine selection as ample as the cicchetti on offer. Arriving on the bacaro scene in 2010, Sbarlefo has expanded to a new location in Dorsoduro, in the calle just behind the church. Making the most of their limited space, owners Alessandro and Andrea have installed counters and stools inside, tables outside, and external banco access for ordering a second round. And order you will, selecting from a spread of delectable cicchetti from classic polpette of meat and tuna to tomino

cheese rounds to speck and robiolo rolls, and more. They've paid equal attention to their wine selection—ask for a recommendation and you're likely to make a new discovery. $ *Average main: €4* ⊠ *Salizzada del Pistor (off Campo Santi Apostoli), Cannaregio 4556/C* 🕾 *041/5233084* ⊟ *No credit cards* Ⓜ *Vaporetto: Ca d'Oro* ⊹ *2:F1.*

$ ✕ **Enoteca Do Colonne.** Venetians from this working-class neighborhood
VENETIAN   frequent this friendly bacaro, not just for a glass of very drinkable wine, but also because of its excellent selection of traditional Venetian cicchetti for lunch. There's not only a large selection of sandwiches and panini, but also luscious tidbits like grilled vegetables, breaded and fried sardines and shrimp, and a superb version of baccalà mantecato. For the more adventurous, there are Venetian working-class specialties such as *musetto* (a sausage made from pigs' snouts served warm with polenta) and *nervetti* (veal tendons with lemon and parsley). These dishes are worth trying at least once when in Venice, and Do Colonne offers the best musetto in town. $ *Average main: €8* ⊠ *Rio Terà Cristo, Cannaregio 1814* 🕾 *041/5240453* ⊕ *www.docolonne.it* ⊟ *No credit cards* ⊘ *Closed Sun.* Ⓜ *Vaporetto: San Marcuola* ⊹ *1:B1.*

$$$ ✕ **La Cantina.** You'll have to look beyond the understated facade to spot
CONTEMPORARY   fresh raw oysters from Normandy, aged Iberian ham and prosciutto hanging from the ceiling, or a pile of artisan cheeses waiting to be paired with a spicy homemade *mostarda* to understand how satisfying a meal here can be. Co-owner and chef Francesco combines the freshest fish (raw or cooked), choicest meats and cheeses, and vegetables to create his *piatti unici* platters. Opt for creative cicchetti at aperitivo time; salad seekers will be supremely satisfied here as well. Though there's an "official" menu, the staff will let you know what's freshest and suggest a wine to pair; just sit back and wait to be supremely satiated. If you're a beer fan, co-owner Andrea makes their own, Morgana. Caveats: no pasta, no risotto; and since Francesco prepares each dish himself, service can be slow on weekend evenings, especially after 8 pm. $ *Average main: €30* ⊠ *Campo San Felice, Cannaregio 3689* 🕾 *041/5228258* ⚲ *Reservations not accepted* ⊘ *Closed Sun. and Mon.* Ⓜ *Vaporetto: Ca' d'Oro* ⊹ *2:E1.*

$ ✕ **Osteria alla Frasca.** For a taste of *tagliata di calimaro* (sliced grilled
VENETIAN   squid) with arugula or *pomodorini* tomatoes with strawberries and violet artichokes, wend your way up quintessential *calli* to La Frasca. Far from the maddening San Marco crowds, this tiny eatery nestled on a remote campiello charms before you even taste the seafood sampler of grilled seppie cuttlefish, *canoce* mantis shrimp, excellent baccalà mantecato, or sarde in saor. Wines are an important part of the meal here; ask for a recommendation from the ample list of predominantly regional selections. With limited indoor seating, La Frasca encloses and heats their outdoor terrace to accommodate winter diners. $ *Average main: €14* ⊠ *Corte de la Carità, Cannaregio 5176* 🕾 *041/2412585* ⊘ *No lunch Mon. and Wed.* Ⓜ *Vaporetto: Fondamente Nove* ⊹ *2:G1.*

$$ ✕ **Ostaria Boccadoro.** Come for the campo, stay for the fare. Bocca-
VENETIAN   doro's spacious patio graces the peaceful Campo Widman; both join forces to provide a most relaxing respite as you dine. Owners Luciano and Monica will do their best to make you feel at home, and they

succeed—many diners are repeat clients. Ask Luciano to suggest a wine from his carefully edited selection, then peruse the menu of classics like succulent *canastrelli* scallops, homemade pasta with *bevarasse* clams, tuna tartare, a crispy frittura, and perfectly grilled *orata* with zucchini sauce; there are plenty of meat options as well. The interior decor is gracious, with traditional linens and contemporary art. [$] *Average main:* €16 ⊠ *Campo Widman, Cannaregio 5405/a* ☎ *041/5211021* ⊕ *www. boccadorovenezia.it* ✛ *2:G1.*

$
WINE BAR

✕**Osteria Ca' D'Oro (alla Vedova).** "The best *polpette* in town," you'll hear fans of the venerable Vedova say, and that explains why it's an obligatory stop on any *giro d'ombra* (bacaro tour). The polpette are always hot and crunchy, and are also gluten-free, as they're made with polenta. Ca' d'Oro is a full-fledged trattoria as well, but make sure to reserve ahead, as it's no secret to locals and travelers alike seeking traditional Venetian fare at a reasonable cost. Vedova is one of the few places that still serves house wine in tiny, traditional *palline* glasses; never fear, if you order a bottled wine you'll get a fancier glass. [$] *Average main:* €12 ⊠ *Calle del Pistor (off the Strada Nova), Cannaregio 3912* ☎ *041/5285324* ▭ *No credit cards* ☉ *Closed Aug.* Ⓜ *Vaporetto: Ca d'Oro* ✛ *2:E1.*

$$
ITALIAN

✕**Osteria Orto dei Mori.** *Un piacere* (a pleasure) might be the best way to describe the dining experience here: from the fanciful, tasteful interior decor to romantic candlelighted tables dotting the Campo dei Mori to the inspired cucina. The attentive expertise of chef and co-owner Lorenzo is evident in every dish: try the *fagotti* (bundles of beef marinated in Chianti with goat cheese) or a seafood version with prawns, zucchini, and ricotta. Risotto with scampi and savory *fenferli* mushrooms won't disappoint, nor will the signature parchment-baked monkfish. Co-owner Micael has artfully created a regional wine list. The osteria is just under the nose of the campo's famous corner statue. [$] *Average main:* €16 ⊠ *Campo dei Mori, Fondamenta dei Mori, Cannaregio 3386* ☎ *041/5235544* ▵ *Reservations essential* ☉ *Closed Tues.* Ⓜ *Vaporetto: Orto, Ca d'Oro, or San Marcuola* ✛ *1:D1.*

$
ITALIAN

✕**Tiziano.** A fine variety of excellent *tramezzini* (sandwiches) lines the display cases at this *tavola calda* (roughly the Italian equivalent of a cafeteria) on the main thoroughfare from the Rialto to Santi Apostoli; inexpensive salad plates and daily pasta specials, are also served. This is a great place for a light meal or snack before a performance at the nearby Teatro Malebran. Whether you choose to sit or stand, it's a handy—and popular—spot for a quick meal or a snack at very modest prices. Service is efficient, if occasionally grumpy. [$] *Average main:* €8 ⊠ *Salizzada San Giovanni Crisostomo, Cannaregio 5747* ☎ *041/5235544* ▭ *No credit cards* Ⓜ *Vaporetto: Rialto* ✛ *2:G2.*

$$$
VENETIAN
Fodor'sChoice
★

✕**Vini da Gigio.** Paolo and Laura, a brother-sister team, run this refined trattoria as if they've invited you to dinner in their home, while keeping the service professional. Deservedly popular with Venetians and visitors alike, it's one of the best values in the city. Indulge in pastas such as rigatoni with duck sauce and arugula-stuffed ravioli. Fish is well represented—try the sesame-encrusted tuna—but the meat dishes steal the show. The steak with red-pepper sauce and the *tagliata di agnello* (sautéed lamb fillet with a light, crusty coating) are both superb, and you'll never enjoy a better *fegato alla veneziana* (Venetian-style liver with onions). This is a place for wine connoisseurs, as the cellar is one of the best in the city. Come at lunch or for the second sitting in the evening for more relaxed service. $ *Average main: €25* ✉ *Fondamenta San Felice, Cannaregio 3628/A* ☎ *041/5285140* ⊕ *www.vinidagigio. com* ⚘ *Reservations essential* ☉ *Closed Mon. and Tues., 2 wks in Jan., and 3 wks in Aug.* Ⓜ *Vaporetto: Ca' d'Oro* ✛ *1:D2.*

CASTELLO

$ ✕ **Aciugheta.** Almost an institution, the "tiny anchovy" (as the name
WINE BAR   translates) doubles as a pizzeria-trattoria, but stick to the tasty cicchetti offered at the bar, like the eponymous anchovy minipizzas, the *arancioni* rice balls, and the *polpette*. The selection of wines by the glass changes daily, but there are always the ubiquitous local whites on hand, as well as some Tuscan and Piedmontese choices thrown in for good measure. Don't miss the *tonno con polenta* (tuna with polenta) if it's offered, but scan the banco (grab a stool to pause a bit longer) and choose whatever appeals. $ *Average main: €12* ✉ *Campo SS. Filippo e Giacomo, Castello 4357* ☎ *041/5224292* Ⓜ *Vaporetto: San Zaccaria* ✛ *2:H4.*

$$$ ✕ **Al Covo.** For years, Diane and Cesare Binelli's Al Covo has set the
VENETIAN   standard of excellence for traditional, refined Venetian cuisine. The Binellis are dedicated to providing their guests with the freshest, highest quality fish from the Adriatic, and vegetables, when at all possible, from the islands of the Venetian lagoon and the fields of the adjacent Veneto region. Although their cuisine could be correctly termed "classic Venetian," it always offers surprises like the juicy crispness of their legendary frito misto—reliant upon a secret, non-conventional ingredient in the batter—or the heady aroma of their fresh anchovies marinated in wild fennel, a herb somewhat foreign to Veneto. The main exception to Al Covo's distinct local flavor is Diane's wonderful Texas-inspired desserts, especially her dynamite chocolate cake. $ *Average main: €28* ✉ *Campiello Pescaria, Castello 3968* ☎ *041/5223812* ⊕ *www.ristorantealcovo. com* ⚘ *Reservations essential* ☉ *Closed Wed. and Thurs.* Ⓜ *Vaporetto: Arsenale* ✛ *1:G4.*

$ ✕ **Al Mascaron.** At the convivial, crowded Al Mascaron, with its paper
VENETIAN   tablecloths and informal atmosphere, you'll likely find locals who drop in to gossip, drink, play cards, and eat cicchetti at the bar—but there are also plenty of travelers who return again and again to take advantage of the food and the hospitality. You can count on delicious fish, pasta, risotto, and seafood salads. Locals complain that the prices have become somewhat inflated, but grudgingly admit that the food is good. $ *Average main: €12* ✉ *Calle Lunga Santa Maria Formosa, Castello 5225* ☎ *041/5225995* ⊕ *www.osteriamascaron.it* ▭ *No credit cards* ☉ *Closed Sun. and mid-Dec.–mid-Jan.* Ⓜ *Vaporetto: Rialto or San Marco* ✛ *2:H3.*

$$$ ✕ **Alle Testiere.** The name is a reference to the old headboards that adorn
VENETIAN   the walls of this tiny, informal restaurant, but the food (and not the
Fodor'sChoice   decor) is undoubtedly the focus. Local foodies consider this one of the
★   most refined eateries in the city thanks to Chef Bruno Cavagni's gently

creative take on classic Venetian fish dishes. The chef's artistry seldom draws attention to itself, but simply reveals new dimensions to familiar fare, creating dishes that stand out for their lightness and balance. A classic black risotto of cuttlefish, for example, is surrounded by a brilliant coulis of mild yellow peppers; tiny potato gnocchi are paired with tender newborn squid. The menu changes regularly to capitalize on the freshest produce of the moment, and the wine selection is top notch. To enjoy a more leisurely meal, be sure to book the second dinner sitting. $ *Average main: €26* ✉ *Calle del Mondo Novo, Castello 5801, Castello* ☎ *041/5227220* ⊕ *www.osterialletestiere.it* ⌕ *Reservations essential* ⊘ *Closed Sun. and Mon., 3 weeks Jan.–Feb., 4 weeks July–Aug.* ✛ *2:H3.*

$$$
ITALIAN
✕ **CoVino.** A charming new concept in Venetian eateries, diminutive CoVino offers a fixed-priced, three-course menu, from which you'll choose among several traditionally inspired antipasti, secondi, and desserts with innovative—and satisfying—twists. At this Slow Food *presidio*, you can watch the cook construct your sliced tuna dressed with Bronte pistachio and eggplant; Bra sausage "imported" from the Piedmont *alla Valpolicella* with tiny green beans; or perhaps even fresh gazpacho. The wine selection is passionately created; if you're looking to be more adventurous on this front, ask enthusiastic owner Andrea for his take. Cash only, for now anyway. $ *Average main: €33* ✉ *Calle del Pestrin, Castello 3829a-3829* ☎ *041/2412705* ⊕ *www.covino venezia.com* ⌕ *Reservations essential* ⊘ *Wed.–Thurs.* Ⓜ *Vaporetto: Arsenale* ✛ *1:G4.*

$
WINE BAR
✕ **El Rèfolo.** At this contemporary cantina in a very Venetian neighborhood, owner Massimiliano pairs enthusiastically chosen wines and artisan beers with select meat, savory cheese, and seasonal vegetable combos. It's a hip hangout named after a play by turn-of-the-20th-century emancipated lady Amalia Rosselli—look for the framed title page inside. With outside-only seating, it's more appropriate for *un aperitivo* and a light meal. In temperate weather, this tiny *enoteca*'s exuberance effervesces out onto the city's broadest street. It's open every day but Sunday from 9:30 am to 12:30 am, with reduced hours in winter. $ *Average main: €6* ✉ *Via Garibaldi, Castello 1580* ⊘ *Closed Sun., hrs limited in winter* Ⓜ *Vaporetto: Arsenale* ✛ *1:G5.*

$
WINE BAR
✕ **Enoiteca Mascareta.** We're just here for the wine. What it lacks in supreme cuisine, Mascareta more than makes up for with its broad and adventurous wine selection (by definition, an enoteca must have more than 100 wines from different varieties), handpicked by owner and brilliant Friuli madman Mauro Lorenzon (you'll know him by his bow tie). Mascareta is also one of the last best bets for a late-night bite, offering mostly cold plates: refined cicchetti, a selection of cured pork and cheeses, and the occasional soup. An offspring of the popular casual restaurant Al Mascaron just down the calle, this place doesn't open until 6 pm, but doesn't close until past midnight—sometimes, way past. $ *Average main: €14* ✉ *Calle Lunga Santa Maria Formosa, Castello 5183* ☎ *041/5230744* ⊕ *www.ostemaurolorenzon.it* ⊘ *Closed Sun., 4 wks over Christmas. No lunch* Ⓜ *Vaporetto: Rialto or San Zaccaria* ✛ *2:H3.*

$$$
MODERN ITALIAN
Fodor'sChoice
★

✕ **Il Ridotto.** Longtime restaurateur Gianni Bonaccorsi (proprietor of the popular Aciugheta nearby) has established an eatery where he can pamper a limited number of lucky patrons with his imaginative cuisine and impeccable taste in wine. Ridotto, "reduced" in Italian, refers to the size of this tiny, gracious restaurant. The innovative menu employing traditional elements is revised daily, with the offerings tending toward lighter, but wonderfully tasty versions of classic dishes. The €60 tasting menus—one meat, one fish—where Gianni "surprises" you with a selection of his own creations, never fail to satisfy. Ask for a wine recommendation from the excellent cantina. $ *Average main: €28* ⊠ *Campo SS Filippo e Giacomo, Castello 4509* ☎ *041/5208280* ⊕ *www.ilridotto.com* ⩘ *Reservations essential* ⊘ *Closed Wed. No lunch Thurs.* Ⓜ *Vaporetto: San Zaccaria* ✛ *2:H4.*

$
VENETIAN
FAMILY

✕ **La Trattoria ai Tosi.** Getting off the beaten track to find good, basic local cuisine isn't easy in Venice, but La Trattoria ai Tosi (aka Ai Tosi Piccoli) fills the bill with its remote (but not too), tranquil location, homey atmosphere, and variety of fine traditional fare at prices that make it worth the walk from anywhere in the city. The baccalà mantecato "sanwicini" are excellent, as are the classic frittura mista and the traditional Venetian *bigoli in salsa* (thick, homemade spaghetti with an anchovy-onion sauce). The fixed-price lunch menu, created for local workers with limited time, is another good deal, and there's even decent pizza. $ *Average main: €12* ⊠ *Seco Marina, Castello 738* ☎ *041/5237102* ⊘ *Closed Mon.* Ⓜ *Vaporetto: Giardini* ✛ *1:H5.*

$$$
VENETIAN
Fodor'sChoice
★

✕ **Osteria di Santa Marina.** The candlelit tables on this romantic campo are inviting enough, but it's this intimate restaurant's imaginative kitchen creations that are likely to win you over. Star dishes include *tortino di baccalà mantecato* (cod torte) with baby arugula and fried polenta; *passatina di piselli* (fresh pea puree with scallops and tiny calamari); scampi *in saor,* a turn on a Venetian classic with leeks and ginger; and fresh ravioli stuffed with mussels and turbot in a creamed celery sauce. You can also opt for one of the rewarding tasting menus (fish or meat, €55–€85). The wine list is ample and well thought out. Service is gracious and cordial—just don't be in a terrible rush, or expect the server to be your new best friend. $ *Average main: €26* ⊠ *Campo Santa Marina, Castello 5911* ☎ *041/5285239* ⊕ *www.osteriadisantamarina.com* ⩘ *Reservations essential* ⊘ *Closed Sun., no lunch Mon.* Ⓜ *Vaporetto: Rialto* ✛ *2:G2.*

LIDO

$
VENETIAN

✕ **Al Vecio Cantier.** The wild scenery of Lido's Alberoni, with intersecting canals and reeds, contributes to the appeal of one of the liveliest places on the Lido, always filled to the gills during the film festival. There's efficient cicchetti service, but the restaurant deserves a longer visit for a relaxing meal in the best Venetian tradition: try whipped baccalà with polenta, or tagliolini *con gamberetti e carciofi* (with shrimp and artichokes) in spring. Homemade desserts include lemon and almond tarts, or you can dip cookies in a glass of *vino passito,* a dessert wine. Outside dining is in a pretty garden. $ *Average main: €14* ⊠ *Via della*

Droma 76, Lido ☎ *041/5268130* ⊕ *www.alveciocantier.com* ⊙ *Closed Mon. No lunch Tues., Nov., or Jan.* Ⓜ *Vaporetto: Lido* ✢ *1:G6.*

$ ╳**Trattoria Bar Trento.** This neat, old-style osteria 10 minutes from Piaz-
VENETIAN zale Santa Maria Elisabetta has a soft spot for meat and innards (one of the owners was a *bechèr,* or butcher). Lunch is the only meal served, but *ombre* (the Venetian term for a glass of wine) and cicchetti are available from 8 to 8. Many of the tasty snacks are made from organ meats (and thus not for squeamish eaters), but there are more familiar options as well, including baccalà *alla vicentina* (stewed with onion, milk, and Parmesan); pasta with seafood; and several seasonal risot-tos. As a secondo, fish can be cooked any way you want. $ *Average main: €12* ⊠ *Via Sandro Gallo 82, Lido* ☎ *041/5265960* ▭ *No credit cards* ⊙ *Closed Sun. No dinner except during Biennale* Ⓜ *Vaporetto: Lido* ✢ *1:G6.*

MURANO

$$ ╳**Acquastanca.** Grab a seat among locals at this charming, intimate
VENETIAN eatery—the perfect place to pop in for a lunchtime primo or embark on a romantic evening. Tasteful decor sets the mood, with exposed brick, iron and glass accents, and charming fish sculptures. Giovanna Arcangeli, changing course after years as an event planner for Harry's Bar, offers up gnocchi with scallops and zucchini, and curried scampi with black *venere* rice; you might even ask for a beef *tagliata* and mush-room plate for the table to share. The name, referring to the tranquility of the lagoon at the turn of the tide, reflects this restaurant's approach to food and service. $ *Average main: €20* ⊠ *Fondamenta Manin, 48* ☎ *041/3195125* ⊕ *www.acquastanca.it* ⌂ *Reservations essential* ⊙ *Sun-day* Ⓜ *Vaporetto: Murano Colonna, Murano Faro* ✢ *1:F1.*

$ ╳**Busa alla Torre da Lele.** A pretty square with olive trees and a well
VENETIAN sets the stage for Da Lele, a favorite of the Muranese and returning travelers. On the ground floor of a dark-red building with a loggia, the restaurant stretches out on the campo, where you eat in the shade of large umbrellas. Check the blackboard for such daily specials as anti-pasto Busa, with granseola and *garusol* (sea snails); *bavette alla busara* (flat spaghetti with a hot, spicy shrimp and tomato sauce); and baked rombo or branzino with potatoes. Homemade cookies are served with *fragolino,* a sweet, sparkling wine redolent of strawberries. $ *Average main: €14* ⊠ *Campo Santo Stefano 3* ☎ *041/739662* ⊙ *Closed Mon. No dinner* Ⓜ *Vaporetto: Faro* ✢ *1:F1.*

$ ╳**La Perla—Ai Bisatei.** A perennial favorite with locals (Murano and oth-
VENETIAN erwise) and a welcome respite for travelers, La Perla offers a relaxed,
FAMILY local atmosphere and lots of delectably prepared standard Venetian fare. Don't even think of arriving late in the lunch hour, or plan on waiting, as everyone else will have reserved or come early. The frittura is not a rare dish in Venice, but you won't find better one—and certainly not at a better price. Choose *spaghetti alle vongole, bigoli in salsa* (spa-ghetti with onions and anchovies), or the fresh catch, served grilled or fried. Don't wait for dinner though; they're only open midday. $ *Aver-age main: €8* ⊠ *Campo San Bernardo 6, Murano* ☎ *041/739528* ▭ *No credit cards* ⊙ *Closed Wed. and Aug.* Ⓜ *Vaporetto: San Stae* ✢ *1:F1.*

$ ╳ **Valmarana.** The most upscale restaurant on Murano is housed in a
SEAFOOD palace on the *fondamenta* (street) across from the Museo del Vetro.
Stucco walls and glass chandeliers complement well-appointed tables,
and although the menu contains no surprises, the cuisine is more refined
than at other places here. Try the baked sea scallops, the crab with fresh
herbs, or the rich risotto *alla pescatora,* containing all kinds of fish.
In warm weather, reserve a table in the back garden or on the terrace
overlooking the canal. ⑤ *Average main: €14* ⊠ *Fondamenta Navagero
31, Murano* ☎ *041/739313* ⊕ *www.ristorantevalmaranamurano.com*
⊘ *Closed 3 wks in Jan.* Ⓜ *Vaporetto: Navagero* ✛ *1:F1.*

BURANO

$$$ ╳ **Al Gatto Nero da Ruggero.** Even cats know that this restaurant dedi-
SEAFOOD cated to one of their own offers the best fish on Burano. It's only been
Fodor's Choice around since 1965, when Ruggero Bovo took it over from its owners
★   of the prior 19 years. "Each day our fisherman return with the best the
lagoon has to offer," says the owner, who upon understanding he could
not pursue his dream of being a musician, instead decided to make the
kitchen sing. The fish is top quality and couldn't get any fresher; all pas-
tas and desserts are made in-house; the *fritto misto* (deep-fried fish) is
outstanding for its lightness and variety of fish. *Risotto de Gò* (*ghiozzo*)
is a *cucina povera* Burano standard that had almost disappeared from
local menus until Anthony Bordain introduced it to travelers. No mat-
ter what you order though, you'll savor the pride Ruggero and his
family have in their lagoon, their island, and the quality of their cucina
(maybe even more so when enjoying it on the picturesque fondamenta).
⑤ *Average main: €26* ⊠ *Fondamenta della Giudecca 88* ☎ *041/730120*
⊕ *www.gattonero.com* ⟨ *Reservations essential* ⊘ *Closed Mon. and 3
wks in Nov.* Ⓜ *Vaporetto: Burano* ✛ *1:F1.*

TORCELLO

$$$ ╳ **Cipriani Restaurant.** A nearly legendary restaurant established by a
VENETIAN nephew of Arrigo Cipriani (the founder of Harry's Bar), this inn prof-
its from its idyllic location on the island of Torcello. Hemingway, who
loved the silence of the lagoon, came here often to eat, drink, and brood
under the green veranda. The food is not exceptional, especially con-
sidering the high-end prices, but dining here is more about getting lost
in Venetian magic. The menu features pastas, *vitello tonnato* (chilled
poached veal in a tuna and caper sauce), baked *orata* (gilthead) with
potatoes, and lots of other seafood. Vaporetto Line 10 runs every 30
minutes until 11:30 pm. Afterward it upon request; service is sporadic.
⑤ *Average main: €34* ⊠ *Piazza Santa Fosca 29* ☎ *041/730150* ⟨ *Reservations essential* ⊘ *Closed Tues. and early Jan.–early Feb.* Ⓜ *Vaporetto:
Torcello* ✛ *1:F1.*

PASTICCERIE (PASTRY SHOPS)

Venetians have always loved pastry, not so much as dessert at the end of a meal, but rather as a nibble that could go well with a glass of sweet wine or a cup of hot milk. Traditional cookies are sold in *pasticcerie* (pastry shops) throughout town, either by weight or by the piece, and often come in attractive gift packages. Search for *zaeleti* (cookies made with yellow corn flour and raisins), *buranelli* (S-shaped cookies from Burano, which also come in heavy, fat rings), and *baicoli* (crunchy cookies made with yeast). Many bakeries also sell pastry by the portion: from apple strudel to *crostate* (jam tarts) and *torta di mandorle* (almond cake)—just point out what you want. After Christmas and through Carnevale, a great deal of frying takes place behind the counter to prepare the tons of pastries annually devoured by Venetians and tourists alike in the weeks preceding Lent: specialties are *frittole* (doughnuts with pine nuts, raisins, and candied orange peel, rolled in sugar), best eaten warm; the ribbonlike *galani* (crunchy, fried pastries sprinkled with confectioners' sugar); and walnut-shaped *castagnole* (fried pastry dumplings rolled in sugar).

SAN MARCO

$ ✕ **Dal Col.** This is a good spot near Piazza San Marco for coffee and
BAKERY pastry on the run, with bar (coffee and beverage) service at the counter. Open every day. ⑤ *Average main: €2* ✉ *Calle dei Fabbri, San Marco 1035* ☎ *041/5205529* ✆ *Closed Aug. 5–20* Ⓜ *Vaporetto: San Marco* ✛ *1:B2* ✛ *2:F4.*

$ ✕ **Rosa Salva.** There are several branches to this venerable pasticceria in
BAKERY town; the headquarters is a small shop on Calle Fiubera in San Marco with a wide selection of pastry and savory snacks as well as bar service at the counter. ⑤ *Average main: €2* ✉ *Calle Fiubera, San Marco 951* ☎ *041/5210544* ✆ *Closed Sun.* Ⓜ *Vaporetto: Rialto* ⑤ *Average main: €2* ✉ *Campo San Luca, San Marco 4589* ☎ *041/2413087* ⊕ *http://www.marchinitime.it/* ✆ *Open daily* ✛ *2:G4.*

DORSODURO

$ ✕ **Pasticceria Tonolo.** Join students and profs from nearby Università di
BAKERY Ca' Foscari at the counter here, which makes for a sweet break while traversing the Frari district. Known for some of the best pastries in the city—try the *krapfen*, which are fresh, cream-filled donuts—Tonolo has been in operation for more than 120 years. ⑤ *Average main: €2* ✉ *Calle San Pantalon, Dorsoduro 3764* ☎ *041/5237209* ▭ *No credit cards* ✆ *Closed Mon. and Aug.* Ⓜ *Vaporetto: San Tomà* ✛ *2:B3.*

SAN POLO

$ ✕ **Rizzardini.** This is the tiniest and prettiest pastry shop in Venice, with
BAKERY a counter dating from the late 18th century. Try the Zurigo (light, flakey apple pastry) and *pastine di riso* (pastry with a creamy rice filling); you'll also find *salatine* (pastry with ham or cheese and vegetables) by 10 am. ⑤ *Average main: €2* ✉ *Calle Papadopoli, San Polo 1415, San Polo* ☎ *041/5223835* ▭ *No credit cards* ✆ *Closed Tues.* Ⓜ *Vaporetto: San Silvestro* ✛ *2:D3.*

SANTA CROCE

$ ✕ **Pasticceria Vio.** Besides the usual selection of small pastries and
BAKERY drinks, enjoy a piece of *crostata di marroni* (chestnut tart) or a bag
of spicy cookies made with chili at one of the tables along a quiet
canal. ⑤ *Average main: €4* ✉ *Fondamenta Rio Marin, Santa Croce 784*
☎ *041/718523* ▭ *No credit cards* ⊘ *Closed Wed.* Ⓜ *Vaporetto: Ferrovia, Riva de Biasio* ✛ *2:B2.*

CANNAREGIO

$ ✕ **Dal Mas.** Crisp croissants, pastries such as *kranz* (a braided pastry
BAKERY filled with almond paste and raisins) and strudel from the Friuli region,
and bar service make this a great place for breakfast. ⑤ *Average main:*
€4 ✉ *Lista di Spagna, Cannaregio 150/A* ☎ *041/715101* ⊘ *Closed Tues.*
Ⓜ *Vaporetto: Stazione* ✛ *1:B2.*

$ ✕ **Panificio Giovanni Volpe.** This is the only place in town that still bakes
BAKERY traditional Venetian-Jewish pastry and delicious *pane azimo* (matzo
bread) all year round, though days of operation give away that the shop
is not kosher. ⑤ *Average main: €4* ✉ *Calle del Ghetto Vecchio, Cannaregio 1143* ☎ *041/715178* ▭ *No credit cards* ⊘ *Closed Sun.* Ⓜ *Vaporetto:*
Guglie ✛ *1:B1.*

CASTELLO

$ ✕ **Didovich.** At this favorite, family-run locale, you'll find all the usual
BAKERY amenities of a pasticceria, and also some sublime vegetable tortes. Enjoy
a primo at lunchtime outside at one of the campo-side tables. ⑤ *Aver-
age main: €8* ✉ *Campo di Santa Marina, Castello 5909* ☎ *041/5230017*
▭ *No credit cards* ⊘ *Closed Sun. June–Sept.; closed Sun. afternoon*
Oct.–May Ⓜ *Vaporetto: Rialto* ✛ *2:G2.*

GIUDECCA

$ ✕ **Harry's Dolci.** With tables offering a spectacular view of the Zattere
BAKERY outside and an elegant room inside, Harry's (of Cipriani fame) makes
for a supremely indulgent stop. While you can linger for lunch or dinner, you can also fill your bag to go with delicious goodies. ⑤ *Average*
main: €10 ✉ *Fondamenta San Biagio, Giudecca 773* ☎ *041/5204844*
⊘ *Closed Tues. and Nov.–Mar.* Ⓜ *Vaporetto: Palanca* ✛ *1:B6.*

THE LIDO

$ ✕ **Pasticceria Maggion.** Since 1958, Venetians have been making the trip
BAKERY to the Lido even in bad weather for celebrated, custom-made fruit tarts
(to be ordered one day ahead; no bar service). ⑤ *Average main: €1*
✉ *Via Dardanelli 46, Lido* ☎ *041/5260836* ▭ *No credit cards* ⊘ *Closed*
Mon. and Tues.; closed 1 pm–4 pm Ⓜ *Vaporetto: Lido* ✛ *1:G6.*

GELATERIE (ICE CREAM SHOPS)

According to Venetians, Marco Polo imported from China a dessert
called *panna in ghiaccio* (literally, "cream in ice"), a brick of frozen
cream between wafers. There's no documentation to support the claim,
but the myth lives on. Several local *gelaterie* (gelato shops) sell panna
in ghiaccio, the supposed "ancestor" of gelato, but you'll have to ask
around for it, because it's almost never kept on display. On a hot summer day, nothing is better than a cup of fruity gelato to restore your

energy: light and refreshing, it will help you go that extra mile before you call it a day.

Newer gelato enterprises, including some chains, are popping up almost daily, many right next to the less flamboyant artisan operations that have been producing their own gelato for decades. The new stuff may or may not be better—but you can almost guarantee it will cost more. Most gelaterie are open nonstop from midmorning to late evening; some keep longer business hours in summer.

SAN MARCO

$ ╳ **Bar Gelateria Paolin.** The morning sun draws crowds of all ages and
BAKERY nationalities to take a seat on busy Campo Santo Stefano and enjoy a little cup at this favorite café-gelateria. A scoop of *limone* (lemon) gelato is particularly refreshing on a hot summer day. $ *Average main: €4* ⊠ *Campo Santo Stefano, San Marco 3464* ☎ *041/5220710* ⊘ *Closed Sat.* Ⓜ *Vaporetto: San Samuele or Sant'Angelo* ✛ *2:D5.*

$ ╳ **Le Café.** On Campo Santo Stefano across from Paolin, Le Café has
CAFÉ see-and-be-seen tables outside year-round. It also has bar service and afternoon tea and offers a variety of hot chocolate drinks and desserts. $ *Average main: €12* ⊠ *Campo Santo Stefano, San Marco 2797* ☎ *041/5237201* ⊕ *www.lecafevenezia.com* ⊘ *Daily 8 am–11 pm, until 8:30 pm in winter* Ⓜ *Vaporetto: San Samuele or Sant'Angelo* ✛ *2:D5.*

$ ╳ **Millevoglie.** The creamy, homemade gelato here satisfies the ad-hoc
CAFÉ *voglie* (yearnings) of *mille* (thousands) passersby as they crisscross between the Frari, Scuola di San Rocco, and San Tomà vaporetto. $ *Average main: €2* ⊠ *Salizzada S Rocco, San Polo 3033* ☎ *041/5244667* Ⓜ *Vaporetto: San Tomà* ✛ *2:C3.*

DORSODURO

$ ╳ **Gelateria Il Doge.** This popular take-away gelateria, just off Campo
CAFÉ Santa Margherita, offers a wide selection of flavors, from a few low-calorie options including yogurt and soy, to the extra-rich *strabon* (Venetian for "more than good," which in this case means made with cocoa, espresso, and chocolate-covered almonds), as well as granitas in summer. It's worth a detour, and it's open late most of the year. $ *Average main: €2* ⊠ *Campo Santa Margherita, Dorsoduro 3058/A* ☎ *041/5234607* ⊘ *Closed Nov.–Feb.* ✛ *2:B4.*

$ ╳ **Nico.** With an enviable terrace on the Zattere, Nico is the city's gelat-
CAFÉ eria with a view. The house specialty is the *gianduiotto*, a brick of dark chocolate ice cream flung into a tall glass filled with freshly whipped cream. There's the more economic bar service if you'd prefer to saunter down the sunny promenade. $ *Average main: €6* ⊠ *Zattere, Dorsoduro 922* ☎ *041/5225293* ⊘ *Closed Thurs. and Dec. 21–Jan. 8* Ⓜ *Vaporetto: Zattere* ✛ *2:C6.*

SANTA CROCE

$ ╳ **Alaska Gelateria-Sorbetteria.** Carlo Pistacchi whips up delicious gelato
BAKERY completely from scratch, and is endlessly experimenting with imaginative flavors. Combine a tried-and-true favorite with, say, asparagus, fennel—or pistacchio, of course. $ *Average main: €2* ⊠ *Calle Larga dei Bari, Santa Croce 1159* ☎ *041/715211* Ⓜ *Vaporetto: Riva de Biasio* ✛ *2:B2.*

CANNAREGIO

$ ✕ **Gelateria Ca' d'Oro.** Here you'll find the usual array of flavors, which
BAKERY change with the seasons, plus a few more-inventive ones. You can also
enjoy a granita (regular and Sicilian), panna in ghiaccio, and some
specialties (chocolate covered and otherwise) in front of the counter.
⑤ *Average main: €2* ✉ *Strada Nova near Campo Santi Apostoli, Cannaregio 4273/B* ☎ *041/5228982* Ⓜ *Vaporetto: Ca' d'Oro* ✛ *2:F1.*

$ ✕ **Gelatone.** Though it's changed hands, new owners try to adhere to
CAFÉ the tradition that kept locals devoted. The flavors are inspired and
the servings ample. ⑤ *Average main: €2* ✉ *Rio Terà della Maddalena,
Cannaregio 2063* ☎ *041/720631* Ⓜ *Vaporetto: San Marcuola* ✛ *1:C1.*

CASTELLO

$ ✕ **Boutique del Gelato.** Even though you'll find newer, shinier gelate-
BAKERY rie all up and down the *salizzada*, good value and marvelous flavors
give this artisanal enterprise a dedicated following. ⑤ *Average main:
€2* ✉ *Salizzada San Lio, Castello 5727* ☎ *041/5223283* ⊙ *Closed Jan.*
Ⓜ *Vaporetto: Rialto* ✛ *2:G3.*

THE LIDO

$ ✕ **Da Titta.** On the Lido, strategically located on the main drag between
CAFÉ the vaporetto stop and the most central beaches, Titta is one of the oldest gelaterie in Venice. Get your receipt at the *cassa* (register) for a cone
to go, or enjoy one of the special combinations while lolling in a swing-
ing chair under the trees that line the Gran Viale. There's also bar service. ⑤ *Average main: €2* ✉ *Gran Viale Santa Maria Elisabetta 61, Lido*
☎ *041/5260359* ⊙ *Closed Nov.–early Mar.* Ⓜ *Vaporetto: Lido* ✛ *1:G6.*

WHERE TO STAY

Updated by
Nan McElroy

Venetian magic can still linger when you retire for the night, whether you're staying in a grand hotel or budget *locanda* (inn). Some of the finest Venetian hotel rooms are lighted with Murano chandeliers and swathed in famed fabrics of Rubelli and Bevilacqua, with gilded mirrors and furnishing styles from baroque to Biedermeier and art deco.

Though more-contemporary decor is working its way into renovation schemes, you still may find the prized Venetian terrazzo flooring and canal views in more-modest *pensioni*. Your window will open, sometimes onto a balcony, so you may enjoy gondoliers' serenades, watch the ebb and flow of city life in the *campo* (square) below, or simply contemplate what the lack of motor traffic permits you to hear, or *not* hear.

Even if well renovated, most hotels occupy very old buildings. Preservation laws prohibit elevators in some, so if climbing stairs is an issue, check before you book. In the lower price categories, hotels may not have lounge areas, and rooms may be cramped, and the same is true of standard rooms in more expensive hotels. Space is at a premium in Venice, and even exclusive hotels have carved out small, dowdy, Cinderella-type rooms in the "standard" category. It's not at all unusual for each room to be different even on the same floor: windows overlooking charming canals and bleak alleyways are both common. En suite bathrooms have become the norm; they're usually well equipped but sizes will range from compact to more than ample; tubs are considered a luxury but are not unheard of, even in less expensive lodging. Carpeted floors are rare, as they're traditionally considered to be unhygienic. Air-conditioning is rarely a necessity until mid-June. A few of the budget hotels make do with fans. Mosquitoes can begin to pester in midsummer; turn lights off in the evening if you leave windows open, and ask the hotel staff for a Vape, an anti-mosquito device. The staff members at most Venetian hotels will be able to converse with you in English, and don't be afraid to ask for anything you need or even to change rooms if you consider it necessary to do so.

WHAT NEIGHBORHOOD TO STAY IN?

"Only a stone's throw from Saint Mark's square" is the standard hotel claim. Whether or not that's the case, it's not necessarily an advantage. In Venice, you can't go terribly wrong in terms of "good" areas in which to stay, and once you get your bearings, you'll find you're never far from anything.

The area in and around San Marco will always be the most crowded and touristy and almost always more expensive: even two- and three-star hotels cost more here than they do in other parts of town. If you want to stay in less trafficked surroundings, consider still convenient but more tranquil locations in Dorsoduro, Santa Croce, and east Cannaregio (though hotels near the train station in Cannaregio can have their own crowd issues), or even Castello in the area beyond the Pietà church. A stay on the Lido in shoulder season offers serenity and beaches for the kids, but it also includes about a half-hour boat ride to the historic center, and in summer it's crowded with beachgoers.

MAKING RESERVATIONS

Venice is saturated with lodging options, but it is also one of the most popular destinations on earth—so book your lodging as far in advance as possible. Planning your trip four to five months (or even farther) ahead will give you a much greater selection. Double-booking is not uncommon, unfortunately, so make sure you take your reservation confirmation along with you, including any special requests you've made (tub or shower, first or top floor, and so on). Almost all hotels can be booked online, either via email or using the booking system on the individual hotel's website—where they often guarantee the lowest rates and even discounts for longer stays or last-minute requests. You can also try larger booking portals such as ⊕ *venere.com* or ⊕ *veniceby.com*.

Venezia Si (☎ *041/5222264* ☉ *Daily 9 am–11 pm* ⊕ *www.veneziasi. it* ✉ *info@veneziasi.com*), the public relations arm of **AVA** (Venetian Hoteliers Association), also offers online booking for almost all hotels in town, and you can make reservations through them by phone or email. If you're in Venice without a room booked, try making same-day reservations at one of the AVA booths, which are at **Piazzale Roma** (☉ *Daily 9 am–10 pm*), **Santa Lucia train station** (☉ *Daily 8 am–9 pm*), and **Marco Polo Airport** (☉ *Daily 9 am–10 pm*).

They also have counters at the San Marco and A.S.M. Parking Garages in Piazzale Roma.

FINDING YOUR HOTEL

It is *essential* to have detailed arrival directions along with the address, including the sestiere and preferably a nearby landmark; conveniently, most hotels include maps on their websites. Even if you choose a pricey water taxi, you may still have a walk, depending on where the boat leaves you. Nothing is obvious on Venice's streets (even if you have GPS); turn-by-turn directions can help you avoid wandering back and forth along side streets and across bridges, luggage in tow.

Hotels are listed alphabetically by neighborhood. Use the coordinate (✚ 1:B2) at the end of each listing to locate a site on the corresponding map.

For expanded hotel reviews, visit Fodors.com.

SAN MARCO

$$
B&B/INN
☷ **Al Teatro.** The renovated home of owners Fabio and Eleonora behind the Fenice Opera House offers three spacious, comfortable, and conscientiously appointed rooms. **Pros:** airy rooms; convenient San Marco location; good for families. **Cons:** the intimacy of a family B&B is not for everyone; canal noise, especially from singing gondoliers. ⑤ *Rooms from: €180* ⊠ *Fondamenta della Fenice, San Marco 2554* ☎ *041/2776191* ⊕ *www.bedandbreakfastalteatro.com* ⬏ *3 rooms* ⦿ *Breakfast* Ⓜ *Vaporetto: Santa Maria del Giglio* ✛ *D4.*

$$$$
HOTEL
Fodor's Choice
★
☷ **Bauer Il Palazzo.** A palazzo with an ornate, 1930s neo-Gothic facade facing the Grand Canal has lavishly decorated guest rooms (large by Venetian standards) featuring high ceilings, tufted walls of Bevilacqua and Rubelli fabrics, Murano glass, marble bathrooms, damask drapes, and imitation antique furniture. **Pros:** pampering service; high-end luxury. **Cons:** in one of the busiest areas of the city; you will pay handsomely for a room with a canal view; Wi-Fi is additional. ⑤ *Rooms from: €700* ⊠ *Campo San Moisè, San Marco 1413/D* ☎ *041/5207022* ⊕ *www.ilpalazzovenezia.com* ⬏ *38 rooms, 34 suites* ⦿ *Breakfast* Ⓜ *Vaporetto: Vallaresso* ✛ *D4.*

$$
HOTEL
☷ **Ca' dei Dogi.** A quiet courtyard secluded from the San Marco melee offers an island of calm in six individually decorated guest rooms (some with private terraces) that feature contemporary furnishings and accessories. **Pros:** some rooms have terraces with views of the Doge's Palace. **Cons:** rooms are on the small side; furnishings are spartan and look a bit cheap; located in the middle of the most tourist-frequented part of Venice. ⑤ *Rooms from: €150* ⊠ *Corte Santa Scolastica, Castello 4242, Castello* ☎ *041/2413751* ⊕ *www.cadeidogi.it* ⬏ *6 rooms* ⊘ *Closed Dec.* ⦿ *Breakfast* Ⓜ *Vaporetto: San Zaccaria* ✛ *F4.*

$$$$
HOTEL
Fodor's Choice
★
☷ **The Gritti Palace.** Re-opened in 2013 after an extensive renovation, the Gritti Palace represents aristocratic Venetian living at its best, complete with hand-blown chandeliers, sumptuous textiles, and sweeping canal views. **Pros:** historic setting; white-glove service; Grand Canal location; classic Venetian experience. **Cons:** major splurge; some extra fees (except for Wi-Fi). ⑤ *Rooms from: €600* ⊠ *Campo Santa Maria del Giglio, San Marco 2467* ☎ *041/794611* ⊕ *www.thegrittipalace.com* ⬏ *61 rooms, 21 suites* ⦿ *No meals* ✛ *D5.*

$$$
HOTEL
Fodor's Choice
★
☷ **Hotel Flora.** The elegant and refined facade announces truly special place; the hospitable staff, the tastefully decorated rooms, and magical garden do not disappoint. **Pros:** central location; lovely garden; fitness center; excellent breakfast; free Wi-Fi. **Cons:** not especially close to a vaporetto stop for those arriving with luggage; some rooms can be on the small side. ⑤ *Rooms from: €240* ⊠ *Calle Bergamaschi, just off Calle Larga XXII Marzo, San Marco 2283/A* ☎ *041/5228217* ⊕ *www. hotelflora.it* ⬏ *40 rooms* ⦿ *Breakfast* Ⓜ *Vaporetto: San Marco (Vallaresso)* ✛ *D5.*

$$
B&B/INN
☷ **Locanda Casa Petrarca.** Neatly decorated and light-filled rooms between St. Marks Square and the Rialto Bridge offer guests something rare in Venice—a central yet quiet base from which to explore the city. **Pros:**

BEST BETS FOR VENICE LODGING

Fodor's provides a selective listing of hotels in every price range, from comfortable, well-maintained bargain finds to luxury pleasure palaces. Here we've compiled our top recommendations, by price category and type of experience. The best of the best earn our Fodor's Choice logo.

Fodor§Choice ★

Al Ponte Antico, $$$, p. 135

Bauer Il Palazzo, $$$$, p. 126

Ca' Maria Adele, $$$$, p. 131

Ca' Sagredo Hotel, $$$$, p. 136

The Gritti Palace, $$$$, p. 126

Hotel al Ponte Mocenigo, $$, p. 134

Hotel Flora, $$$, p. 126

La Calcina, $$, p. 131

Metropole, $$$$, p. 139

Pensione Accademia Villa Maravege, $$$, p. 132

Westin Europa & Regina, $$$$, p. 130

Best by Price

$

Al Palazzetto, p. 135

$$

3749 Ponte Chiodo, p. 135

Alla Vite Dorata, p. 135

Hotel al Ponte Mocenigo, p. 134

La Calcina, p. 131

Locanda Casa Petrarca, p. 126

$$$

Al Ponte Antico, p. 135

Hotel Flora, p. 126

Palazzo Abadessa, p. 137

Pensione Accademia Villa Maravege, p. 132

$$$$

Bauer Il Palazzo, p. 126

Ca' Maria Adele, p. 131

Ca' Sagredo Hotel, p. 136

The Gritti Palace, p. 126

Metropole, p. 139

Best by Experience

AWAY FROM THE CROWDS

3749 Ponte Chiodo, $$, p. 135

Ca' Maria Adele, $$$$, p. 131

Hotel al Ponte Mocenigo, $$, p. 134

La Calcina, $$, p. 131

Pensione Accademia Villa Maravege, $$$, p. 132

CANAL VIEWS

3749 Ponte Chiodo, $$, p. 135

Al Palazzetto, $, p. 135

Ca' Sagredo, $$$$, p. 136

The Gritti Palace, $$$$, p. 126

La Calcina, $$, p. 131

ROMANTIC

Ca' Sagredo, $$$$, p. 136

Hotel Flora, $$$, p. 126

La Calcina, $$, p. 131

Locanda Orseolo, $$, p. 130

Oltre il Giardino, $$$, p. 134

Pensione Accademia Villa Maravege, $$$, p. 132

Ruzzini Palace Hotel, $$$$, p. 139

CLASSIC VENETIAN DESIGN

Al Ponte Antico, $$$, p. 135

Ca' Sagredo Hotel, $$$$, p. 136

The Gritti Palace, $$$$, p. 126

Locanda Ca' Amadi, $$, p. 137

Palazzo Abadessa, $$$, p. 137

CONTEMPORARY DESIGN

Aman Canal Grande Venice, $$$$, p. 133

Ca' Maria Adele, $$$$, p. 131

Charming House DD 724, $$$$, p. 131

Hotel UNA Venezia, $$$, p. 137

GOOD FOR FAMILIES

Al Teatro, $$, p. 126

Casa Rezzonico, $$, p. 131

Hotel Flora, $$$, p. 126

PERSONAL SERVICE

Al Ponte Antico, $$$, p. 135

Ca' dei Dogi, $$, p. 126

Hotel al Ponte Mocenigo, $$, p. 134

Locanda Ca' Amadi, $$, p. 137

4

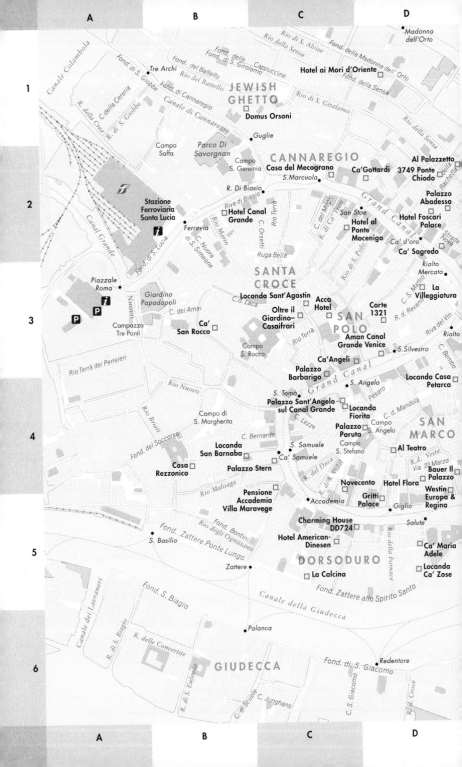

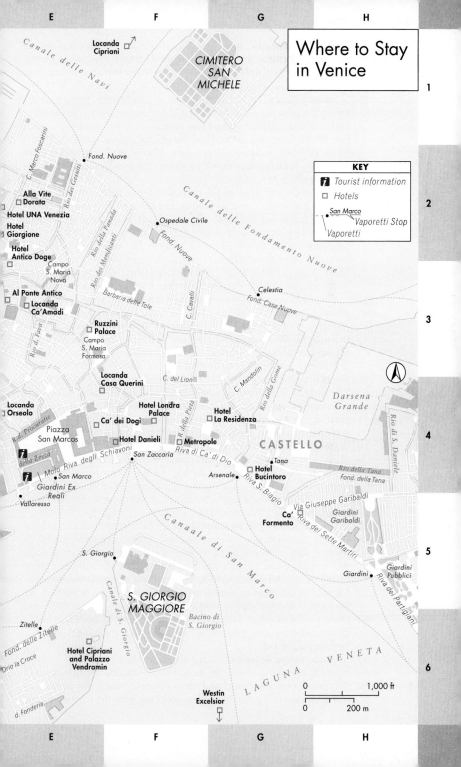

Where to Stay in Venice

E   F   G   H

Canale delle Navi

Locanda
Cipriani

CIMITERO
SAN
MICHELE

1

C. Marco Foscarini

Fond. Nuove

Canale delle Fondamento Nuove

2

Alla Vite
Dorata

Hotel UNA Venezia

Hotel
Giorgione

Rio dei Mendicanti

Rio della Panada

Ospedale Civile

Fond. Nuove

C. Cavalli

Hotel
Antico Doge

Campo
S. Maria
Nova

Celestia
Fond. Case Nuove

Al Ponte Antico

Locanda
Ca'Amadi

Rio d. Fava

Barbaria delle Tole

3

Ruzzini
Palace

Campo
S. Maria
Formosa

C. del Lion

C. Mandolin

Rio della Gorne

Darsena
Grande

Rio di S. Daniele

Locanda
Casa Querini

Locanda
Orseolo

R. d. Procuratie

Piazza
San Marcos

R. d. Zecca

Moto Riva degli Schiavoni

Hotel Londra
Palace

Ca' dei Dogi

Hotel Danieli

San Zaccaria

R. della Pieta

Hotel
La Residenza

Metropole

Riva di Ca' di Dio

CASTELLO

Hotel
Bucintoro

4

Giardini Ex
Reali

Vallaresso

San Marco

Tana

Arsenale

Riva S. Biagio

Rio della Tana
Fond. della Tana

Ca'
Formento

Via Giuseppe Garibaldi

Riva dei Sette Martiri

Giardini
Garibaldi

Canale di San Marco

S. Giorgio

Giardini

Giardini
Pubblici

Riva dei Partigiani

5

S. GIORGIO
MAGGIORE

Canale di S. Giorgio

Bacino di
S. Giorgio

LAGUNA   VENETA

Zitelle

Fond. delle Zitelle

Drio la Croce

Hotel Cipriani
and Palazzo
Vendramin

d. Fonderia

Westin
Excelsior

6

0   1,000 ft
0   200 m

KEY

🛈 Tourist information

☐ Hotels

<u>San Marco</u>
● *Vaporetti Stop*
Vaporetti

E   F   G   H

gentle prices and quiet for a central location. **Cons:** credit cards are not accepted; difficult to find. $ *Rooms from: €130* ✉ *Calle de le Schiavine, San Marco 4386, San Marco* ☎ *041/5200430* ⊕ *www.casapetrarca.com* ⇨ *7 rooms* ▭ *No credit cards* ❝◎❞ *Breakfast* Ⓜ *Vaporetto: Rialto* ⊹ *D4.*

$$
B&B/INN
🏨 **Locanda Fiorita.** Tucked behind Campo San Stefano in a charming little courtyard, this oasis offers small but peaceful rooms decorated in 18th-century Venetian style. **Pros:** central location; romantic setting; free Wi-Fi. **Cons:** rooms and bathrooms are indeed small. $ *Rooms from: €200* ✉ *Campiello Novo, San Marco 3457* ☎ *041/5234754* ⊕ *www.locandafiorita.com* ⇨ *10 rooms* ❝◎❞ *Breakfast* Ⓜ *Vaporetto: Sant'Angelo* ⊹ *D4.*

$$
HOTEL
🏨 **Locanda Orseolo.** Traditional, tasteful Venetian decor takes on a Carnevale theme in cozy, well-appointed, and comfortable rooms are enlivened by fanciful wall murals. **Pros:** intimate and romantic; friendly staff; Wi-Fi is free. **Cons:** no elevator; canal-side rooms can be noisy (think singing gondoliers); rooms without a canal view can be small and dark. $ *Rooms from: €180* ✉ *Corte Zorzi, off Campo San Gallo, San Marco 1083* ☎ *041/5204827* ⊕ *www.locandaorseolo.com* ⇨ *12 rooms* ☾ *Closed Jan.* ❝◎❞ *Breakfast* Ⓜ *Vaporetto: Rialto or Vallaresso* ⊹ *E4.*

$$$
HOTEL
🏨 **Novecento.** A stylish yet intimate retreat tucked away on a quiet *calle* midway between Piazza San Marco and the Accademia Bridge offers exquisite rooms decorated with original furnishings and tapestries from the Mediterranean and Far East. **Pros:** intimate, romantic atmosphere; free Wi-Fi. **Cons:** Some rooms are small, and some can be noisy. $ *Rooms from: €240* ✉ *Calle del Dose, off of Campo San Maurizio, San Marco 2683/84* ☎ *041/2413765* ⊕ *www.novecento.biz* ⇨ *9 rooms* ❝◎❞ *Breakfast* Ⓜ *Vaporetto: Santa Maria del Giglio* ⊹ *C4.*

$$$$
HOTEL
🏨 **Palazzo Paruta.** Steeped in lavish Venetian ambience, junior suites are palatial, superior rooms comfortably sized, bright, and well appointed, and ornate frescoes, pastel bas-reliefs, and splendid coffered and carved beamed ceilings abound. **Pros:** few small lodgings compare in terms of comfort and opulence. **Cons:** standard rooms are quite small; not handy to the best values for dining; no Wi-Fi in rooms. $ *Rooms from: €300* ✉ *Campo Sant'Angelo, San Marco 3824* ☎ *041/2410835* ⊕ *www.palazzoparuta.com* ⇨ *8 rooms, 5 junior suites* ❝◎❞ *No meals* Ⓜ *Vaporetto: Sant'Angelo* ⊹ *D4.*

$$$$
HOTEL
🏨 **Palazzo Sant'Angelo sul Canal Grande.** This elegant palazzo is large enough to deliver expected facilities and services but small enough to pamper its guests; rooms have red-and-gold tapestry-adorned walls and carpeting and Carrara and Alpine marble in the bath, and those facing the Grand Canal have balconies. **Pros:** distinguished yet comfortable; convenient to vaporetto stop. **Cons:** modest breakfast; fee for Wi-Fi, and Internet available only in common areas. $ *Rooms from: €420* ✉ *Campo Sant'Angelo, San Marco 3488* ☎ *041/2411452* ⊕ *www.palazzosantangelo.com* ⇨ *14 rooms* ❝◎❞ *Breakfast* Ⓜ *Vaporetto: Sant'Angelo* ⊹ *D4.*

$$$$
HOTEL
Fodor'sChoice
★
🏨 **Westin Europa & Regina.** Spread across five historic palazzi (is there anything else in Venice?) in the lee of San Marco, this amalgamation of the former Hotel Britannia and Hotel Regina is easily one of Venice's still-undiscovered gems. **Pros:** ideal location, with the über-boutiques

of via XXII Marzo and the Piazza San Marco a stone's throw away. **Cons:** slightly dated public areas and restaurants. $ *Rooms from: €550* ✉ *Corte Barozzi, San Marco 2159* ☎ *041/240–0001* ⊕ *www. westineuropareginavenice.com* ⤳ *185 rooms* ⧫ *No meals* ✛ *D5.*

DORSODURO

$$$$
HOTEL
Fodor'sChoice
★
⬚ **Ca' Maria Adele.** One of the city's most intimate and elegant getaways immerses guests in a mix of classic style (terrazzo floors, dramatic Murano chandeliers, antique-style furnishings) and touches of the contemporary, found in the African-wood reception area and breakfast room. **Pros:** quiet and romantic; imaginative contemporary decor; free Wi-Fi; tranquil yet convenient spot near Santa Maria della Salute. **Cons:** small rooms, even for Venice; few good restaurants nearby. $ *Rooms from: €420* ✉ *Campo Santa Maria della Salute, Dorsoduro 111* ☎ *041/5203078* ⊕ *www.camariaadele.it* ⤳ *12 rooms, 4 suites* ⧫ *Breakfast* Ⓜ *Vaporetto: Salute* ✛ *D5.*

$$
B&B/INN
⬚ **Casa Rezzonico.** Some pleasant if generic guest rooms overlook a sunny fondamenta and canal, and others a spacious private garden, where breakfast is served in good weather. **Pros:** canal views at a reasonable rate; two lively squares nearby; great for families. **Cons:** must reserve well in advance; some rooms are quite small; ground-floor rooms are dark; air-conditioning and heating not totally reliable. $ *Rooms from: €150* ✉ *Fondamenta Gherardini, Dorsoduro 2813* ☎ *041/2770653* ⊕ *www.casarezzonico.it* ⤳ *6 rooms* ⧫ *Breakfast* Ⓜ *Vaporetto: Ca' Rezzonico* ✛ *B4.*

$$$$
HOTEL
⬚ **Charming House DD 724.** These ultramodern surroundings abandon all things traditionally Venetian, opting instead to create the air of a stylish residence with impeccable, minimalist decor and a contemporary, warmly romantic, and occasionally even dramatic atmosphere. **Pros:** unique decor; variety of lodging options. **Cons:** not traditional Venetian style. $ *Rooms from: €350* ✉ *Ramo da Mula off Campo San Vio, Dorsoduro 724* ☎ *041/2770262* ⊕ *www.thecharminghouse.com* ⤳ *5 rooms, 2 junior suites, 2 suites* ⧫ *Breakfast* Ⓜ *Vaporetto: Accademia* ✛ *D5.*

$$$
HOTEL
⬚ **Hotel American–Dinesen.** The exceptional service here will help you feel at home in spacious guest rooms furnished in Venetian brocade fabrics with lacquered Venetian-style furniture; some front rooms have terraces with canal views. **Pros:** high degree of personal service; on a bright, quiet, exceptionally picturesque canal; free Wi-Fi. **Cons:** no elevator; rooms with a canal view are more expensive; some rooms could stand refurbishing. $ *Rooms from: €300* ✉ *San Vio, Dorsoduro 628* ☎ *041/5204733* ⊕ *www.hotelamerican.com* ⤳ *28 rooms, 2 suites* ⧫ *Breakfast* Ⓜ *Vaporetto: Accademia, Salute, and Zattere* ✛ *C5.*

$$
HOTEL
Fodor'sChoice
★
⬚ **La Calcina.** Time-burnished and elegant rooms with parquet floors, original 19th-century furniture, and firm beds enjoy an enviable position along the sunny Zattere, with front rooms offering vistas across the wide Giudecca Canal; a few have private terraces. **Pros:** panoramic views from some rooms; elegant, historic atmosphere. **Cons:** not for travelers who prefer ultramodern surroundings; no elevator; rooms with views are appreciably more expensive. $ *Rooms from: €180* ✉ *Zattere,*

4

Dorsoduro 780 ☎ *041/5206466* ⊕ *www.lacalcina.com* ⤵ *27 rooms, 26 with bath; 5 suites* ¶⊚¶ *Breakfast* Ⓜ *Vaporetto: Zattere* ✛ *C5.*

$$ ⬚ **Locanda Ca' Zose.** The idea that the Campanati sisters named the 15
HOTEL   rooms in their renovated 17th-century locanda after the stars and con-
stellations of the highest magnitude in the Northern Hemisphere says
something about how personally this place is run. **Pros:** quiet but con-
venient location; efficient, personal service. **Cons:** no outdoor garden
or terrace; no Wi-Fi in rooms (but free in lounge, as is computer use);
unimpressive breakfast. ⑤ *Rooms from: €165* ✉ *Calle del Bastion, Dor-
soduro 193/B* ☎ *041/5226635* ⊕ *www.hotelcazose.com* ⤵ *10 rooms, 1
junior suite, 1 suite* ¶⊚¶ *Breakfast* Ⓜ *Vaporetto: Salute* ✛ *D5.*

$$ ⬚ **Locanda San Barnaba.** This family-run, value-for-money establishment
HOTEL   is housed in a 16th-century palazzo and, if you're lucky, you'll bag one
of the superior rooms or the double that have original 18th-century
frescoes; one junior suite has two small balconies and is exceptionally
luminous. **Pros:** garden and terrace; close to vaporetto stop; traditional
furnishings make spacious rooms attractive and welcoming. **Cons:** no
elevator, minibar, or Internet access. ⑤ *Rooms from: €175* ✉ *Calle del
Traghetto, Dorsoduro 2785–2786* ☎ *041/2411233* ⊕ *www.locanda-
sanbarnaba.com* ⤵ *11 rooms, 2 junior suites* ¶⊚¶ *Breakfast* Ⓜ *Vaporetto:
Ca' Rezzonico* ✛ *C4.*

$$$$ ⬚ **Palazzo Stern.** This opulently refurbished neo-Gothic palazzo features
HOTEL   marble-columned arches, terrazzo floors, frescoed ceilings, mosaics,
and a majestic carved staircase and some rooms have tufted walls and
parquet flooring, but the gracious terrace that overlooks the Grand
Canal is almost reason alone to stay here. **Pros:** excellent service; lovely
views from many rooms; modern renovation retains historic ambience; steps from vaporetto stop. **Cons:** multiple renovations may turn
off some Venetian architectural purists; rooms with a Grand Canal
view are much more expensive; terrace bar and service are substan-
dard. ⑤ *Rooms from: €400* ✉ *Calle del Traghetto, Dorsoduro 2792*
☎ *041/2770869* ⊕ *www.palazzostern.com* ⤵ *18 rooms, 5 junior suites,
1 suite* ¶⊚¶ *Breakfast* Ⓜ *Vaporetto: Ca' Rezzonico* ✛ *C4.*

$$$ ⬚ **Pensione Accademia Villa Maravege.** Behind iron gates in one of the
HOTEL   most densely packed parts of the city you'll find yourself in front of a
Fodor's Choice   large and elegant garden and Gothic-style "villa" where accommoda-
★   tions are charmingly decorated with a connoisseur's eye. **Pros:** a unique
"villa" in the heart of Venice; one of the city's most enchanting hotels.
Cons: standard rooms are smaller than is usual in Venice, and seem to
be more sparsely decorated than the more expensive options. ⑤ *Rooms
from: €290* ✉ *Fondamenta Bollani, Dorsoduro 1058* ☎ *041/5210188*
⊕ *www.pensioneaccademia.it* ⤵ *27 rooms, 2 suites* ¶⊚¶ *Breakfast*
Ⓜ *Vaporetto: Accademia* ✛ *C4.*

SAN POLO

$ ⬚ **Acca Hotel.** One of Venice's more economical options offers bright,
HOTEL   well-appointed rooms and attentive service. **Pros:** lots of amenities for
its category; excellent value. **Cons:** no views; not terribly handy to a
vaporetto stop. ⑤ *Rooms from: €100* ✉ *Calle Pezzana, San Polo 2160*

☎ *041/2440126* ⊕ *www.accahotel.com* 🛏 *8 rooms, 1 suite* ⊙ *Breakfast* Ⓜ *Vaporetto: San Silvestro* ✛ *C3.*

$$$$ 🏨 **Aman Canal Grande Venice.** The restored Palazzo Papdopoli provides
RESORT   its guests with extravagant period details alongside elegant contemporary design, an expansive private garden, a rooftop terrace, and light-
filled and spacious rooms with garden or canal views. **Pros:** excellent
facilities; stunning views from common areas. **Cons:** breakfast not
included; basic rooms don't offer much historical detail; a bit distant
from San Marco; level of service may not meet expectations. ⑤ *Rooms
from: €1000* ✉ *Palazzo Papadopoli, Calle Tiepolo, San Polo 1364*
☎ *041/2707333*   ⊕ *www.amanresorts.com/amancanalgrandevenice/
home.aspx* 🛏 *24 rooms* ⊙ *No meals* Ⓜ *Vaporetto: San Silvestro* ✛ *D3.*

$$ 🏨 **Ca' Angeli.** The heirs of an important Venetian architect have trans-
B&B/INN   formed his former residence, on the third and top floors of a palace
along the Grand Canal, into an elegant lodging with views of either the
Grand Canal or a side canal—or in the case of the smallish Room 6,
rooftops from a terrace twice the size of the room. **Pros:** historic resi-
dence with Grand Canal views; helpful staff. **Cons:** a bit of a walk from
the vaporetto stop; credit cards accepted only for stays of two or more
nights. ⑤ *Rooms from: €200* ✉ *Calle del Traghetto de la Madoneta,
San Polo 1434* ☎ *041/5232480* ⊕ *www.caangeli.it* 🛏 *6 rooms, 1 suite,
1 apartment* ⊙ *Breakfast* Ⓜ *Vaporetto: San Silvestro* ✛ *D3.*

$$ 🏨 **Ca' San Rocco.** A former doctor's residence has been transformed into
B&B/INN   an exceptionally quiet oasis by the Cuogo sisters, with guest rooms that
are modestly decorated but spacious and bright. **Pros:** lots of greenery
and outdoors areas; just off main thoroughfare from Piazzale Roma to
the San Tomà vaporetto stop. **Cons:** no elevator or porter (so you have
to carry your own bags upstairs to your room); definitely not for people
with mobility problems; three bridges with steps to the bus or train station; Wi-Fi is extra. ⑤ *Rooms from: €165* ✉ *Ramo Cimesin, San Polo
3078* ☎ *041/716744* ⊕ *www.casanrocco.it* 🛏 *6 rooms* ⊙ *Breakfast*
Ⓜ *Vaporetto: Piazzale Roma or San Tomà* ✛ *B3.*

$$ 🏨 **Corte 1321.** If you're looking to escape the 18th-century-style decor
B&B/INN   that predominates Venetian lodging, check out these spacious, carefully
renovated rooms where ceramic lamps, tapestries, and carved platform
beds are combined with standard Venetian features such as beamed ceil-
ings and parquet flooring. **Pros:** contemporary decor; convivial, eclectic
atmosphere. **Cons:** all rooms but one open onto the courtyard—and
the occasionally lively conversations of its guests. ⑤ *Rooms from: €200*
✉ *Campiello Ca' Bernardi, San Polo 1321* ☎ *041/5224923* ⊕ *www.
corte1321.com* 🛏 *4 rooms, 1 apartment* ☾ *Closed Jan.* ⊙ *Breakfast*
Ⓜ *Vaporetto: San Silvestro* ✛ *D3.*

$$ 🏨 **La Villeggiatura.** If eclectic Venetian charm is what you seek, this
HOTEL   luminous residence offers six individually decorated rooms, each with
its own original, theatrically themed fresco by a local artist. **Pros:**
relaxed atmosphere; meticulously maintained; well-located. **Cons:**
positioned high over a popular and busy thoroughfare; no elevator and lots of stairs; modest breakfast; no view to speak of, despite
the climb. ⑤ *Rooms from: €195* ✉ *Calle dei Botteri, San Polo 1569*

4

☎ *041/5244673* ⊕ *www.lavilleggiatura.it* 🛏 *6 rooms* ❙❂❙ *Breakfast*
Ⓜ *Vaporetto: Rialto Mercato* ✢ *D3.*

$$ ⛫ **Locanda Sant'Agostin.** You'll find enough classic Venetian charac-
B&B/INN   teristics to remind of you where you are, but not so many as to be
stuffy or ostentatious. **Pros:** tranquil atmosphere; attentive service;
authentic period renovation; good location near the Frari. **Cons:** a
bit of a walk from the vaporetto stop; no Wi-Fi in rooms. ⑤ *Rooms*
from: €195 ✉ *Campo Sant'Agostin, San Polo 2344* ☎ *041/2759414*
⊕ *www.locandasantagostin.com* 🛏 *9 rooms, 1 junior suite* ❙❂❙ *Breakfast*
Ⓜ *Vaporetto: San Stae, San Silvestro, or San Tomà* ✢ *C3.*

$$$ ⛫ **Oltre il Giardino–Casaifrari.** It's easy to overlook—and it can be a chal-
HOTEL   lenge to find—this secluded palazzo, sheltered as it is behind a brick wall
just over the bridge from the Frari church, but the search is well worth
it: airy, individually decorated guest rooms face a large garden, an oasis
of peace (especially in high season). **Pros:** a peaceful, gracious, and convenient setting; walled garden. **Cons:** a beautiful, but not particularly
Venetian, ambience. ⑤ *Rooms from: €250* ✉ *Fondamenta Contarini,*
San Polo 2542 ☎ *041/2750015* ⊕ *www.oltreilgiardino-venezia.com*
🛏 *6 rooms* ❙❂❙ *Breakfast* Ⓜ *Vaporetto: San Tomà* ✢ *C3.*

$$$ ⛫ **Palazzo Barbarigo.** It is not unusual to find an opulent hotel along
HOTEL   the Grand Canal; it *is* unusual to discover black marble, matte lac-
quer, indirect lighting, and 1940s design perfectly ensconced in a
16th-century Venetian palace. **Pros:** small; lavish; an uncommon ambi-
ence. **Cons:** standard rooms have pleasant side canal, but not Grand
Canal, views; at times, unpleasant odors waft from the side canal.
⑤ *Rooms from: €300* ✉ *Calle Cormer, San Polo 3765* ☎ *041/74072*
⊕ *www.palazzobarbarigo.it* 🛏 *8 rooms, 6 junior suites* ❙❂❙ *Breakfast*
Ⓜ *Vaporetto: San Tomà* ✢ *C4.*

SANTA CROCE

$$ ⛫ **Hotel al Ponte Mocenigo.** A columned courtyard welcomes you to this
HOTEL   elegant, charming palazzo, former home of the Santa Croce branch of
Fodor's Choice   the Mocenigo family (which has a few doges in its past), and the cano-
★   pied beds, striped damask fabrics, lustrous terrazzo flooring, and gilt-
accented furnishings keep the sense of Venice's past strong in the guest
rooms. **Pros:** enchanting courtyard; water access; friendly and helpful
staff; free Wi-Fi. **Cons:** beds are on the hard side; standard rooms are
small; rooms in the annex can be noisy. ⑤ *Rooms from: €145* ✉ *Fonda-*
mento de Rimpeto a Ca' Mocenigo, Santa Croce 2063 ☎ *041/5244797*
⊕ *www.alpontemocenigo.com* 🛏 *10 rooms, 1 junior suite* ❙❂❙ *Breakfast*
Ⓜ *Vaporetto: San Stae* ✢ *C2.*

$$$$ ⛫ **Hotel Canal Grande.** A convenient location near the train station yet off
HOTEL   the beaten tourist path couples 18th-century elegance with modern amenities, and the decoration, inspired by Venetian history, includes lush
damasks, gold-framed mirrors, and plenty of Murano glass and Rez-
zonico-style floors. **Pros:** excellent position for those traveling by train;
Grand Canal views; helpful and informative staff; free Wi-Fi. **Cons:**
far from Piazza San Marco; a little on the pricey side. ⑤ *Rooms from:*
€310 ✉ *Campo San Simeone Grande, Santa Croce 932* ☎ *041/2440148*

⊕ *www.hotelcanalgrande.it* ➫ *22 rooms* |◎| *Breakfast* Ⓜ *Vaporetto: Riva di Biasio* ⊕ *C2.*

CANNAREGIO

$$
B&B/INN
⊡ **3749 Ponte Chiodo.** Attractively appointed guest rooms handy to the Ca' d'Oro vaporetto stop look past geranium-filled windows to the bridge leading to its entrance (one of the few without hand railings remaining) and canals below or the spacious enclosed garden. **Pros:** highly attentive service; warm, relaxed atmosphere; private garden; excellent value. **Cons:** no elevator; some bathrooms are smallish. Ⓢ *Rooms from: €180* ⊠ *Calle Racchetta, Cannaregio 3749, Cannaregio* ☏ *041/2413935* ⊕ *www.pontechiodo.it* ➫ *6 rooms* |◎| *Breakfast* Ⓜ *Vaporetto: Ca' d'Oro* ⊕ *D2.*

$$
B&B/INN
⊡ **Alla Vite Dorata.** Newly restored and thoughtfully appointed lodgings at the end of a narrow calle have beamed ceilings, large windows that invite in light and provide canal views, and space-liberating iron and glass furniture. **Pros:** canal views; handy for sightseeing; lots of restaurant and *bàcari* (wine bars) options nearby; no stairs. **Cons:** ground-level lodgings might not appeal to everyone. Ⓢ *Rooms from: €140* ⊠ *Rio Terà Barba Frutariol, Cannaregio 4690/B, Cannaregio* ☏ *041/2413018* ⊕ *www.allavitedorata.com* ➫ *6 rooms* |◎| *Breakfast* Ⓜ *Vaporetto: Ca' d'Oro, Fondamente Nove* ⊕ *C2.*

$
B&B/INN
Fodor'sChoice
★
⊡ **Al Palazzetto.** Understated yet gracious Venetian decor, original open-beam ceilings and terrazzo flooring, spotless marble baths, and friendly, attentive service are hallmarks of this intimate, family-owned locanda. **Pros:** standout service; owner on-site; quiet; free Wi-Fi. **Cons:** not for amenity seekers or lovers of ultramodern decor. Ⓢ *Rooms from: €100* ⊠ *Calle delle Vele, Cannaregio 4057, Cannaregio* ☏ *041/2750897* ⊕ *www.guesthouse.it* ➫ *6 rooms, 1 suite* |◎| *Breakfast* Ⓜ *Vaporetto: Ca' d'Oro* ⊕ *D2.*

$$$
HOTEL
Fodor'sChoice
★
⊡ **Al Ponte Antico.** This 16th-century palace inn has lined its Gothic windows with tiny white lights, creating an inviting glow that's emblematic of the hospitality and sumptuous surroundings that await you inside: rich brocade-tufted walls, period-style furniture, and hand-decorated beamed ceilings. **Pros:** upper-level terrace overlooks Grand Canal; family run; superior service; Internet is free. **Cons:** in one of the busiest areas of the city. Ⓢ *Rooms from: €315* ⊠ *Calle dell'Aseo, Cannaregio 5768, Cannaregio* ☏ *041/2411944* ⊕ *www.alponteantico.com* ➫ *12 rooms, 1 junior suite* |◎| *Breakfast* Ⓜ *Vaporetto: Rialto* ⊕ *E3.*

$$$
HOTEL
⊡ **Ca' Gottardi.** Traditional Venetian style mixes with contemporary design: the clean white-marble entrance leading up to the luminous *piano nobile* (main floor) of the 15th-century palace gracefully contrasts with the opulent Murano chandeliers and rich wall brocades. **Pros:** great location; mix of old and new styles; canal views. **Cons:** no outdoor garden or terrace; standard rooms are quite small. Ⓢ *Rooms from: €250* ⊠ *Strada Nova, Cannaregio 2283, Cannaregio* ☏ *041/2759333* ⊕ *www.cagottardi.com* ➫ *7 rooms, 2 suites* |◎| *Breakfast* Ⓜ *Vaporetto: Ca' d'Oro* ⊕ *D2.*

$
B&B/INN
⊡ **Casa del Melograno.** This renovated classic Venetian residence is modestly appointed, but you'll still find features like Venetian terrazzo

flooring and tiled baths, and it offers its guests an ample garden in which they can relax with a good book or have breakfast. **Pros:** simple, handy, and inexpensive for Venice; beautiful and spacious garden for breakfast in the summer; handy to the train station for day trips. **Cons:** extra charge for Internet; decor is spartan, so not the ideal place for a romantic Venetian vacation. $\boxed{S}$ *Rooms from: €115* ✉ *Fondamenta del Ponte Storto, Cannaregio 2023, Cannaregio* ☎ *041/5208807* ⊕ *www. locandadelmelograno.it* ⇆ *6 rooms* ⦿*| Breakfast* Ⓜ *Vaporetto: San Marcuola* ✛ *C2.*

$$$$
HOTEL
Fodor's Choice
★
🖼 **Ca' Sagredo Hotel.** A study in Venetian opulence, this expansive palace has been the Sagredo family residence since the mid-1600s and has the decor to prove it: the massive staircase has Longhi frescoes soaring above it and the large common areas are adorned with original art by Tiepolo, Longhi, and Ricci, among others. **Pros:** excellent location; authentic yet comfortable renovation of Venice's patrician past. **Cons:** more opulent than intimate. $\boxed{S}$ *Rooms from: €400* ✉ *Campo Santa Sofia, Cannaregio 4198/99, Cannaregio* ☎ *041/2413111* ⊕ *www. casagredohotel.com* ⇆ *42 rooms, 2 junior suites, 3 suites* ⦿*| Breakfast* Ⓜ *Vaporetto: Ca' d'Oro* ✛ *D2.*

$$
B&B/INN
🖼 **Domus Orsoni.** The grounds of the famous Orsoni Mosaics factory provides the setting for these five rooms that have been uniquely decorated with color and gold mosaics accenting furniture, fixtures, and baths. **Pros:** a fine option for anyone looking for a unique experience in lodging; no bridges and few steps to deal with. **Cons:** near vaporetto stops but a bit removed from the action (which can be a plus); no sweeping views. $\boxed{S}$ *Rooms from: €200* ✉ *Sottoportego dei Vedei, Cannaregio 1045, Cannaregio* ☎ *041/2759538* ⊕ *www.domusorsoni.it* ⇆ *5 rooms* ⦿*| Breakfast* Ⓜ *Vaporetto: Guglie, Tre Archi, or Crea* ✛ *B1.*

$$
HOTEL
🖼 **Hotel ai Mori d'Oriente.** Though the atmosphere harkens back to Venice's connection with the exotic East, the surroundings and amenities are everything you'd expect from a 21st-century establishment, and the staff is highly accommodating. **Pros:** quiet area; modern structure; nice for families; canal-side bar for breakfast or cocktails. **Cons:** a bit remote from San Marco; fee for Wi-Fi. $\boxed{S}$ *Rooms from: €200* ✉ *Fondamenta della Sensa, Cannaregio 3319, Cannaregio* ☎ *041/711001* ⊕ *www. morihotel.com* ⇆ *19 rooms, 2 junior suites* ⦿*| Breakfast* Ⓜ *Vaporetto: San Marcuola or Madonna dell'Orto* ✛ *D1.*

$$
HOTEL
🖼 **Hotel Antico Doge.** Once the home of Doge Marino Falier, this *palazzo* has been attentively modernized in elegant Venetian style: all rooms are adorned with brocades, damask tufted walls, gilt mirrors, and parquet floors and even the breakfast room comes fitted out with a stuccoed ceiling and Murano chandelier. **Pros:** romantic, atmospheric decor; convenient to the Rialto and beyond. **Cons:** on a busy thoroughfare; no outdoor garden or terrace; no elevator. $\boxed{S}$ *Rooms from: €170* ✉ *Campo Santi Apostoli, Cannaregio 5643, Cannaregio* ☎ *041/2411570* ⊕ *www. anticodoge.com* ⇆ *19 rooms, 1 suite* ⦿*| Breakfast* Ⓜ *Vaporetto: Ca' d'Oro or Rialto* ✛ *E3.*

$$$
HOTEL
🖼 **Hotel Foscari Palace.** Rooms in this extensively renovated palace overlook the Grand Canal or the bustling Campo Santo Sofia, and plush, traditional furnishings and extensive use of marble and blond

wood trim contribute to a relaxed yet gracious ambience. **Pros:** lovely view over the rooftops and Grand Canal from the terrace; handy for walking, vaporetto, and gondola traghetto. **Cons:** on a busy square; has a less distinctively Venetian feel than some other options. Ⓢ *Rooms from: €270* ✉ *Campo Santo Sofia, Cannaregio 4200/1/2, Cannaregio* ☎ *041/5297611* ⊕ *www. hotelfoscaripalace.com* ⇄ *23 rooms, 1 junior suite, 2 suites* |○| *Breakfast* Ⓜ *Vaporetto: Ca' d'Oro* ✛ *D2.*

> **WORD OF MOUTH**
>
> "I don't think you can select a 'wrong place' to stay in Venice. Each district or sestiere is unique. All are safe and delightful to be in." —Mormor

$$$ 🛏 **Hotel Giorgione.** Comfortably appointed rooms in a quiet corner of
HOTEL Cannaregio charm guests with their traditional Venetian fabric and furnishings, along with the original terrazzo flooring, gracious courtyard and marble fountain, fanciful Murano chandeliers, and billiard salon. **Pros:** family-run; unique ambience; elegant garden. **Cons:** no canal views. Ⓢ *Rooms from: €240* ✉ *Off Campo Santi Apostoli, Cannaregio 4587, Cannaregio* ☎ *041/5225810* ⊕ *www.hotelgiorgione. com* ⇄ *76 rooms* |○| *Breakfast* Ⓜ *Vaporetto: Ca' d'Oro or Fondamente Nove* ✛ *E2.*

$$$ 🛏 **Hotel UNA Venezia.** Up a narrow calle and across the bridge from the
HOTEL bustling Strada Nova, this 15th-century palazzo lingers silently over a tranquil canal and an evocative little campo; inside you'll find traditional Venetian decor and guest rooms featuring silk damasks tufted onto multiwindowed walls. **Pros:** an intimate, boutique hideaway still handy for exploring the city; substantial rate reduction for stays of three days or longer. **Cons:** classic rooms are quite small; extra charge for Internet. Ⓢ *Rooms from: €260* ✉ *Ruga Do Pozzi, Cannaregio 4173, Cannaregio* ☎ *041/2442711* ⊕ *www.unahotels.com* ⇄ *28 rooms, 3 junior suites, 3 suites* |○| *Breakfast* Ⓜ *Vaporetto: Ca' d'Oro* ✛ *E2.*

$$ 🛏 **Locanda Ca' Amadi.** A historic palazzo is a welcome retreat on a tran-
HOTEL quil *corte,* and individually decorated rooms have tufted walls and views of a lively canal or a quiet courtyard. **Pros:** classic Venetian style; personal service; free Wi-Fi; handy for sightseeing. **Cons:** standard rooms are small; not ideal for guests with mobility issues; staff present only during hours of reception (though always available by phone and on request). Ⓢ *Rooms from: €140* ✉ *Corte Amadi, Cannaregio 5815, Cannaregio* ☎ *041/5285210* ⊕ *www.caamadi.it* ⇄ *6 rooms* |○| *Breakfast* Ⓜ *Vaporetto: Rialto* ✛ *E3.*

$$$ 🛏 **Palazzo Abadessa.** At this late-16th-century palazzo, you can experi-
HOTEL ence gracious hospitality, a luxurious atmosphere, and unusually spa-
Fodor's Choice cious guest rooms well appointed with antique-style furniture, frescoed
★ or stuccoed ceilings, and silk fabrics. **Pros:** enormous walled garden, a rare and delightful treat in crowded Venice; superb guest service. **Cons:** some bathrooms are small. Ⓢ *Rooms from: €295* ✉ *Calle Priuli off Strada Nova, Cannaregio 4011, Cannaregio* ☎ *041/2413784* ⊕ *www. abadessa.com* ⇄ *10 rooms, 5 suites* |○| *Breakfast* Ⓜ *Vaporetto: Ca' d'Oro* ✛ *E2.*

CASTELLO

$$
HOTEL
⛨ **Ca' Formenta.** In a residential area off the tourist track, a thoroughly renovated 15th-century building offers pleasant accommodations and plenty of service. **Pros:** Castello still feels like authentic Venice; convenient to the piazza, the Lido, and the north lagoon islands. **Cons:** a bit removed from some sights. $ *Rooms from: €215* ✉ *Via Garibaldi, Castello 1650* ☎ *041/5285494* ⊕ *www.hotelcaformenta.it* ↪ *12 rooms, 2 suites* ⦿ *Breakfast* Ⓜ *Vaporetto: Arsenale or Giardini* ✛ *G5.*

$$$$
HOTEL
⛨ **Hotel Bucintoro.** "All rooms with a view" touts this *pensione*-turned-four-star-hotel—and the views are indeed expansive: from the hotel's waterfront location near lively Via Garibaldi, your windows swing open to a panorama that sweeps from the Lido across the basin to San Giorgio and San Marco; upper-floor vistas are particularly inspiring. **Pros:** recent, tasteful renovation; lagoon views from all rooms; waterfront without the San Marco crowds; reduced rates for stays of more than one night. **Cons:** yachts and huge cruise ships sometimes dock outside, blocking lagoon views, and without those views the hotel is really overpriced. $ *Rooms from: €400* ✉ *Riva degli Schiavoni, Castello 2135/A* ☎ *041/5209909* ⊕ *www.hotelbucintoro.com* ↪ *20 rooms, 6 junior suites* ⦿ *Breakfast* Ⓜ *Vaporetto: Arsenale* ✛ *G4.*

$$$$
HOTEL
⛨ **Hotel Danieli.** Welcoming guests with one of the most sumptuous, quintessentially Venetian loggias-lobbies (part of the late-14th-century Palazzo Dandolo, built by the family of the doge who conquered Constantinople), this fabled and meticulously maintained monument of Venetian history sets the standard for premium luxury: marble columns here; carved archways there, and plush furniture everywhere. **Pros:** beautiful, well-maintained rooms; a sense of history; spectacular views; lower rates available for rooms without views. **Cons:** the restaurant, though acceptable, isn't of the standard of the rest of the hotel; breakfast is not included, and expensive. $ *Rooms from: €820* ✉ *Riva degli Schiavoni, Castello 4196* ☎ *041/5226480* ⊕ *www.danielihotelvenice. com* ↪ *225 rooms* ⦿ *No meals* Ⓜ *Vaporetto: San Zaccaria* ✛ *F4.*

$$
HOTEL
⛨ **Hotel La Residenza.** Most rooms at this renovated Gothic-Byzantine *palazzo* are spacious and elegant, with period furnishings and 18th-century paintings as well as modern amenities. **Pros:** free Wi-Fi; quiet, residential area. **Cons:** not super close to a vaporetto stop; a few of the rooms are indeed small; not the warmest staff. $ *Rooms from: €190* ✉ *Campo Bandiera e Moro (or Bragora), Castello 3608* ☎ *041/5285315* ⊕ *www.venicelaresidenza.com* ↪ *15 rooms* ⦿ *Breakfast* Ⓜ *Vaporetto: Arsenale* ✛ *G4.*

$$$$
HOTEL
⛨ **Hotel Londra Palace.** A wall of windows soaks up extraordinary, sweeping views of the lagoon and the island of San Giorgio, enjoyed from many of the individually decorated guest rooms and suites, which have fine fabric, damask drapes, Biedermeier furniture, and Venetian glass. **Pros:** superlative views; professional service. **Cons:** area is one of the most touristy in Venice, and the Riva's liveliness can extend late into the evening. $ *Rooms from: €430* ✉ *Riva degli Schiavoni, Castello 4171* ☎ *041/5200533* ⊕ *www.londrapalace.com* ↪ *35 rooms, 18 junior suites* ⦿ *Breakfast* Ⓜ *Vaporetto: San Zaccaria* ✛ *F4.*

$ 🏨 **Locanda Casa Querini.** Pastel lacquered furnishings pay tribute to 18th-
B&B/INN   century Venetian style, and deep blue carpeting helps keep rooms quiet;
ask for one that overlooks the campo in front. **Pros:** strategic location
between San Zaccaria and Campo Santa Maria Formosa. **Cons:** no
elevator. $ *Rooms from: €160* ✉ *Campo San Giovanni Novo, Cas-
tello 4388* ☎ *041/2411294* ⊕ *www.locandaquerini.com* ⤳ *6 rooms*
⎟◎⎟ *Breakfast* Ⓜ *Vaporetto: San Zaccaria* ✛ *F4.*

$$$$ 🏨 **Metropole.** Atmosphere prevails in this labyrinth of intimate, opulent
HOTEL   spaces featuring classic Venetian decor combined with exotic Eastern
Fodor's Choice   influences: the owner—a lifelong collector of unusual objects—fills
★   common areas and the sumptuously appointed guest rooms with an
assortment of antiques and curiosities. **Pros:** hotel harkens back to a
gracious Venice of times past; fine bar. **Cons:** one of the most densely
touristed locations in the city; rooms with views are considerably more
expensive; air-conditioning not completely reliable; restaurant is very
expensive. $ *Rooms from: €400* ✉ *Riva degli Schiavoni, Castello 4149*
☎ *041/5205044* ⊕ *www.hotelmetropole.com* ⤳ *67 rooms, 13 junior
suites, 9 suites* ⎟◎⎟ *Breakfast* Ⓜ *Vaporetto: San Zaccaria* ✛ *F4.*

$$$$ 🏨 **Ruzzini Palace Hotel.** Public rooms are Renaissance- and baroque-style,
HOTEL   with soaring spaces, Venetian terrazzo flooring, frescoed and open-
beamed ceilings, and Murano chandeliers, while guest rooms are essays
in historic style but come integrated with contemporary furnishings and
appointments. **Pros:** excellent service; a luminous, aristocratic ambience. **Cons:** the walk from San Zaccaria or Rialto includes two bridges
and can be cumbersome for those with mobility issues or significant
amounts of luggage; relatively far from a vaporetto stop; no restaurant.
$ *Rooms from: €380* ✉ *Campo Santa Maria Formosa, Castello 5866*
☎ *041/2410447* ⊕ *www.ruzzinipalace.com* ⤳ *19 rooms, 6 junior suites,
3 suites* ⎟◎⎟ *Breakfast* Ⓜ *Vaporetto: San Zaccaria or Rialto* ✛ *F3.*

THE GIUDECCA

$$$$ 🏨 **Hotel Cipriani and Palazzo Vendramin by Orient-Express.** An oasis in the
HOTEL   midst of the hustle and bustle of Venice embodies the glamour and
elegance of the mid-20th century: excellent service, elegant, peaceful
rooms that blend historic and contemporary styles, some with spectacular views of the lagoon, and a heated saltwater swimming pool.
Pros: obliging staff; beautiful setting. **Cons:** reachable only by the
hotel's shuttle or taxi service; you could forget you're in Venice, which
might appeal to some guests. $ *Rooms from: €1,100* ✉ *Giudecca
10, Giudecca* ☎ *041/240801* ⊕ *www.hotelcipriani.com* ⤳ *95 rooms*
⎟◎⎟ *Breakfast* ✛ *E6.*

THE LIDO

$$$$ 🏨 **Westin Excelsior.** The Excelsior's imposing, Moorish-style building
RESORT   with its green cupolas and inner courtyard comes complete with pot-
ted lemon trees, a reflecting pool; and dramatic windows overlooking the Adriatic Sea; the feel is decidedly Mediterranean. **Pros:** private
beach with classic European beach facilities; pool June–September;
superb service. **Cons:** removed from Venice proper; no Wi-Fi in rooms.

Ⓢ *Rooms from: €350* ✉ *Lungomare Marconi 17* ☎ *041/5260201* ⊕ *www.hotelexcelsiorvenezia.com* ⤳ *178 rooms, 19 suites* ⊘ *Closed Nov.–Mar.* ⦿ *Breakfast* Ⓜ *Vaporetto: Lido* ✣ *G6.*

TORCELLO

$$$
B&B/INN

▦ **Locanda Cipriani.** Founded by Giuseppe Cipriani in the late 1920s, this intimate *locanda* on the island of Torcello remains in the Cipriani family and retains the simple, classy character of the period, and the lovingly furnished rooms have large beds, plush armchairs, vaulted ceilings, and modern amenities—but absolutely no televisions! **Pros:** charming ambience; pure tranquility. **Cons:** very isolated, yet Torcello is a delight. Ⓢ *Rooms from: €260* ✉ *Piazza Santa Fosca 29, Torcello* ☎ *041/730150* ⊕ *www.locandacipriani.com* ⤳ *5 rooms* ⦿ *Breakfast* Ⓜ *Vaporetto: Torcello* ✣ *F1.*

NIGHTLIFE
AND THE ARTS

Updated by
Nan McElroy

Your first impression may well be that Venice doesn't have a nightlife. As the last rays of daylight slip away, so, too, do most signs of a bustling town. Boat traffic drops to the occasional vaporetto, shutters roll down, and signs go dark. Even though *bacari* (wine bars) would seem to be natural after-hours gathering spots, most close before 9 pm.

But boulevardiers, flaneurs, and those who simply enjoy a little after-dinner entertainment can take heart. Sprinkled judiciously around the city's residential-looking *calli* and *campi* (streets and squares), you'll stumble upon *locali* (nightspots) that stay open until 1 or 2 am. Some even offer live music, though rarely past midnight—a city noise ordinance prohibits too much wildness except during Carnevale. Though there are no suitable venues for rock shows, Piazza San Marco has hosted some less-rambunctious concerts on summer evenings. Except for a few lounge bars with dancing, nightlife tends to be student oriented.

Both private and city museums regularly host major traveling art exhibits, from ancient to contemporary. Classical music buffs can rely on a rich season of concerts, opera, chamber music, and some ballet. Smaller venues and churches offer lower-priced, occasionally free performances that often highlight Venetian and Italian composers. Though the city has no English-language theater, during Carnevale you'll find foreign companies that perform in their mother tongue. All films screened at the Venice Film Festival (some in an ad-hoc amphitheater constructed in Campo San Polo) in late summer are shown in the original language, with subtitles in English, Italian, or both.

There is a variety of resources for finding what's on in Venice. Both the city and the province have tourism offices and associated websites with English versions, ⊕ *turismovenezia.com* and ⊕ *comune.venezia.it*, respectively. (For the second, click on the "Tourism" tab.) The calendar publication available at the APT tourist offices on the Piazza San Marco and in the Pavilion near the Vallaresso vaporetto stop provides extensive, current information on museums, churches, exhibitions, events day-by-day, useful phone numbers, gondola and taxi fares, opening hours, and more. *A Guest in Venice,* a monthly bilingual booklet, free at hotels, also includes information about pharmacies, vaporetto and bus lines, and main trains and flights; ⊕ *aguestinvenice.com* lists musical, artistic, and sporting events, as does Agenda Venezia (⊕ *agendavenezia. org*). *Venezia News,* available at newsstands, has similar information but also includes in-depth articles about noteworthy events; listings are bilingual, but most articles are in Italian. *Venezia da Vivere* is a bilingual guide that comes out seasonally listing nightspots and live music. Try ⊕ *venicexplorer.com* for a fantastic map function to find any address in Venice, and ⊕ *venicebanana.com* and the ⊕ *2night.it* listings for lots of insider restaurant and entertainment goings-on. Look to ⊕ *music-invenice.com* for a comprehensive calendar of musical events that you can also reserve (they even have a 24-hour phone service). Last but not least, don't ignore the posters you see everywhere in the streets; they're often as current as you can get.

NIGHTLIFE

Nightspots in and around Venice can be difficult to categorize. Pubs, of the English or Irish variety, with beer on tap and occasional live music, are easy enough to identify and are especially popular with local and traveling youth. When you're looking to dance, things get murkier: lounge-type piano bars generally have small dance floors, while dance clubs are scarce but may serve snacks and even late-night meals. Bars and cafés are even harder to classify, as availability of snacks, meals, beverages, and music varies with the time of day and the season. Many also decorate their walls with works by local artists, whose paintings are for sale.

The proximity to the university makes Campo Santa Margherita and the surrounding area one of the livelier gathering places in town after dark. The Erbaria, a wide open campo running along the Grand Canal at the foot of the Rialto Bridge on the San Polo side, and the Fondamenta Misericordia in Cannaregio are two other areas that have a happening evening scene.

It's worth noting that during Carnevale many ordinary bars, which close around dinnertime the rest of the year, stay open around the clock. ⇨ *For more about Carnevale, see the feature in the Experience Venice.*

SAN MARCO

BARS

B Bar Lounge. This room in the Hotel Bauer is multipurpose: it functions more like a lounge on weekdays and an intimate dance club complete with a DJ on the weekends, though it really depends on the clientele's mood. Cocktail prices are high, but so are your chances of seeing a celebrity. ⊠ *Hotel Bauer, San Marco 1459* ☎ *041/5207022* ⊘ *Mon. and Tues.* Ⓜ *Vaporetto: San Marco.*

Caffè Baglioni. Just outside Piazza San Marco (near Museo Correr), Hotel Luna Baglioni's pleasant café is perfect for an intimate chat in

the cold winter months. There's live piano (or guitar) music from 6 pm until midnight Fridays and Saturdays, as well as on Thursdays during the summer. ⊠ *Calle Larga de l'Ascension, San Marco 1243* ☎ *041/5289840* Ⓜ *Vaporetto: Vallaresso.*

Caffè Centrale. A late-night, chilled-out crowd that looks more Hollywood than Venice assembles in this former movie theater. You'll find classic (if overpriced) wines and mojitos and other mixed drinks; black leather couches, dim lighting, and a DJ set the lounge mood. There's occasional live music. Late-night dinner is also an option. ⊠ *Piscina Frezzeria, San Marco 1659/B* ☎ *041/2960664* ⊕ *www. caffecentralevenezia.com/.*

Corte dell'Orso. It is easy to see why this place is popular with the locals: you cannot go wrong with fairly priced cocktails, excellent *cicchetti* (snacks), and a good selection of Italian wine, along with a warm ambience, a friendly staff, and live music every Wednesday (beginning around 8 pm). The kitchen stays open until midnight if you care for a late-night dinner. ⊠ *Just tucked away behind Campo San Bartolomeo, San Marco 5495* ☎ *041/5224673* Ⓜ *Vaporetto: Rialto.*

DORSODURO

BARS

Al Chioschetto. Although this popular place consists only of a kiosk set up to serve some outdoor tables, it is located on the Zattere, and hence provides panoramic views. It's a handy meet-up for locals and a stop-off for tourists in nice weather for a *spritz*, late-night *panini* (sandwiches), or a sunny read as the Venetian world eases by. ⊠ *Near Ponte Lungo, Dorsoduro 1406/A* ☎ *338/1174077* Ⓜ *Vaporetto: Zattere.*

Fodor'sChoice
★ **Il Caffè.** Commonly called "Bar Rosso" for its bright-red exterior, Il Caffè has far more tables outside than inside. A favorite with students and faculty from the nearby university, it's a good place to enjoy a *spritz*—the preferred Venetian aperitif of white wine, Campari or Aperol, soda water, an olive, and a slice of orange. It has excellent tramezzini (among the best in town) and panini, and a hip, helpful staff. Its closing time depends on the always-changing noise laws, but typically around 1 am. ⊠ *Campo Santa Margherita, Dorsoduro 2963* ☎ *041/5287998* ☾ *Closed Sun.*

Fodor'sChoice
★ **Imagina.** Just off Campo Santa Margherita toward the Porte dei Pugni, this bar draws a more mature and sophisticated Venetian clientele than the student-oriented places in the campo itself. The friendly fellows running the place make an excellent (and generous) spritz, serve decent wine, and some American regulars have taught them to make a rather palatable martini. Sandwiches and snacks are limited, but what's offered is fresh and tasty. Outdoor and indoor seating is available. The bar hosts regular art exhibitions by local, yet-to-be-established artists. ⊠ *Campo Santa Margherita, Dorsoduro 3126* ☾ *Closed Sun.* Ⓜ *Vaporetto: Ca' Rezzonico.*

Impronta. One of the rare locales that has a kitchen serving until midnight also offers a bar menu until 2. It's also a good spot for nightcap—you

The Biennale gives a contemporary look to its classic Venetian setting.

can expect a fairly lively atmosphere right up until closing time. ✉ *Calle Crosera, Dorsoduro 3815* ☎ *041/2750386* 🌐 *www.improntacafevenice.com* ⏲ *Closed Sun.* Ⓜ *Vaporetto: San Tomà.*

Margaret Duchamp. The French-sounding name befits this artfully minimalist café-brasserie in Campo Santa Margherita. Classic Venetian cocktails are served alongside warm sandwiches and light salads all day until 2 am. ✉ *Campo Santa Margherita, Dorsoduro 3019* ☎ *041/5286255* Ⓜ *Vaporetto: Ca' Rezzonico.*

Orange. Modern, hip, and complemented by a nice internal garden, this welcoming bar anchors the south end of Campo Santa Margherita, the liveliest campo in Venice. You can have *piadine* sandwiches, salads, and drinks while watching soccer games on a massive screen inside, or sit at the tables in the campo. Despite being close to the university, Orange is frequented primarily by young working people from the mainland and tourists. ✉ *Campo Santa Margherita, Dorsoduro 3054/A* ☎ *041/5234740.*

Senso Unico. This popular neighborhood hangout is decorated in wood and brick and has a couple of tables that have a great view of the canal. There are beers on tap and plenty of wine and sandwich choices from 10 am to 1 am. ✉ *Past Campo San Vio before the Guggenheim, Dorsoduro 684* ☎ *348/3720847* ⏲ *Closed Tues.* Ⓜ *Vaporetto: Accademia.*

Sotto Sopra. On two warmly decorated floors that resemble an old ship, you can enjoy one of 30 different beers, 20 aged whiskeys, or a glass of Italian wine. It opens at 10 am weekdays, 5 pm Saturday, and serves light dishes until 1:30 am every night. There is karaoke by request until 11 pm nightly. ⊠ *San Pantalon, Dorsoduro 3740* ☎ *041/5242177* Ⓜ *Vaporetto: San Tomà.*

JAZZ CLUBS

Venice Jazz Club. This spot hosts the only live jazz concerts in town; the cover gets you a concert, a table, and your first drink. They also serve cold cuts and sandwiches from when the doors open at 7 pm until the music begins at 9 pm. It's best to reserve a table (and you can book through the website). ⊠ *Near Ponte dei Pugni, Dorsoduro 3102* ☎ *041/5232056, 340/1504985* ⊕ *www.venicejazzclub.com* ☉ *Closed Dec., Jan., and Aug., and occasionally on Thurs. and Sun.* Ⓜ *Vaporetto: Ca' Rezzonico.*

SAN POLO

BARS

Naranzaria. At the friendliest of the several bar-restaurants that line the Erbaria, enjoy a cocktail outside along the Canal Grande or at a cozy table inside of the renovated 16th-century palazzo. After the kitchen closes at 10:30, light snacks are served until midnight, and live music (usually jazz, Latin, or rock) plays on Sunday evenings. ⊠ *L'Erbaria, along the Canal Grande, San Polo 130* ☎ *041/7241035* Ⓜ *Vaporetto: Rialto Mercato.*

CANNAREGIO

BARS

The Irish Pub. Guinness and gab flow freely from 5 pm to 1 am. There are typically four Irish brews, plus cider, on tap, as well as sports on TV and occasional live music, either Irish or rock. Small sandwiches are available until late (the *segalini* are divine). ⊠ *Corte dei Pali, off Strada Nova, Cannaregio 3847* ☎ *041/5239930* Ⓜ *Vaporetto: Ca' d'Oro.*

CASINOS

Palazzo Vendramin-Calergi. The city-run gambling casino in splendid Palazzo Vendramin-Calergi is a classic scene of well-dressed high rollers playing French roulette, Caribbean poker, chemin de fer, 30–40, and slots. You must be at least 18 to enter, and men must wear jackets. ⊠ *Campiello Vendramin, Cannaregio 2040* ☎ *041/5297111* 💶 *€10 entry includes €10 in chips* ☉ *Slots daily 11 am–2:30 am, tables daily 3:30 pm–2:30 am* Ⓜ *Vaporetto: San Marcuola.*

CASTELLO

BARS

Fodor's Choice ★ **El Réfolo Wine Bar.** Tiny dimensions notwithstanding, this popular stop is inviting to anyone on their way up or down Via Garibaldi, owing to its savory snacks, wine selection, and live music on some Friday nights when the weather's fine. There's no set closing hour—they'll tell you when it's time to leave. ⊠ *Via Garibaldi, Castello 1580* Ⓜ *Vaporetto: Arsenale.*

Enoiteca Mascareta. Wander the long *calle* from Santa Maria Formosa to find this welcome spot where you're sure to find the light on. Choose from one of the best wine selections in the city, and opt for a late-night snack if you prefer. They're open until 2 am. ⊠ *Calle Lurga Santa Maria Formosa, Castello 5138* ☎ *041/5230744* ⊘ *Tues. and Wed.* Ⓜ *Vaporetto: San Zaccaria.*

Inishark. The popular Italo-Irish pub Inishark, located midway between San Marco and Rialto, is known for its variety of international beers. It's open until 1:30 am. ⊠ *Calle Mondo Novo near San Lio, Castello 5787* ☎ *041/5235300* ⊘ *Closed Mon.* Ⓜ *Vaporetto: Rialto.*

Fodor's Choice
★

Serra dei Giardini. By day this grand, Liberty-style greenhouse sells plants and gardening equipment and serves as a well-placed café for Biennale visitors. By night, it is a great place to come for a prosecco cocktail (blended with fresh, seasonal fruit juice) and a light snack while taking in the greenery—a rarity in Venice. There is live music on Saturday nights, from 8 to midnight, where bands play everything from jazz to reggae to rockabilly. The space also occasionally hosts art exhibitions. ⊠ *Viale Giuseppe Garibaldi, Castello 1254* ☎ *041/2960360* ⊕ *www. serradeigiardini.org* ⊘ *Mon.* Ⓜ *Vaporetto: Giardini.*

Zanzibar. This kiosk bar that's very popular on warm summer evenings offers food but that is mostly limited to sandwiches and ice cream. The most delicious thing about the place is its location along the canal near Chiesa di Santa Maria Formosa, which makes it a truly pleasant place for a drink. ⊠ *Campo Santa Maria Formosa, Castello 5840* ☎ *041/962640* Ⓜ *Vaporetto: San Zaccaria.*

THE ARTS

Art has been a way of life in Venice for so many centuries that it seems you need only inhale to enjoy it. From mid-June to early November in odd-numbered years, the Biennale dell'Arte attracts a whirlwind of contemporary arts, showcasing several hundred contemporary artists from around the world. During Carnevale, masks and costumes let revelers dance with history. Costumed musicians will entice you to performances in the finest churches, palaces, and *scuole grande*, but don't ignore the bel canto wafting through the canals or the opera issuing from open windows of conservatory practice halls.

MUSIC

The band Pink Floyd made rock history with a 1989 concert staged aboard a pontoon floating near Piazza San Marco. Fans made such a mess of the piazza and loud music stirred up such antipathy that the show was destined to become the city's first and last rock happening. Nearby Parco San Giuliano, Mestre, Padua, Verona, Trieste, and Treviso sometimes host artists on their European tours. Though the Biennale Musica and some clubs in Venice do spotlight contemporary music, the vast majority of the city's concerts are classical. *For more about the Biennale, see the feature in Experience Venice.*

The highlight of the Festa del Redentore is a spectacular midnight fireworks display over the Bacino di San Marco. *For more about this and other festivals, see the feature in Experience Venice.*

Numerous orchestras perform pricey "greatest hits" classical music programs marketed toward tourists—you'll easily spot ticket vendors in period costume. Groups may have a semipermanent venue, such as an ex-church or *scuola,* although they can change frequently. You'll find these promoted at your hotel, in tourist offices, in travel agencies, and in many of the previously mentioned websites and local publications. It's not usually necessary to book in advance, however, as these performances rarely sell out.

In addition to these commercial groups, there are professional orchestras that perform less regularly, usually in museums or palazzi. Churches, scuole, palazzi, and museums sometimes sponsor concerts of their own, especially around the holidays, often featuring touring musicians. Keep an eye out for notices plastered on walls along walkways for last-minute, often free concerts offered by local musicians, choirs, and city-sponsored groups.

Contemporary music options are at their richest during Biennale Musica (⇨ *See Experience Venice for more information about the Biennale),* when concerts are held throughout Venice, these events are advertised on the Biennale website and on billboards in all principal campi, and materials are available in tourist offices.

Cini Foundation. Concerts sponsored by this cultural foundation, located on the island of San Giorgio, are well worth attending, if only to visit the lovely Benedictine monastery, which is normally closed to the public. ⊠ *Isola di San Giorgio* ☎ *041/5289900* ⊕ *www.cini.it.*

Museo Querini-Stampalia. This palazzo/museum occasionally stays open late on Friday and Saturday evenings to host curated evenings of music, from jazz to centuries-old music played on antique instruments. Your museum ticket includes the concert, and the Florian Art e Caffè on the premises has food and drink available. ⊠ *Campo Santa Maria Formosa, Castello 5252* ☎ *041/2711411* 🎟 *€6.*

OPERA AND BALLET

The city's main venues are Teatro La Fenice and Teatro Malibran; you can review the calendar and buy tickets for performances at both at ⊕ *www.teatrolafenice.it*, or *contact* **HelloVenezia** (☎ *041/2424* ⊕ *www. hellovenezia.com* ⊙ *8 am–8 pm*), or visit one of their **sales offices** (⊠ *Piazzale Roma or Ferrovia*). It's worth a try to head for the theater box office an hour before showtime to see if any last-minute tickets are available.

Teatro Malibran. La Fenice's more intimate sister venue was built by the powerful Grimani family in 1677, opening as the Teatro Grimani a San Grisostomo and soon becoming one of Europe's most famous theaters. The theater at first hosted theatrical productions, including many works by Metastasio and, later, Goldoni. It became an opera house in the early 19th century and was renamed Malibran in 1835, after Maria Garcia Malibran, the great soprano of her day. It was converted into a movie theater in 1927 and then reopened for live performances in 2001 after lengthy restoration. ⊠ *Campiello del Teatro Malibran, Cannaregio 5870* ☎ *041/786511 La Fenice* Ⓜ *Vaporetto: Rialto.*

Teatro La Fenice. One of Italy's oldest opera houses has witnessed many memorable operatic premieres, including, in 1853, the dismal first-night flop of Verdi's *La Traviata*. It has also witnessed its share of disasters: the most recent being a horrific fire that burned most of the interior; it was deliberately set in January 1996, and was followed by endless delays in a complicated reconstruction. In keeping with its name (which translates as The Phoenix, coined when it was built over the ashes of its predecessor in 1792), La Fenice rose again. It was restored and once again hosts seasons of symphony, opera, and dance. The acoustics of the reconstructed theatre have received mainly positive reviews, but attitudes expressed toward the decoration (replicated based on the style of the early 19th century, but using cheaper, less exacting techniques) have been mixed. According to music critics, in recent years less well known and accomplished artists have been booked, the production quality has deteriorated somewhat, and some operas (because of budget cuts) are presented in *concertante* (just sung, without staging). Daily audio-guided tours through the theatre are available in several languages, from 9:30 to 6. ⊠ *Campo San Fantin, San Marco 1965* ⊕ *www.teatrolafenice. it* 🎟 *€8 for audio guide tour* Ⓜ *Vaporetto: Sant'Angelo, Giglio.*

SHOPPING

WHAT TO SHOP FOR IN VENICE

Colorful Murano glass may be the most obvious thing to shop for in Venice—you can't avoid encountering a mind-boggling variety of it in shop windows, often in kitschy displays, but the city has many other artisan traditions.

Ceramics

Venice may be known for glass, but there is also lovely pottery to be found. Look for replicas of 19th-century chocolate cups, usually cream-white and delicately gilded (not for daily use); pottery from Bassano, typically decorated with reliefs of fruit and vegetables; and some modern, handmade plates and mugs.

GLASS

Glass, much of it made in Murano, is Venice's trademark product. Bear in mind that the value of any piece—signature and shape apart—is also based on the number and quality of colors, the presence of gold, and, in the case of goblets, the thinness of the glass. Prices are about the same all over, but be warned: some shops sell glass made in Taiwan. Most shops will arrange shipping.

GOLDWORK

Venice's passion for glittering golden objects, which began with the decoration in the Basilica di San Marco and later spread into the finest noble palaces, kept specialized gold artisans (called *doradori*) busy throughout the city's history. They still produce lovely cabinets, shelves, wall lamps, lanterns, candleholders, banisters, headboards, frames, and the like by applying gold leaf to wrought iron and carved wood.

JEWELRY

Venetians have always liked gold, and the city is packed with top-of-the-line jewelry stores, as well as more modest shops found, most notably, around the Rialto district. A typical piece of inexpensive jewelry is the *murrina*, a thin, round slice of colored glass (imagine a bunch of colored spaghetti firmly held together and sliced) encircled with gold and sold as pendants or earrings.

LACE

Burano is the traditional home of Venetian lace-making and, although most of the lace sold in town is machine made in China or Taiwan, you can still find something that more closely resembles the real thing in the best shops. Surprisingly, period lace (made between 1900 and 1940) is easier to find and less expensive than contemporary lace, even though the former is a finer product, made *ad ago* (with the needle), while the latter is made with thicker threads or *a fusello* (with the bobbin). Consider that a 10-inch doily takes about 400 hours to make, and the price will reflect it.

LEATHER GOODS

In Venice you'll find a good assortment of leather goods, especially shoes and women's bags. There are plenty of boutiques selling upmarket designer articles; for less fancy items, explore the areas of Rialto and Campo San Polo.

MASKS

The boom in Venetian mask shops started in the late 1970s when the Carnevale tradition was resurrected. Now almost every shop and street vendor offers some version of the mask, in countless sizes, colors, designs, and materials, from cheap, mass-produced ceramics to the original white papiermâché to more recent ornate designs and handcrafted leather inspired by the Commedia dell'Arte. Prices go up dramatically for leather and gilded masks, and you might come across expensive *pezzi da collezione* (collectors' items)—unique pieces whose casts are destroyed. You'll get better value direct from producers, so make a point to visit several of the largest workshops.

PAPER GOODS

In 1482 Venice was the printing capital of the world, and nowadays you'll find dozens of *legatori* (bookbinderies) around town. Hand-printed paper and ornate leather-bound diaries make great souvenirs.

6

Updated by
Nan McElroy

It's no secret that Venice offers some excellent shopping opportunities, but the best of them are often not the most conspicuous. Look beyond the ubiquitous street vendors and the hundreds of virtually indistinguishable purse, glass, and lace shops that line the calli, and you'll discover a bounty of unique and delightful treasures—some might be kitschy, but much will show off the high level of craftsmanship for which Venice has long been known.

Alluring shops abound. You'll find countless vendors of trademark Venetian wares such as Murano glass and Burano lace; the authenticity of some goods can be suspect, but they're often pleasing to the eye regardless of their heritage. For more sophisticated tastes (and deeper pockets), there are jewelers, antiques dealers, and high-fashion boutiques on a par with those in Italy's larger cities but often maintaining a uniquely Venetian flair. Don't ignore the contemporary, either: Venice's artisan heritage lives on in the hand and eye of the today's designers—no matter where they hail from.

While the labyrinthine city center can seem filled with imposing high-fashion emporiums and fancy glass shops, individual craftspeople often working off the main thoroughfares produce much of what is worth taking home from Venice. In their workshops artful stationery is printed with antique plates; individual pairs of shoes are adroitly constructed; jewelry is handcrafted; fine fabrics are skillfully woven; bronze is poured to make gondola décor, and iron is worked into fanali lanterns; paper is glued, pressed, and shaped into masks; and oars and forcola oarlocks are hewn and sculpted in the workshops of remér wood craftsmen.

PLANNING

STORE HOURS

Regular store hours are usually 9–12:30 and 3:30 or 4–7:30 PM; some stores are closed Saturday afternoon or Monday morning. Food shops are open 8–1 and 5–7:30, and are closed all day Sunday and Wednesday afternoon. However, many tourist-oriented shops are open all day, every day, especially those in the San Marco area. Some privately owned shops close for both a summer and a winter vacation.

It's always a good idea to mark the location of a shop that interests you on your map; even better, ask for their business card as you pass (they often have maps printed on the back); otherwise, you may not be able to find it again in the maze of tiny streets.

TAX REFUNDS

If you make a major purchase, take advantage of tax-free shopping with the value-added tax (V.A.T., or IVA in Italian) refund. On clothing and luxury-goods purchases totaling more than €155 made at a single store, non-EU residents are entitled to get back the up to 20% tax included in the purchase price. *(For details, see "Taxes" in the Travel Smart chapter at the end of this book.)*

WHERE TO SHOP

The rule here is simple: the closer you are to Piazza San Marco, the higher the prices. The serious jewelry and glasswork in the windows of the shops of the Procuratie Vecchie and Nuove make for a pleasant browse; in summer your stroll will be accompanied by the music from the bands that set up in front of Caffè Quadri and Florian. In the shade of the arcades of the Piazza San Marco you'll also find Murano glass vendors like Pauly and Venini, the Galleria Ravagnan, old-fashioned shops selling kitschy souvenirs, and an assortment of lace, linen blouses, silk ties, and scarves.

The area of San Marco west of the piazza (in the Frezzeria and beyond the Fenice) has a concentration of boutiques, jewelry shops, antiques dealers, and the most important art galleries in the city, including Bugno.

The Rialto district, surrounding the famous bridge on both sides of the Grand Canal in San Marco and San Polo, is the mecca for buyers of traditional, inexpensive souvenirs: *pantofole del gondoliere,* velvety slippers with rubber soles that resemble the traditional gondoliers' shoes; 18th-century-style wooden trays and coasters that look better after a little wear; and glass "candies," which make a nice, inexpensive (if inedible) gift. Clothing and shoe shops are concentrated between the Rialto Bridge and Campo San Polo, along Ruga Vecchia San Giovanni and Ruga Ravano, and around Campo Sant'Aponal. From the Rialto heading toward Campo Santi Apostoli in Cannaregio, you'll find the elegant Murano glass and jewelry purveyor Rose Douce, along with the department store Coin, is just across the bridge from Campo San Bartolomeo (they don't close for lunch).

6

SAN MARCO

ART AND ANTIQUES DEALERS

Kleine Galerie. This is a good address for antique books and prints, majolica, and other ceramics. ⊠ *Calle delle Botteghe, San Marco 2972* ☎ *338/7389194* Ⓜ *Vaporetto: Sant'Angelo or San Samuele.*

Linea d'Acqua. Fine antique print and book aficionados will fall in love with this gem of a store run by the extremely knowledgeable Luca Zentilini. His focus is on Venetian culture and limited editions with special interest in illustrated books from the 18th century. A large selection of Venetian maps are on offer, as well as etchings by masters including Piranesi, Visentini, Tiepolo, and Carlevarijs. ⊠ *Calle della Mandola, San Marco 3717/D* ☎ *041/5224030* ⊕ *www.lineadacqua.it* Ⓜ *Vaporetto: Sant'Angelo.*

ART GALLERIES

Bugno. This retailer of modern and contemporary art, along with photography, puts together windows representative of the whole gallery. ⊠ *Campo San Fantin, San Marco 1996/D* ☎ *041/5231305* ⊕ *www.bugnoartgallery.it* Ⓜ *Vaporetto: Sant'Angelo, San Giglio.*

Caterina Tognon Arte Contemporanea. Contemporary visual artists who employ glass as their medium are featured by Caterina in her marvelous piano nobile. ⊠ *Calle del Dose, San Marco 2746* ☎ *041/5207859* ⊕ *www.caterinatognon.com* Ⓜ *Vaporetto: San Giglio.*

Le Sculture di Livio de Marchi. Signor De Marchi's swift hands turn wood into outstanding full-scale sculptures that perfectly reproduce everyday objects such as hats, laundry hung out to dry, telephones, jackets, books, fruit, lace—even underwear. The shop is closed weekends. ⊠ *Salizzada San Samuele near Palazzo Grassi, San Marco 3157/A* ☎ *041/5285694* ⊕ *www.liviodemarchi.com* Ⓜ *Vaporetto: Sant'Angelo or San Samuele.*

BOOKSTORES

Studium. Studium is a good stop for books in English, especially guidebooks and books on Venetian culture and food. It's also particularly strong on English-language fiction with Italian, mostly Venetian, settings and themes; in addition, it has a small but worthy collection of recent hardcover fiction. ⊠ *Calle della Canonica, San Marco 337* ☎ *041/5222382* Ⓜ *Vaporetto: San Marco.*

CLOTHING

Al Duca d'Aosta. The most stylish of Venetians and visitors alike come here for women's and men's designer labels for every taste. Brands include Burberry, Ralph Lauren, Jil Sander, Lanvin, Moncler, and many others; be prepared to be wowed. ⊠ *Marzaria del Capitelo, San Marco 4946, San Marco* ☎ *041/5204079* ⊕ *www.alducadaosta.com* Ⓜ *Vaporetto: Rialto.*

Boutique Marly's. You need only step off the vaporetto to find tiny Boutique Marly's, which has a highly appealing collection of classic Italian women's wear. ⊠ *Calle Vallaresso, San Marco 1321* ☎ *041/5203851* Ⓜ *Vaporetto: San Marco Vallaresso.*

Caberlotto. This shop has cornered the market on fabulous fur coats and hats. They sell interesting wool blazers and pashmina shawls by Rosenda Arcioni Meer, along with a complete line of luxurious cashmere clothing. ☒ *Larga Mazzini, San Marco 5114* ☏ *041/5229242* ⊕ *www.caberfurs.com* Ⓜ *Vaporetto: Rialto.*

Camiceria San Marco. The town's top custom shirtmaker counts Hemmingway and the Duke of Windsor among its former customers. Only the finest fabrics are used (they can also be bought by the meter). As well as elegant, made-to-measure shirts, they also make blouses, pajamas, gowns, and ladies' dresses. ☒ *Calle de la Mandola at Campo Sant'Angelo, San Marco 3627* ☏ *041/5221432* ⊕ *www. camiceriasanmarco.it* Ⓜ *Vaporetto: Sant'Angelo.*

Élite. The source for not-so-casual Italian outdoor menswear carries the Canali line as well as the quintessentially English Aquascutum coats that so many Italians favor. Silk ties and cashmere scarves complete the English country look. ☒ *Calle Larga San Marco, San Marco 284, San Marco* ☏ *041/5230145* Ⓜ *Vaporetto: San Marco.*

Fiorella Mancini Gallery. Your best bet for original creations and the craziest looks in town. ☒ *Campo Santo Stefano, San Marco 2806* ☏ *041/5209228* ⊕ *www.fiorellagallery.com* Ⓜ *Vaporetto: Accademia or San Samuele.*

G. Bee 1920. Located in the heart of San Marco amidst important designer names and trinket shops, G. Bee 1920 stocks fine men's and women's knitwear, all proudly made in Italy. Each season brings new items from classic to contemporary, and prices are reasonable while the quality remains impeccable. ☒ *Spadaria, San Marco 675* ☏ *041/5229681* Ⓜ *Vaporetto: San Marco.*

Fodor'sChoice ★ **Godi Fiorenza.** At Godi Fiorenza, Patrizia Fiorenza's designs in silk chiffon appear more sculpted than sewn—they're highly tailored pieces that both conceal and expose. Her sister Samanta is a jewelry designer and silversmith whose unique pieces compliment any outfit. ☒ *Rio Terà San Paternian, San Marco 4261* ☏ *041/2410866* ⊕ *www.fiorenzadesign. com* Ⓜ *Vaporetto: Rialto.*

La Coupole. Two shops a stone's throw from one another offer an excellent selection of name-brand *alta moda* (high fashion) for men and women. ☒ *Calle Larga XXII Marzo, San Marco 2366 and 2414* ☏ *041/5224243.*

La Perla. The extremely elegant lingerie in this boutique is comfortable, too. ☒ *Campo San Salvador, San Marco 4828* ☏ *041/5226459* Ⓜ *Vaporetto: Rialto.*

Malo. One of Italy's highest-quality producers of cashmere garments features styles for men and women that are tasteful and refined, designed and made to be worn for many years. ☒ *Calle de le Ostreghe, San Marco 2359* ☏ *041/5232162* ⊕ *www.malo.it* Ⓜ *Vaporetto: San Marco or Santa Maria del Giglio.*

Max Mara. A name synonymous with luxurious quality, Max Mara delights season after season with a line of classic women's apparel that seamlessly incorporates today's trends with well-made pieces that

you'll enjoy for a lifetime. ⊠ *Marziale Due Aprile, San Marco 5033* ☎ *041/5226688* ⊕ *www.maxmara.com* Ⓜ *Vaporetto: Rialto.*

COSTUMES AND ACCESSORIES

Venetia. Antonia Sautter's opulent, fanciful display of 18th-century Venetian gowns often causes passersby pause and ponder. She is the atelier of the prestigious Ballo del Doge Carnevale ball, along with many other extraordinarily fantastically coutured Venetian events. You also find medieval-style garments, masks, and accessories behind the curtains inside. ⊠ *Frezzeria, San Marco 1286* ☎ *041/5224426* Ⓜ *Vaporetto: San Marco.*

GIFTS

Atmosfera Veneziana. One stop might fit the bill when you've got last-minute gifts to buy. American Theresa works only with Murano artisans, and offers an abundant, tasteful selection of reasonably priced beads, vases, goblets, and jewelry, even mirrors and chandeliers. ⊠ *Calle dei Fuseri, San Marco 4340* ☎ *041/2413256* ⊕ *www.atmosferaveneziana.com* Ⓜ *Vaporetto: San Marco Vallaresso.*

Giuliana Longo. A hat shop that's been around since 1901 offers an assortment of Venetian and gondolier straw hats, Panama hats from Ecuador, caps and berets, and some select scarves of silk and fine wool; even a special corner dedicated to accessories for antique cars. ⊠ *Calle del Lovo, San Marco 4813* ☎ *041/5226454* ⊕ *www.giulianalongo.com* Ⓜ *Vaporetto: San Marco.*

Materialmente. Artists Maddalena Venier and Alessandro Salvadori of Materialmente envision "balancing the precious with the everyday." They succeed with a fascinating collection of fanciful, light-as-air sculpture, lamps, jewelry, and housewares. ⊠ *Ramo Marzaria San Salvador, San Marco 4850* ☎ *041/5286881* ⊕ *www.materialmente.it* Ⓜ *Vaporetto: Rialto.*

GLASS

L'Isola. Vhic, contemporary glassware is signed by Carlo Moretti. ⊠ *Calle delle Botteghe, San Marco 2970* ☎ *041/5231973* ⊕ *www.lisola.com.*

Ma.Re. Collectors head here for the one-of-a-kind objects created by leading glass artists. If you've broken a piece out of a set of out of production Venetian glasses, the friendly staff will try to help you replace it, either by finding a substitute, or having one made for you. A visit to this shop will give you a good overview of premium Venetian production. ⊠ *Via XXII Marzo, San Marco 2088* ☎ *041/5231191* 🖷 *041/5285745* ⊕ *www.mareglass.com* Ⓜ *Vaporetto: San Marco.*

Paropàmiso. Aside from stunning Venetian glass beads, jewelry from all over the world is available. ⊠ *Frezzeria, San Marco 1701* ☎ *041/5227120.*

Fodor'sChoice ★ **Pauly & C.** Established in 1866, Pauly & C features a truly impressive selection of authentic Murano art glass (both traditional and contemporary styles) by the most accomplished masters—and at better prices than on the island. The showroom at No. 73 houses the more traditional collection; at No. 77 you can find works by artists and designers. ⊠ *Pi-*

azza San Marco, San Marco 73 and 77 ☎ *041/5235484, 041/2770279* ⊕ *www.pauly.it.*

Tre Erre. This reliable and respected firm offers both traditional and contemporary glass designs. ⊠ *Piazza San Marco, San Marco 79/B* ☎ *041/5201715* Ⓜ *Vaporetto: San Marco Vallaresso.*

Venini. An institution since the 1930s attracts some of the foremost names in glass design. To see some of the best offerings, visit the Venini Showroom at Fondamenta Vetrai 47 on Murano. ⊠ *Piazzetta dei Leoncini, San Marco 314* ☎ *041/5224045* ⊕ *www.venini.com.*

GOLD, WOOD, AND METALWORK

Valese Fonditore. This studio has been casting brass, bronze, copper, and pewter into artistic handles, menorahs, Carnevale masks, and real gondola decorations (which make great paperweights, bookends, or shelf pieces) since 1913. The coups de grâce are the brass chandeliers, exactly like those that hang in the Oval Office in the White House. Call to arrange a visit to the stuido in Cannaregio when they pour. ⊠ *Shop: Calle Fiubera, San Marco 793* ☎ *041/5227282* ⊕ *www.valese. it* Ⓜ *Vaporetto: San Marco.*

JEWELRY

Bastianello. Classic jewelry here includes pieces made with semiprecious stones. ⊠ *Via Due Aprile off Campo San Bartolomio, San Marco 5041* ☎ *041/5226751* Ⓜ *Vaporetto: Rialto.*

Cartier. Your special trip to Venice might just require a unique keepsake. Why not head to Cartier? The renowned French jeweler and fine watchmaker is located in the heart of the city and merits a visit, even if you're only window-shopping. ⊠ *Ramo San Zulian, San Marco 506* ☎ *041/5222071* ⊕ *www.cartier.com* Ⓜ *Vaporetto: San Zaccaria or Rialto.*

Missiaglia. A landmark in Piazza San Marco sells fabulous jewelry and a few silver accessories. ⊠ *Procuratie Vecchie, San Marco 125* ☎ *041/5224464* ⊕ *www.missiaglia.com* Ⓜ *Vaporetto: San Marco.*

Nardi. Exquisite *moretti*—earrings and brooches in the shape of Moors' heads—are studded with diamonds, rubies, or emeralds. ⊠ *Under Procuratie Nuove, Piazza San Marco, San Marco 69* ☎ *041/5225733* ⊕ *www.nardi-venezia.com* Ⓜ *Vaporetto: San Marco Vallaresso.*

Salvadori. Watches are the specialty, as are sparkling diamonds and other precious stones set in the shop's own designs. ⊠ *Merceria San Salvador, San Marco 5022* ☎ *041/5230609* ⊕ *www.salvadori-venezia. com* Ⓜ *Vaporetto: Rialto.*

LACE, LINEN, AND FABRIC

Fodor's Choice ★ **Bevilacqua.** This renowned studio has kept the weaving tradition alive in Venice since 1875, using 18th-century hand looms for its most precious creations. Its repertoire of 3,500 different patterns and designs yields a ready-to-sell selection of hundreds of brocades, Gobelins, damasks, velvets, taffetas, and satins. You'll also find tapestry, cushions, and braiding. Fabrics made by this prestigious firm have been used to decorate the Vatican, the Royal Palace of Stockholm, and the White House. This listing is for the main retail outlet of the Bevilacqua establishment;

Colorful fabrics are among Venice's trademark wares.

there's another behind the San Marco Basilica. ■ TIP→ **If you're interested in seeing the actual 18th-century looms in action making the most precious fabrics, request an appointment at the Luigi Bevilacqua production center in Santa Croce.** ⊠ *Campo di Santa Maria del Giglio, San Marco 2520* ☎ *041/2410662 main retail outlet, 041/5287581 retail outlet (behind the Basilica), 041/721566 Santa Croce production center* ⊕ *www.bevilacquatessuti.com* Ⓜ *Vaporetto: Giglio.*

Frette. High-quality sheets and bath towels are the hallmarks of this international luxury brand—lace and embroidery are machine-made, but the general effect is nonetheless luxurious and elegant. ⊠ *Calle Larga XXII Marzo, San Marco 2070/A* ☎ *041/5224914* ⊕ *www.frette. com* Ⓜ *Vaporetto: San Marco.*

Gaggio. You need to ring the bell to be admitted inside one of Venice's most prestigious fabric shops. Bedcovers, cushions, tapestry, and the like are available, plus a line of delightful small bags made in silk velvet with dark wooden frames. The colors of the fabric are never garish—they tend toward mellow autumnal tones. ⊠ *Calle delle Botteghe near Campo Santo Stefano, San Marco 3451* ☎ *041/5228574* ⊕ *www.gaggio.it* Ⓜ *Vaporetto: Sant'Angelo or San Samuele.*

Il Merletto. The best of Burano's renowned lace-making tradition is rarely represented by the examples you'll see on display. However, at Il Merletto, you can ask for the authentic, handmade lace safeguarded in drawers behind the counter. This is the only place in Venice connected with the students of the Scuola del Merletto in Burano, who, officially, do not sell to the public. Hours of operation are daily 10 to 5. ⊠ *Piazza*

San Marco, Sotoportego del Cavalletto under the Procuratie Vecchie, San Marco 95 ☎ *041/5208406.*

Jesurum. A great deal of so-called "Burano-Venetian" lace is now made in China; so, unless you're an expert—and experts really can tell the difference—you're best off going a trusted place. Jesurum has been the major producer of handmade Venetian lace since 1870. Its lace is, of course, all modern production, but if you want an antique piece, the people at Jesurum can point you in the right direction. ⊠ *Calle Larga XII Marzo, San Marco 2401* ☎ *041/5238969* ⊕ *www.jesurum.it.*

Rubelli. Founded in1858, Rubelli offers the same sumptuous brocades, damasks, and cut velvets used by the world's most prestigious decorators. ⊠ *Palazzo Corner Spinelli, San Marco 3877* ☎ *041/5236110* ⊕ *www.rubelli.com.*

LEATHER GOODS

Bottega Veneta. This prestigious Italian chain sells bags typically made with intertwined strips of leather, plus smooth bags and elegant low-heeled shoes. Menswear is on offer as well. ⊠ *Salizada San Moise, San Marco 1473* ☎ *041/5228489* ⊕ *www.bottegaveneta.com/* Ⓜ *Vaporetto: San Marco.*

Daniela Ghezzo, Segalin a Venezia. Custom shoemakers follow in the footsteps of the shop's founder, Rolando Segalin. This artisan team can give life to your wildest shoe fantasy as well as make the most classic designs. ⊠ *Calle dei Fuseri, San Marco 4365* ☎ *041/5222115* ⊕ *www. danielaghezzo.it.*

Emporium. Traveling bags and suitcases by Alviero Martini are typically decorated with maps in light colors; Trussardi accessories are also available. ⊠ *Spadaria, San Marco 670/695* ☎ *041/5235911* Ⓜ *Vaporetto: San Marco.*

Fratelli Rossetti. The selection of bags, boots, leather jackets, and shoes of the Rossetti brothers is better there than in the Rome shop. ⊠ *Campo San Salvador, San Marco 4800* ☎ *041/5230571* ⊕ *www.fratellirossetti. com/* Ⓜ *Vaporetto: San Marco.*

Gucci. Their signature products are so much fun to peruse, even if under the watchful eyes of the salespeople. Gucci is an Italian institution, but if the prices are too deep for your pockets, the vast window displays will lend an overview on the season's hottest and newest accessories. You'll find another Gucci store under the porticos in Piazza San Marco. ⊠ *Calle XXII Marzo, San Marco 2102, San Marco* ☎ *041/2413968* ⊕ *www.gucci.com* Ⓜ *Vaporetto: San Giglio or San Marco.*

La Parigina. A Venetian institution shows off its leather goods in five large windows in two neighboring shops. You'll find the house collection plus a dozen lesser-known designers. ⊠ *Merceria San Zulian, San Marco 727* ☎ *041/5226743.*

René Caovilla. René Caovilla's shoes are meant for showing off, not walking around town (especially in Venice). The evening shoes here are so glamorous and over-the-top that you might feel compelled to buy a pair and then create an occasion to wear them. ⊠ *Calle Seconda*

6

a l'Ascensione, San Marco 1296 ☎ *041/5238038* ⊕ *www.caovilla.com* Ⓜ *Vaporetto: San Marco.*

PAPER GOODS

Antica Legatoria Piazzesi. One of the oldest bookbinderies in Venice is known for its historic *stampi,* hand-printed paper using carved wood plates, which artisans carefully filled with colored inks. Don't let the sporadic opening times discourage you from trying to visit or purchase their exquisite papers. ✉ *Campo della Feltrina near Campo Santa Maria del Giglio, San Marco 2511* ☎ *041/5221202* ⊕ *www.legatoriapiazzesi. it* Ⓜ *Vaporetto: Santa Maria del Giglio.*

Ebrû. The name is a Turkish word meaning "cloudy" and refers to the technique that Alberto Valese uses to decorate paper, as well as silk ties and paperweights. ✉ *Campo Santo Stefano, San Marco 3471* ☎ *041/5238830* ⊕ *www.albertovalese-ebru.it* Ⓜ *Vaporetto: Accademia.*

Fabriano Boutique. The name has been synonymous with high-quality paper since 1264 and is esteemed by publishers, writers, and artists. The boutique offers a glimpse into their full range of products from luxurious stationery to journals and specialized notebooks. They also offer a line of writing instruments and leather items. ✉ *Calle del Lovo, San Marco 4816* ☎ *041/5286988* ⊕ *www.fabrianoboutique.com* Ⓜ *Vaporetto: Rialto.*

La Ricerca. A broad assortment of writing materials, bound journals and albums, book covers, medieval sketchbooks and handmade marble paper are made in a nearby laboratory. New products are introduced often so that no two visits to the store are ever the same. ✉ *Ponte delle Ostreghe near Campo Santa Maria del Giglio, San Marco 2431* ☎ *041/5212606* ⊕ *venicemarbledpaper.com* Ⓜ *Vaporetto: Santa Maria del Giglio.*

WINE

Fodor's Choice ★ **Millevini.** Lorenzo will be more than happy to assist you in exploring the broad selection of wines from across the region, the entire Italian landscape, and beyond. You'll also find liquors and brandies, lovely bubblies, and even a few microbrews. ✉ *Ramo del Fontego dei Turchi, just off the Rialto Bridge, San Marco 5362* ☎ *041/5206090* ⊕ *www. millevini.it* Ⓜ *Vaporetto: Rialto.*

DORSODURO

ANTIQUES AND ART DEALERS

Antichità Pietro Scarpa. This distinguished shop next to the Gallerie dell'Accademia sells old master paintings—originals, not copies—with accordingly rarified prices. ✉ *Campo della Carità, Dorsoduro 1023/A* ☎ *041/5239700* ⊕ *www.scarpa1953.com* Ⓜ *Vaporetto: Accademia.*

Claudia Canestrelli. In her tasteful shop, Claudia has amassed a limited choice of antiques, small paintings, and plenty of interesting-looking bric-a-brac, including silver ex-votos and period souvenirs, such as brass ashtrays in the shape of lions' heads. ✉ *Campiello Barbaro, near the Peggy Guggenheim Collection, Dorsoduro 364/A* ☎ *041/5227072, 340/5776089* Ⓜ *Vaporetto: Accademia or Salute.*

Le Forcole de Saverio Pastor preserves the Venetian craft of handmade gondola oars and oarlocks.

BOOKSTORES

Ca' Foscarina. The bookstore of Università di Venezia Ca' Foscari has a reasonable selection of titles in English. Shelves teem with literature and history, but there's also a handful of travel books, as well as the latest best sellers. ⊠ *Campiello Squelini, Dorsoduro 3259* ☎ *041/2404802* ⊕ *www.cafoscarina.it* Ⓜ *Vaporetto: Ca' Rezzonico.*

Libreria Toletta. A linchpin in the city's literary history, Libreria Toletta offers a varied selection of English books and numerous volumes about the city of Venice in addition to their vast literary, art, and architecture offerings in Italian. Their staff is friendly and knowledgeable. ⊠ *Saca de la Toleta, Dorsoduro 1213* ☎ *041/5232034* Ⓜ *Vaporetto: Ca' Rezzonico or Accademia.*

CLOTHING

Arras. Scarves, as well as blouses and jackets, are all hand woven in wool or silk. The store also occasionally organizes weaving workshops. ⊠ *Campiello Squelini, Dorsoduro 3235* ☎ *041/5226460* ⊕ *www.arrastessuti.wordpress.com* Ⓜ *Vaporetto: Ca' Rezzonico.*

GIFTS

Madera. Craftswoman and architect Francesca Meratti and a team of local and international artisans combine traditional and contemporary design to create a mix of most appealing objects, including dishware, carved wooden bowls, jewelry, and ceramic pieces. ⊠ *Campo San Barnaba, Dorsoduro 2762* ☎ *041/5224181* ⊕ *www.maderavenezia.it* Ⓜ *Vaporetto: Ca' Rezzonico.*

Signor Blum. Solid, large-piece jigsaw puzzles (painted or in natural wood colors) depict animals, views of Venice, and trompe l'oeil scenes. Ideal for toddlers, the puzzles also look nice hanging on a wall. ⊠ *Fondamenta Gherardini off Campo San Barnaba, Dorsoduro 2840* ☎ *041/5226367* ⊕ *www.signorblum.com* Ⓜ *Vaporetto: Ca' Rezzonico.*

GLASS

Angolo del Passato. Giordana Naccari collects tempting 20th-century glassware, and produces her own intriguing Venetian *gotò* cups, plates, and pitchers at high-end prices. ⊠ *Campiello dei Squelini, Dorsoduro 3276, Dorsoduro* ☎ *041/5287896* ⊕ *Vaporetto: Ca'Rezzonico.*

Genninger Studio. This is the retail outlet for Leslie Ann Genninger, an American from Ohio who was the first woman to enter the male-dominated world of Murano master bead makers. She established her own line of jewelry, called Murano Class Act, in 1994 using period glass beads, and when she could no longer find antique beads she started designing her own. ⊠ *Campiello Barbaro, Dorsoduro 364* ☎ *041/5225565* ⊕ *www.genningerstudio.com* Ⓜ *Vaporetto: Accademia or Salute.*

Marina and Susanna Sent. The beautiful and elegant glass jewelry of Marina and Susanna Sent has been featured in *Vogue.* Look also for vases and other exceptional design pieces. Other locations are near San Moise in San Marco and on Murano on the Fondamenta Serenella. ⊠ *Campo San Vio, Dorsoduro 669* ☎ *041/5208136 Dorsoduro, 041/5204014 San Marco, 041/5274665 Murano* ⊕ *www.marinaesusannasent.com/* Ⓜ *Vaporetto: Accademia/Zattere, Giglio, Murano Serenella.*

Trina Tygrett. American-born but Venetian by choice, glass bead artist Trina Tygrett opened her studio after completing her studies at the Academy of Fine Arts. She married into one of the oldest surviving families of traditional Venetian glassblowing and was able to study some of the older techniques founded on Murano. Her signature jewelry is a breath of fresh air as she mixes her beads with materials such as metal fabric, silver, and precious stones to create unique and eclectic pieces. ⊠ *Calle del Bastion, Dorsoduro 188* ☎ *041/5239426* ⊕ *www. nasontygrett.com* Ⓜ *Vaporetto: Salute, Accademia.*

GOLD, WOOD, AND METALWORK

Cornici Trevisanello. Byzantine and rich Renaissance handcrafted frames are made of gold-leafed wood and inset with antique glass beads, mosaic tesserae, and small ceramic tiles. The more-elaborate pieces look their best when used to frame an old mirror. ⊠ *Fondamenta Bragadin off Campo San Vio, Dorsoduro 662* ☎ *041/5207779* Ⓜ *Vaporetto: Accademia.*

Fodor's Choice ★ **Le Forcole di Saverio Pastor.** The sculpted walnut-wood oarlocks (*forcole*) used exclusively by Venetian rowers may be utilitarian, but they are beautiful, custom-made objects that make for uniquely Venetian gifts or souvenirs. Saverio Pastor (along with Paolo Brandolisio) is one of the few remaining oar and forcola makers left in Venice. ⊠ *Fondamenta Soranzo, Dorsoduro 341* ☎ *041/5225699* ⊕ *www.forcole.com* Ⓜ *Vaporetto: Salute.*

6

JEWELRY

Gualti. Creative earrings, broaches, and necklaces are done in colored resin that looks as fragile as glass but is as strong and soft as rubber. Silk shoes can be custom "garnished" with jewelry. ⊠ *Rio Terà Canal near Campo Santa Margherita, Dorsoduro 3111* ☎ *041/5201731* ⊕ *www. gualti.it* Ⓜ *Vaporetto: Ca' Rezzonico.*

LACE, LINEN, AND FABRIC

Annelie. A highly appealing selection—from Venice and beyond—includes fine cotton and linen tablecloths, baby clothing, shirts, nightgowns, sheets, and curtains, as delightful and unique as the proprietor herself. Ask to see antique lace. ⊠ *Calle Lunga San Barnaba, Dorsoduro 2748* ☎ *041/5203277* Ⓜ *Vaporetto: Ca' Rezzonico.*

LEATHER GOODS

Fodor's Choice ★ **Il Grifone.** Very few artisan leather shops remain in Venice, and Il Grifone is the standout with respect to quality, tradition, and a guarantee for an exquisite product. For more than 30 years, Antonio Peressin has been making bags, purses, belts, and smaller leather items that have a worldwide following because of his precision and attention to detail. His store is a feast for the eyes while his prices remain reasonable and accessible. ⊠ *Fondamenta del Gaffaro, Dorsoduro 3516, Dorsoduro* ☎ *041/5229452* ⊕ *www.ilgrifonevenezia.it* Ⓜ *Vaporetto: Piazzale Roma.*

MARKETS

Campo Santa Margherita food market. Dorsoduro's liveliest square is the setting for a colorful morning food market. ⊠ *Campo Santa Margherita, Dorsoduro* Ⓜ *Vaporetto: Ca' Rezzonico.*

MASKS

Ca' Macana. A large showroom offering lots of gilded creations, both traditional and new, is a must-see. Ask about mask-making workshops. ⊠ *Calle delle Botteghe off Campo San Barnaba, Dorsoduro 3172* ☎ *041/2776142* ⊕ *www.camacana.com* Ⓜ *Vaporetto: San Tomà.*

PAPER GOODS

Il Pavone. The name aptly translates as "The Peacock," and the shop offers a great selection of *coda di pavone,* a kind of paper with colors and patterns resembling peacock feathers. Artisans here are particularly proud of their hand-painted paper. ⊠ *Fondamenta Venier, Dorsoduro 721* ☎ *041/5234517* ⊕ *www.ilpavonevenezia.it* Ⓜ *Vaporetto: Zattere.*

WINE

Cantinone Già Schiavi. One of Venice's finest wine bars is just as popular for the ample choice of excellent bottled wines and spirits sold to go. ⊠ *Ponte San Trovaso, Dorsoduro 992* ☎ *041/5285137* Ⓜ *Vaporetto: Accademia.*

Venice's Signature Crafts: Masks

When Carnevale was revived in the late 1970s, mask making returned as well, with travelers inspiring its evolution to its current ornate form. Although many workshops stick to centuries-old techniques, none have been in business for more than 40 years.

A key date in the history of Venetian masks is 1436, when the *mascareri* (mask makers) founded their guild. By then the techniques were well established: a mask is first modeled in clay, then a chalk cast is made from it and lined with papier-mâché, glue, gauze, and wax.

Masks were popular well before the mascareri's guild was established. Local laws regulating their use appeared as early as 1268, often intended to prevent people from carrying weapons when masked or in an attempt to prohibit the then-common practice of masked men disguised as women entering convents to seduce nuns. Even on religious holidays—when masks were theoretically prohibited—they were used by Venetians going to the theater or attempting to avoid identification at the city's brothels and gaming tables.

In the 18th century actors started using masks for the traditional roles of the commedia dell'arte. Arlecchino, Pantalone, Pulcinella, and company would wear leather masks designed to amplify or change their voices. It's easy to spot these masks in stores today: Arlecchino (Harlequin) has the round face and surprised expression, Pantalone has the curved nose and long mustache, and Pulcinella has the protruding nose.

The least expensive mask is the white *larva*, smooth and plain with a long upper lip and no chin, allowing the wearer to eat and drink without having to remove it. In the 18th century it was an integral part of the *Bauta* costume, composed of the *larva*, a black tricornered hat, and a black mantled cloak. The *Moretta* is the *Bauta's* female counterpart; she kept her oval mask on by biting down on a button inside it, thus rendering her mute.

The pretty Gnaga, which resembles a cat's face, was used by gay men to "meow" compliments and proposals to good-looking boys. The most interesting of the traditional masks is perhaps the Medico della Peste (the Plague Doctor), with glasses and an enormous nose shaped like a bird's beak. During the plague of 1630 and 1631, doctors took protective measures against infection: as well as wearing masks, they examined patients with a rod to avoid touching them and wore waxed coats that didn't "absorb" the disease. Inside the nose of the mask they put medical herbs and fragrances thought to filter the infected air, while the glasses protected the eyes.

Following the boom of mask shops, numerous costume rental stores opened in the 1990s. Here you'll find masks and simplified versions of 18th-century costumes. If you plan to rent a costume during Carnevale, it's a good idea to reserve several months in advance.

6

SAN POLO

ART GALLERIES

Scriba. A delightful husband-and-wife team sells exclusive Italian-made crafts, along with maps, fine prints, and paintings by Italian and international artists. ⊠ *Campo dei Frari, San Polo 3030* ☎☎ *041/5236728* Ⓜ *Vaporetto: San Tomà.*

CLOTHING

Kirikù. This is the place for trendy girl's (0–14 years) and women's wear, with all the latest names from Italian and French designers and all very special and unique. ⊠ *Calle de la Madoneta, San Polo 1463* ☎ *041/2960619* Ⓜ *Vaporetto: San Silvestro.*

Queen of Casablanca. Classy, neutral trends in men's and women's clothing, from jeans to linen to silk and fine wool, are for the young and young-at-heart. ⊠ *Ruga Rialto, San Polo 773* ☎ *041/5223917* Ⓜ *Vaporetto: San Silvestro.*

Zazù. Clothing and accessories here have a definite Eastern feel. Owner Federica Zamboni is also a jewelry expert; ask to see her collection of antique Indian necklaces and earrings. ⊠ *Calle dei Saoneri, San Polo 2750* ☎ *041/715426* Ⓜ *Vaporetto: San Tomà.*

COSTUMES AND ACCESSORIES

Atelier Pietro Longhi. Costumes for sale or rent are inspired by 18th- and 19th-century models, with masks (for sale only) to match. Large sizes are available for both sexes. By appointment only, but well worth the effort. ⊠ *Rio terà dei Frari (near the Frari), San Polo 2608* ☎ *041/714478* ⊕ *www.pietrolonghi.com* Ⓜ *Vaporetto: San Tomà.*

Laboratorio Arte & Costume. If you are making your own costume, Monica Daniele at Laboratorio Arte & Costume can offer you professional sartorial assistance while you browse hundreds of hats and bags and an array of vintage clothing. ⊠ *Calle del Scaleter near Campo San Polo, San Polo 2235* ☎ *041/5246242* Ⓜ *Vaporetto: San Tomà.*

GIFTS

Il Baule Blu. *Orsi artistici,* mohair teddy bears, are made to collect and treat with great care. Painstakingly handmade in many sizes and colors with articulated paws and glass eyes, when squeezed they can either grumble or play a carillon tune. Some are stark naked; others are dressed in old baby garments trimmed with lace and ribbons. ⊠ *Calle del Mandoler off Campo San Tomà, San Polo 2916/A* ☎ *041/719448* Ⓜ *Vaporetto: San Tomà.*

Sabbie e Nebbie. The Japanese aesthetic is quite apparent in the ceramic and porcelain bowls, plates, vases, and teapots, with inviting clean, natural lines and muted colors, of artist-owner Maria Theresa Laghi and her collaborators. Her silk scarves are just as appealing. ⊠ *Calle dei Nomboli, San Polo 2768/A* ☎ *041/719073* Ⓜ *Vaporetto: San Tomà.*

GOLD, WOOD, AND METALWORK

Gilberto Penzo. The gondola and lagoon boat expert in Venice creates scale models and real gondola *forcole* in his *laboratorio* (workshop) nearby. (If the retail shop is closed, a sign posted on the door will explain how to find Signor Penzo.) When he's not busy sawing and sanding, Mr. Penzo writes historical and technical books about gondola building. Here you'll also find gondola model kits, a great gift for the boatbuilder in your life. ⊠ *Calle Seconda dei Saoneri, San Polo 2681* ☎ *041/719372* ⊕ *www.veniceboats.com* Ⓜ *Vaporetto: San Tomà.*

JEWELRY

Attombri. Celebrated brothers Daniele and Stefano blend and weave copper and silver wire with Murano glass beads to render stylish, contemporary pieces with a timeless feel. There's a second location in San Marco on the Frezzeria. ⊠ *Sottoportego degli Oresi, San Polo 74* ☎ *041/5212524* ⊕ *www.attombri.com* Ⓜ *Vaporetto: Rialto Mercato or Rialto.*

Fodor's Choice
★

Laberintho. A tiny *bottega* near Campo San Polo is run by a team of young goldsmiths and jewelry designers specializing in inlaid stones. The work on display in their shop is exceptional, and they also create customized pieces. ⊠ *Calle del Scaleter, San Polo 2236* ☎ *041/710017* ⊕ *www.laberintho.it* Ⓜ *Vaporetto: San Stae or San Tomà.*

Mercante di Sabbia. French-born owner-designer Claudia Puschi travels across Europe to fill her store with eclectic and intriguing home accessories and jewelry. Her unique items can't be found anywhere else in the city; in fact, she herself designed many of the purses you'll find in the store—which she deftly and stylishly transformed from a former butcher shop. ⊠ *Calle dei Saoneri, San Polo 2724* ☎ *041/5243865* Ⓜ *Vaporetto: San Tomà.*

LACE, LINEN, AND FABRIC

La Bottega di Cenerentola. "Cinderella's Workshop" creates unique handmade lampshades out of silk, old lace, and real parchment, embroidered and decorated with gold braids and cotton or silk trim. It also sells restored lace and embroidered vintage clothing. The pieces on display are a perfect match for country- and antique-style furniture. The owner, Lidiana Vallongo, and her daughter will be happy to discuss special orders. ⊠ *Calle dei Saoneri, San Polo 2718/A* ☎ *041/5232006* ⊕ *www. cenerentola.eu* Ⓜ *Vaporetto: San Tomà.*

LEATHER GOODS

Fanny. Run by a family of market stall sellers, Fanny combines good value, friendly service, and cheerful design. Come here for leather and suede bags and soft leather gloves. ⊠ *Calle dei Saoneri, San Polo 2723* ☎ *041/5228266* Ⓜ *Vaporetto: San Tomà.*

Francis Model. A tiny workshop specializes in superb handmade leather bags in all shapes and sizes. The craftsmanship is exceptional; get Bottega Veneta look-alikes at half the price. ⊠ *Ruga Rialto, San Polo 773/A* ☎ *041/5212889* Ⓜ *Vaporetto: San Silvestro.*

Vladi. These sassy shoes have just enough fantasy to be stylish, but not too much to be over the top. ⊠ *Ruga dei Speziati, San Polo 247/48* ☎ *041/5222831* ⊕ *www.vladishoes.it* Ⓜ *Vaporetto: Rialto Mercato.*

MARKETS

Rialto markets. The Rialto fish, fruit, and vegetable markets have been operational in this same location effectively since Venice has been in existence. It's a food potpourri; scan the stalls to see what all you'll be dining on during your stay (or better yet, rent an apartment and experiment yourself). Look for the word "nostrano" when shopping to identify the most local fish and produce. ⊠ *Campiello della Pescheria, San Polo* ☎ *No phone* Ⓜ *Vaporetto: Rialto Mercato.*

MASKS

Fodor's Choice
★

La Bottega dei Mascareri. Despite the great popularity of the Venetian Carnevale, mask making is sadly a dying art in the city. The large majority of masks for sale in the shops and kiosks of Venice are kitsch made in Asia and have little (if any) relationship to the popular local tradition. A shining exception to this sorry situation is Sergio and Massimo Boldrin's Bottega dei Mascareri. Staunch traditionalists, the Boldrin brothers recreate beautiful and historically accurate versions of the masks of the Venetian *Commedia dell'Arte*. They have also carefully extended their repertoire to include masks inspired by characters in Tiepolo's paintings, thereby inventing new masks while remaining true to the spirit of 18th-century Carnevale. A mask from Bottega is about as close to the "real thing" as you can get. ⊠ *Ruga dei Oresi at the foot of the Rialto Bridge, San Polo 80 (Rialto Bridge), San Polo 2720 (Calle dei Saoneri), San Polo* ☎ *041/5223857, 041/5242887* ⊕ *www.mascarer.com* ☾ *Daily 9–6* Ⓜ *Vaporetto: San Silvestro.*

Tragicomica. A good mask selection comes with a lot of information for Carnevale parties. The shop also turns out a limited number of costumes made from hand-printed cotton fabric. ⊠ *Calle dei Nomboli, San Polo 2800* ☎ *041/721102* ⊕ *www.tragicomica.it* Ⓜ *Vaporetto: San Tomà.*

PAPER GOODS

Legatoria Polliero. Beautiful leather-bound blank books, desk accessories, and picture frames are available at some of Venice's most reasonable prices. ⊠ *Campo dei Frari, San Polo 2995* ☎ *041/5285130* Ⓜ *Vaporetto: San Tomà.*

SANTA CROCE

CERAMICS

La Margherita Venezia. Unique, deliciously appealing faience-style majolica on a white background feature figures of animals, flowers, and fruit as well as abstract designs. Margherita also fashions handmade greeting cards that are one-of-a-kind works of art in themselves. ⊠ *Calle Canal off Campo de la Lana, Santa Croce 659* ☎ *041/2100272* ⊕ *www.lamargheritavenezia.com* Ⓜ *Vaporetto: Riva de Biasio or Piazzale Roma.*

The Rialto market shows off exceptional produce from Sant'Erasmo, the Veneto mainland, and beyond.

CANNAREGIO

ART GALLERIES

Melori & Rosenberg. On view are established and young Italian artists on their way up, including Luigi Rocca (hyper-realist scenes of modern life), Miria Malandri (views of Venice, portraits, still lifes), and Norberto Moretti (glass designer). ✉ *Campo del Ghetto Nuovo, Cannaregio 2919* ☎ *041/2750039* ⊕ *www.melori-rosenberg.com* Ⓜ *Vaporetto: San Marcuola.*

BOOKSTORES

Libreria Marco Polo. Finished your book midway through your vacation? Not a problem; trade it in for another from Libreria Marco Polo's vast selection of new and used books in English and Italian. The owners are always hosting authors on interesting topics, especially about the challenges facing the city of Venice. ✉ *Calle Teatro Malibran, Cannaregio 5886a* ☎ *041/5226343* ⊕ *www.libreriamarcopolo.com* Ⓜ *Vaporetto: Rialto.*

COSTUMES AND ACCESSORIES

Laboratorio Parrucche Carlotta. Wig maker Carlotta Carisi believes that at Carnevale details count, and her sensational creations are the ideal way to top off an elegant costume. Note that quality comes at a price, and credit cards are not accepted. ✉ *Campo Widman, Cannaregio 5415* ☎ *041/5207571* Ⓜ *Vaporetto: Ca' d'Oro.*

Nicolao Atelier. The largest costume-rental showroom in town has outfitted many a period film (including *Casanova*). They have nearly 7,000 choices ranging from the historical to the fantastic, including thematic costumes ideal for group masquerades. By appointment only. ✉ *Fondamenta Misericordia, Cannaregio 2590* ☎ *041/5207051* ⊕ *www.nicolao. com* Ⓜ *Vaporetto: Ca d'Oro.*

DEPARTMENT STORES

Coin. The upscale chain department store with four floors is Venice's largest store. ✉ *Salizzada San Giovanni Crisostomo, Cannaregio 5787, Cannaregio* ☎ *041/5203581* ⊕ *www.coin.it* Ⓜ *Vaporetto: Rialto.*

GIFTS

Fusetti Diego Baruch. All manner of handmade Jewish handicrafts are available, including copies of antique menorahs, in glass, bronze, gold, silver, and mosaic. It's closed Saturday. ✉ *Ghetto Vecchio, Cannaregio 1218* ☎ *041/720092* ⊕ *www.shalomvenice.com* Ⓜ *Vaporetto: San Marcuola or Guglie.*

La Stamperia del Ghetto. Black-and-white prints of the old Ghetto are beautiful keepsakes. It's closed Saturday. ✉ *Ghetto Vecchio, Cannaregio 1185/A* ☎ *041/2750200* Ⓜ *Vaporetto: San Marcuola or Guglie.*

Do Maghi. Do Maghi means "two magicians" but in fact there are three glass masters at work here. The store is balanced with a mix of items steeped in Murano tradition complemented by whimsical and humorous creations from goldfish in bowls to single long-stemmed red roses. ✉ *Calle Dolfin, Cannaregio 5621* ☎ *041/5208535* Ⓜ *Vaporetto: Ca' d'Oro.*

JEWELRY

Rose Douce. An enticing selection of tasteful Murano glass accessories, figures, and chalices includes jewelry made with Murano antique beads and braided gold. ✉ *Salizzada San Giovanni Crisostomo, Rialto area, Cannaregio 5782* ☎ *041/5227232* Ⓜ *Vaporetto: Rialto.*

MARKETS

Canale Cannaregio food market. This neighborhood market stretches along the busy canal, where many of the stalls often sell fresh fish. ✉ *Canale Cannaregio, Cannaregio* ⊕ *Vaporetto: Guglie.*

WINE

Midora Vini. Enjoy a wine tasting, at a nominal charge, or just ask for advice before purchasing a bottle or two from the carefully honed selection of regional and mostly Italian wines. ✉ *Salizzada San Cassiàn, Cannaregio 5905* ☎ *041/5205669* ⊕ *www.midoravenezia.it.*

CASTELLO

CLOTHING

Fodor's Choice
★
Barbieri-Arabesque. Scarves and shawls for women come in myriad colors and textures; you can also pick up fine men's ties while you're here. They've been a perennial favorite of Venetians and travelers alike since they opened in 1945. ✉ *Ponte dei Greci, Castello 3403* ☎ *041/5228177* Ⓜ *Vaporetto: San Zaccaria.*

Ceriello. The only place in town that sells Brioni suits for men features Amina Rubinacci and Mazzi for men and women as well. ✉ *Campo*

CLOSE UP

Venice's Signature Crafts: Glass

Perhaps it's a matter of character that Venice, a city whose beauty depends so much upon the effects of shimmering, reflected light, also developed glass—a material that seems to capture light in solid form—as an artistic and expressive medium. There's not much in the way of a practical explanation for the affinity, since the materials used to make glass, even from earliest days, have not been found in the Venetian lagoon. They've had to be imported, frequently with great difficulty and expense.

Glass production in the city dates back to the earliest days of the Republic; evidence of a seventh- or eighth-century glass factory has been found on Torcello. Glass was already used as an artistic medium, employing techniques imported from Byzantine and Islamic glassmakers, by the 11th century. You can see surviving examples of early Venetian glass in the tiles of the mosaics of San Marco.

By 1295 the secrets of Venetian glassmaking were so highly prized that glassmakers were forbidden to leave the city. Venice succeeded in keeping the formulas of Venetian glass secret until the late 16th century, when some renegades started production in Bohemia. In 1291, to counter the risk of fire in Venice proper, the glass furnaces were moved to the then underpopulated island of Murano, which has remained the center of Venetian glassmaking to the present.

The fall of Damascus in 1400 and of Constantinople in 1435 sent waves of artisans to Venice, who added new techniques and styles to the repertoire of Venetian glass factories, but the most important innovation was developed by a native Venetian, Angelo Barovier. In the mid-15th century he discovered a way of making pure, transparent glass, *cristallo veneziano*. This allowed for the development of further decorative techniques, such as filigree glass, which became mainstays of Venetian glass production.

Glass studios such as Venini, Pauly, Moretti, and Berengo make up the premium line of Venetian glass production. These firms all have factories and showrooms on Murano, but they also have showrooms in Venice. Although their more elaborate pieces can cost thousands of dollars, you can take home a modest but lovely piece bearing one of their prestigious signatures for about $100, or even less.

On Murano you can visit a factory and watch Venetian glass being made, but among the premium manufacturers only Berengo allows visitors to its factory and they are quite dedicated to educating the public about glass. At minor factories, you'll generally get an adequate demonstration of Venetian glassmaking, as well as a high-pressure sales pitch.

Venice and Murano are full of shops selling glass, of varying taste and quality. Some of it is made on the Venetian mainland, or even in Eastern Europe or China. Many minor producers on Murano have formed a consortium and identify their pieces with a sticker, which guarantees that the piece was made on Murano. The premium glass manufacturers, however, do not belong to the consortium—so the sticker guarantees only where the piece was made, not necessarily its quality or value.

6

SS. Filippo e Giacomo, Castello 4275 ☎ *041/5222062* ⊕ *www.ceriello. it* Ⓜ *Vaporetto: San Zaccaria.*

GLASS

Al Campanil. Jewelry designer Sabina taught at the International School of Glass on Murano and still makes beads on-site in her store. In addition to her own creations, she now sources new products from an array of international designers and proudly sells items that have been created from materials including glass, metal, fabric, and paper. ⊠ *Calle Lunga Santa Maria Formosa, Castello 5184* ☎ *041/5235734* Ⓜ *Vaporetto: Rialto, San Zaccaria, or Ospedale.*

GOLD, WOOD, AND METALWORK

Cose Antiche di Luca Sumiti. Luca Sumiti carries on the work of his father, Maurizio; traditional wrought-iron chandeliers and lamps come unadorned, gilded, or tastefully enameled in bright colors. Here you'll also find conspicuous, 5-foot-tall wooden sculptures of *mori veneziani* (Venetian Moors). ⊠ *Calle delle Bande, Castello 5274* ☎ *041/5205621* ⊕ *coseantiche.eu* Ⓜ *Vaporetto: Rialto or San Zaccaria.*

Jonathan Ceolin. Carrying on the traditions of his adopted city, this craftsman makes traditional wrought-iron chandeliers, wall lamps, and Venetian lanterns, either plain black or gilded (like in the old days), in his tiny workshop near Campo Santa Maria Formosa. ⊠ *Ponte Marcello off Campo Santa Marina, Castello 6106* ☎ *041/5200609* ⊕ *www. ceolinjonathan.com* Ⓜ *Vaporetto: Rialto.*

Paolo Brandolisio. Paolo Brandolisio's workshop is a lofty tribute to his craft; this is where Brandolisio apprenticed with his famous mentor, Giuseppe Carlì (spot photos of him and a youthful Paolo dotting the walls). Gondoliers' oars await pickup, piled underneath the skylight; you can purchase a tiny hand-carved oarlock as a very special souvenir. ⊠ *Calle Corte Rota, Castello 4725* ☎ *041/5224155* ⊕ *paolobrandolisio. altervista.org* Ⓜ *Vaporetto: San Zaccaria.*

LACE, LINEN, AND FABRICS

Scarpa Ricambi. A charmingly old-fashioned shop has no dressing room: you'll have to make do in a tiny corner behind a folding screen. The top-of-the-line silk lace shirts, are well worth the trouble, as are the lace cooking aprons. ⊠ *Campo San Zaccaria, Castello 4683* ☎ *041/5287883* Ⓜ *Vaporetto: San Zaccaria.*

MARKETS

Via Garabaldi food market. Fresh foods, including farm fresh cheeses and other dairy products, are available at the morning market near the Giardini della Biennale. ⊠ *Via Garabaldi, Castello* ⊕ *Vaporetto: Arsenale.*

MASKS

Il Canovaccio. This is a treasure trove of papier-mâché objects, panels, and masks designed for the theater stage. Mask-making classes are offered by appointment. ⊠ *Calle delle Bande, Castello 5369/70* ☎ *041/5210393* ⊕ *www.ilcanovaccio.com* Ⓜ *Vaporetto: Rialto or San Marco.*

Scheggi di Arlecchino. What distinguishes family-owned-and-operated Scheggi di Arlecchino is that many of their masks are inspired by the works of famous painters, including Picasso, Klimt, and de Chirico, to name but a few. ✉ *Calle Lunga Santa Maria Formosa, Castello 6185* ☎ *041/5225789* Ⓜ *Vaporetto: Rialto.*

WINE

Bottiglieria Colonna. Regional wines are handpicked from small producers, and the shop also stocks an ample selection of unusual wines from central Italy. You'll find sparkling wines and liquor, too. ✉ *Calle de la Fava, Castello 5595* ☎ *041/5285137* Ⓜ *Vaporetto: Rialto.*

Vino e . . . Vini. In-store experts offer advice in choosing from an extensive selection of the excellent regional wines they stock, and happily help you choose Italian and international wines as well. ✉ *Salizzada del Pignater, Castello 3566* ☎ *041/5210184* Ⓜ *Vaporetto: Arsenale.*

CASTELLO

LEATHER GOODS

Fodor'sChoice
★
Giovanna Zanella. Cobbler-designer Giovanna Zanella Caeghera creates whimsical contemporary footwear in a variety styles and colors. She was a student of the famous Venetian master cobbler Rolando Segalin. ✉ *Calle Carminati off Campo San Lio, Castello 5641* ☎ *041/5235500* ⊕ *www.giovannazanella.it* Ⓜ *Vaporetto: Rialto.*

6

Kalimala. This shop should not be missed if you are looking for soft leather bags, a perfect match for almost any outfit, or very pretty, inexpensive copper jewelry. ✉ *Salizzada San Lio, Castello 5387* ☎ *041/5283596* Ⓜ *Vaporetto: Rialto.*

La Venexiana. This narrow store is overflowing with a sea of colorful and unique bags, wallets, iPad covers, and durable luggage. They carry the full line of the sought-after Gabs bags from Florence as well as one-of-a-kind pieces from Caterina Lucchi and Gianni Segatta. A purchase here is like taking home a practical, portable work of art. ✉ *Ruga Giuffa S. Apollonia near the Ponte della Canonica, Castello 4322, Castello* ☎ *041/5233558* Ⓜ *Vaporetto: San Zaccaria.*

Mariani. A longtime favorite destination for shoe shopping in Venice has reasonable prices. ✉ *Ponte de la Canonica, Castello 4313, Castello* ☎ *041/5222967* Ⓜ *Vaporetto: San Zaccaria.*

GIUDECCA

LACE, LINEN, AND FABRIC

Fortuny Tessuti Artistici. The original Fortuny textile factory has been converted into a showroom. Prices are over-the-top at €150 a meter, but it's worth a trip to see the extraordinary colors and textures of their hand-printed silks and velvets. ✉ *Fondamenta San Biagio, Giudecca 805* ☎ *041/5224078* ⊕ *fortuny.com* Ⓜ *Vaporetto: Palanca.*

MURANO

GLASS

Berengo Studio. In addition to contemporary fine-art glass, this high-end manufacturer gives tours of its Murano factory, something that most studios in this elite category do not do. ✉ *Fondamenta Vetrai, Murano 109/A* ☎ *041/739453* ⊕ *www.berengo.com* Ⓜ *Vaporetto: Murano Colonna or Murano Faro.*

Domus. Vases, sculpture, objects and jewelry from Murano's best glassworks are on offer. ✉ *Fondamenta dei Vetrai, Murano 82* ☎ *041/739215.*

SIDE TRIPS
FROM VENICE

WELCOME TO SIDE TRIPS FROM VENICE

TOP REASONS TO GO

★ **Giotto's frescoes in the Cappella degli Scrovegni:** In this Padua chapel, Giotto's expressive and innovative frescoes foreshadowed the painting techniques of the Renaissance.

★ **Villa Barbaro in Maser:** Master architect Palladio's graceful creation meets Veronese's splendid frescoes in a onetime-only collaboration.

★ **Opera in Verona's ancient arena:** The performances may not be top-notch, but even serious opera fans can't resist the spectacle of these shows.

★ **Roman and early-Christian ruins at Aquileia:** Aquileia's ruins offer an image of the transition from pagan to Christian Rome, and are almost entirely free of tourists.

1 Padua. A city of both high-rises and history, Padua is most noted for Giotto's frescoes in the Cappella degli Scrovegni, where Dante's contemporary painted with a human focus that foreshadowed the Renaissance.

Capella degli Scrovegni, Padua

AUSTRIA

Tarvisio

Tolmezzo

52

CARNIA

A23   Gemona
       del Friuli

FRIULI-VENEZIA
GIULIA

Tagliamento

Udine   Cormóns

Pordenone   13

                      Gorizia

A28   A4

53   A4   14   SLOVENIA

Piave   354   Monfalcone

              Lignano   Grado   Trieste
              Sabbiadoro

           Caorle

Lido di Jesolo

Mare Adriatico

CROATIA

GETTING ORIENTED

The Venetian Arc is the sweep of land curving north and east from the River Adige to the Slovenian border. It's made up of two Italian regions—the Veneto and Friuli–Venezia Giulia— that were once controlled by Venice, and the culture is a mix of Venetian, Alpine, and Central European sensibilities.

7

2 Verona. Shakespeare placed Romeo, Juliet, and a couple of gentlemen in Verona, one of the oldest, best-preserved, and most beautiful cities in Italy. Try to catch *Aïda* at the gigantic Roman arena.

3 Vicenza. This elegant art city, on the green plain reaching inland from Venice's lagoon, bears the signature of the great 16th-century architect Andrea Palladio, including several palazzi and other important buildings.

4 Friuli–Venezia Giulia. Set between the Adriatic Sea and Slovenia in the eastern corner of Italy, this is a region where menus run from gnocchi to goulash. Friuli's elegant principal city, Udine, is the birthplace of Venice's great 18th-century painter Gianbattista Tiepolo. Sleepy little Aquileia's Roman and early-Christian remains offer an image of the transition from pagan to Christian Rome. The port city of Trieste has a mixed Venetian-Austrian heritage and an important literary and political history that comes alive in Belle Epoque cafés and palaces built for Habsburg nobility.

EATING AND DRINKING WELL IN THE VENETO AND FRIULI–VENEZIA GIULIA

With the decisive seasonal changes of the Venetian Arc, it's little wonder that many restaurants shun printed menus. Elements from field and forest define much of the local cuisine, including white asparagus, herbs, chestnuts, radicchio, and wild mushrooms.

Restaurants here tend to cling to tradition, not only in the food they serve but in how they serve it. This means that from 3 in the afternoon until about 7:30 in the evening most places other than bars are closed tight, and on Sunday afternoon restaurants are packed with Italian families and friends indulging in a weekly ritual of lunching out. Meals are still sacred for most Italians in this region, so don't be surprised if you get disapproving looks when you gobble down a sandwich or a slice of pizza while seated on the church steps or a park bench. In many places it's actually illegal to do so. Likewise, your waiter will likely be very upset if you order just one course at a meal. If you want to dine lightly yet fit in with the locals, eat while standing at a bar.

THE BEST IN BEANS

Pasta e fagioli, a thick bean soup with pasta, served slightly warm or at room temperature, is made all over Italy. Folks in Veneto, though, take a special pride in their version. It features particularly fine beans that are grown around the village of Lamon, near Belluno.

Even when they're bought in the Veneto, the beans from Lamon cost more than double the next most expensive variety, but their rich and delicate taste is considered to be well worth the added expense. You never knew that bean soup could taste so good.

PASTA, RISOTTO, POLENTA

For *primi* (first courses), the Veneto dines on *bigoli* (thick whole-wheat pasta) generally served with an anchovy-onion sauce delicately flavored with cinnamon, and risotto flavored either with local fish, sausage, or vegetables. *Polenta* (corn meal gruel) is everywhere, whether it's a stiff porridge topped with Gorgonzola or stew, or a patty grilled alongside meat or fish, *as in the photo below.*

FISH

The catch of the day is always a good bet, whether sweet and succulent Adriatic shellfish, sea bream, bass, or John Dory, or freshwater fish from Lake Garda near Verona. A staple in the Veneto is *baccalà*, dried salt cod, soaked in water or milk, and then prepared in a different way in each city. In Vicenza, baccalà *alla vicentina, pictured at left,* is cooked with onions, milk, and cheese, and is generally served with polenta.

MEAT

Because grazing land is scarce in the Veneto, beef is a rarity, but pork and veal are standards, while goose, duck, and guinea fowl are common poultry options. Lamb is available mostly in spring, when it's young and delicate. In Friuli–Venezia Giulia, menus show the influences of Austria-Hungary: you may find deer and hare on the menu, as well as Eastern European–style goulash.

Throughout the Veneto an unusual treat is *nervetti*—cubes of gelatin from a cow's knee prepared with onions, parsley, olive oil, and lemon.

RADICCHIO DI TREVISO

In fall and winter be sure to try the radicchio di Treviso, *pictured above,* a red endive grown near that town but popular all over the region. Cultivation is very labor intensive, so it can be a bit expensive. It's best in a stew with chicken or veal, in a risotto, or just grilled or baked with a drizzle of olive oil and perhaps a little taleggio cheese from neighboring Lombardy.

WINE

Wine is excellent here: the Veneto produces more D.O.C. (Denominazione di Origine Controllata) wines than any other region in Italy. Amarone, the region's crowning achievement, is a robust and powerful red with an alcohol content as high as 16%. Valpolicella and Bardolino are other notable appellations.

The best of the whites are Soave, sparkling Prosecco, and *pinot bianco* (pinot blanc). In Friuli–Venezia Giulia the local wines par excellence are *tocai friulano*, a dry, lively white made from the sauvignon vert grape, which has attained international stature, and piccolit, perhaps Italy's most highly prized dessert wine.

Updated
by Bruce
Leimsidor

Much of the pleasure of exploring the arc around Venice—stretching from Verona to Trieste, encompassing the Veneto and Friuli–Venezia Giulia regions—comes from discovering the variations on the Venetian theme that give a unique character to each of the towns.

Some of the cities outside Venice, such as Verona and Udine, have a solid medieval look. Padua, with its narrow arcaded streets, is romantic; Vicenza, ennobled by the architecture of Palladio, is elegant. Udine is a genteel, intricately sculpted city that's home to the first important frescoes by Giambattista Tiepolo. Trieste shows off its past as a port of the Austro-Hungarian Empire in its Viennese-inspired coffeehouses and great palaces. Wherever you go, the emblem of Venice, Saint Mark's winged lion, is emblazoned on palazzi or poised on pedestals, and the art, architecture, and way of life all in some way reflect Venetian splendor.

PLANNING

PLANNING AHEAD

Reservations are required to see the Giotto frescoes in Padua's Cappella degli Scrovegni—though if there's space, you can "reserve" on the spot.

On the outskirts of Vicenza, Villa della Rotonda, one of star-architect Palladio's masterpieces, is open to the public only from mid-March through mid-November, and only on Wednesday and Saturday. (Hours for visiting the grounds are less restrictive.)

Another important Palladian villa, Villa Barbaro near Maser, is open weekends and several days during the week from March to October. From November to February, it's open only on weekends.

If you plan to take in an opera at the Arena di Verona, buy tickets as early as you can, since they sell out quickly. Also, book a room for the evening in Verona, as you are likely to miss the last train back to Venice.

For details about Cappella degli Scrovegni, look in this chapter under "Top Attractions" in Padua. For the villas, see "Top Attractions" in

Vicenza and Palladio Country. For the Arena di Verona, see "Nightlife and the Arts" in Verona.

MAKING THE MOST OF YOUR TIME

Lined up in a row west of Venice are Padua, Vicenza, and Verona—three prosperous small cities that are each worth at least a day on a trip out of Venice. Verona has the greatest charm, and it's probably the best choice if you're going to visit only one of these cities, even though it also draws the biggest crowds of tourists.

East of Venice, the region of Friuli–Venezia Giulia is off the main tourist circuit, but you may be drawn by its caves and castles, its battle-worn hills, and its mix of Italian and Central European culture. The port city of Trieste, famous for its elegant cafés, has quiet character that some people find dull and others find alluring.

GETTING HERE AND AROUND

BUS TRAVEL

There are interurban and interregional connections throughout the Veneto and Friuli, handled by nearly a dozen private bus lines. To figure out which line will get you where, the best strategy is to get assistance from local tourist offices.

CAR TRAVEL

Padua, Vicenza, and Verona are on the highway and train line between Venice and Milan. Seeing them without a car isn't a problem; in fact, having a car can complicate matters. The cities sometimes limit access, permitting only cars with plates ending in an even number on even days, odd on odd, or prohibiting cars altogether on weekends. The only place in which a car would be really useful is Aquileia, since public transportation there is somewhat limited, although still possible.

The A4, the primary route from Milan to Venice and Trieste, skirts Verona, Padua, and Udine along the way. Driving time, in normal traffic, from Venice to Padua is 30 minutes; Venice to Vicenza, 60 minutes, and to Verona 90 minutes. Heading east out of Venice, Aquileia is about 90 minutes, Udine about 90 minutes, and Trieste 120 minutes.

TRAIN TRAVEL

Trains on the main routes from Venice stop almost hourly in Verona, Vicenza, and Padua.

To the west of Venice, the main line running across the north of Italy stops at Padua (30 minutes from Venice), Vicenza (1 hour), and Verona (1½ hours); to the east is Trieste (2 hours).

Be sure to take express trains whenever possible—a local "milk run" that stops in every village along the way can take considerably longer. The fastest trains are the Eurostars, but reservations are obligatory and fares are much higher than on regular express trains.

Train Information FS. You can check schedules on the Italian national railway's website. ☎ *892021* ⊕ *www.trenitalia.com.*

RESTAURANTS

Prices in the reviews are the average cost of a main course at dinner or, if dinner is not served, at lunch.

7

HOTELS

There's a full range of accommodations throughout the region. Ask about weekend discounts, often available at hotels catering to business clients. Rates tend to be higher in Padua and Verona; in Verona especially, seasonal rates vary widely and soar during trade fairs and the opera season. There are fewer good lodging choices in Vicenza, perhaps because more overnighters are drawn to the better restaurant scene in Verona and Padua. *Agriturismo* (farm stay) information is available at tourist offices and sometimes on their websites.

Prices in the reviews are the lowest cost of a standard double room in high season.

PADUA

42 km (25 miles) west of Venice.

A romantic warren of arcaded streets, Padua has long been one of the major cultural centers of northern Italy. Its university, founded in 1222 and Italy's second oldest, attracted such cultural icons as Dante (1265–1321), Petrarch (1304–74), and Galileo Galilei (1564–1642), thus earning the city the sobriquet *La Dotta* (The Learned). Padua's Basilica di Sant'Antonio, begun around 1238, attracts droves of pilgrims, especially on his feast day, June 13. Three great artists—Giotto (1266–1337), Donatello (circa 1386–1466), and Mantegna (1431–1506)—left significant works in Padua, with Giotto's Scrovegni Chapel being one of the best-known, and most meticulously preserved, works of art in the country. Today, a cycle-happy student body—some 50,000 strong—flavors every aspect of local culture. Don't be surprised if you spot a *laurea* (graduation) ceremony marked by laurel leaves, mocking lullabies, and X-rated caricatures.

GETTING HERE AND AROUND

The train trip between Venice and Padua is short, and regular bus service originates from Venice's Piazzale Roma. By car from Venice, Padua is on the Autostrada Torino–Trieste A4/E70. Take the San Carlo exit and follow Via Guido Reni to Via Tiziano Aspetti into town. Regular bus service connects Venice's Marco Polo airport with downtown Padua.

Padua is a walker's city. If you arrive by car, leave your vehicle in one of the parking lots on the outskirts or at your hotel. Unlimited bus service is included with the Padova Card (€16 or €21, valid for 48 or 72 hours), which allows entry to all the city's principal sights (€1 extra for a Scrovegni Chapel reservation). It's available at tourist information offices and at some museums and hotels.

VISITOR INFORMATION

Padua Tourism Office ⊠ *Padova Railway Station* ☎ *049/8752077* ⊕ *www. turismopadova.it* ⊠ *Galleria Pedrocchi* ☎ *049/8767927.*

EXPLORING PADUA

TOP ATTRACTIONS

Basilica di Sant'Antonio (*Basilica del Santo*). Thousands of faithful make the pilgrimage here each year to pray at the tomb of Saint Anthony, while others come to admire works by the 15th-century Florentine master Donatello. His equestrian statue (1453) of the *condottiere* (mercenary general) Erasmo da Narni, known as Gattamelata, in front of the church is one of the great masterpieces of Italian Renaissance sculpture, inspired by the ancient statue of Marcus Aurelius in Rome's Campidoglio. Donatello also sculpted the beautiful series of bronze reliefs in the imposing interior illustrating the miracles of Saint Anthony, as well as the bronze statues of the Madonna and saints, on the high altar.

The huge church, which combines elements of Byzantine, Romanesque, and Gothic styles, was probably begun around 1238, seven years after the death of the Portuguese-born saint. It was completed in 1310, with structural modifications added from the end of the 14th century into the mid-15th century. Because of the site's popularity with pilgrims, masses are held in the basilica almost constantly, which makes it difficult to see these works. More accessible is the restored **Cappella del Santo** (housing the tomb of the saint), which dates from the 16th century. Its walls are covered with impressive reliefs by various important Renaissance sculptors, including Jacopo Sansovino (1486–1570), the architect of the library in Venice's Piazza San Marco, and Tullio Lombardo (1455–1532), the greatest in a family of sculptors who decorated many churches in the area, among them Venice's Santa Maria dei Miracoli. ✉ *Piazza del Santo* ☎ *049/8225652* ⊕ *www.santantonio.it* ☉ *Oct.–Apr., daily 6:20 am–7 pm; May–Sept., daily 6:20 am–7:45 pm.*

Fodor's Choice
★ **Cappella degli Scrovegni** (*The Arena Chapel*). The spatial depth, emotional intensity, and naturalism of the frescoes illustrating the lives of Mary and Jesus in this world-famous chapel—note the use of blue sky instead of the conventional, depth-destroying gold background of medieval painting—broke new ground in Western art. Enrico Scrovegno commissioned these frescoes to atone for the sins of his deceased father, Reginaldo, the usurer condemned to the Seventh Circle of the Inferno in Dante's *Divine Comedy.* Giotto and his assistants executed the frescoes from 1303 to 1305, arranging them in tiers to be read from left to right. Opposite the altar is a *Last Judgment,* most likely designed and painted by Giotto's assistants, where Enrico offers his chapel to the Virgin, celebrating her role in human salvation—particularly appropriate, given the penitential purpose of the chapel.

Mandatory reservations are for a specific time and are nonrefundable. They can be made well in advance at the ticket office, online, or by phone. Payments online or by phone by credit card must be made one day in advance; payments by bank transfer (possible by phone only) should be made four days in advance. Reservations are necessary even if you have a Padova Card. In order to preserve the artwork, doors are opened only every 15 minutes. A maximum of 25 visitors at a time must spend 15 minutes in an acclimatization room before making a 15-minute (20-minute in winter, late June, and July) chapel visit.

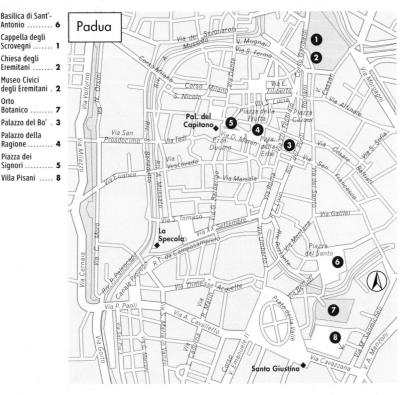

Punctuality is essential; tickets should be picked up at least one hour before your reservation time. If you don't have a reservation, it's sometimes possible to buy your chapel admission on the spot—but you might have to wait a while until there's a group with an opening. You can see fresco details as part of a virtual tour at Musei Civici degli Eremitani. A good place to get some background before visiting the chapel is the multimedia room, which offers films and interactive computer presentations. ⊠ *Piazza Eremitani 8* ☏ *049/2010020 for reservations* ⊕ *www.cappelladegliscrovegni.it* ✉ *€13 includes Musei Civici, or €1 with PadovaCard* ☉ *Early Nov.–early Mar. and mid-June–early Aug., daily 9–7; early Mar.–mid-June and early Aug.–early Nov., Mon. 9–7, Tues.–Sun. 9 am–10 pm; entry by reservation only.*

Palazzo della Ragione. Also known as Il Salone, the spectacular arcaded reception hall in Padua's original law courts is as notable for its grandeur—it's 85 feet high—as for its colorful setting, between the Piazza delle Frutta and surrounded by shops, cafés, and open-air fruit and vegetable markets. Niccolò Miretto and Stefano di Ferrara, working from 1425 to 1440, painted the frescoes, following the plan of frescoes by Giotto destroyed by a fire in 1420. The stunning space hosts art shows, and an enormous wooden horse, crafted for a 15th-century public tournament, commands pride of place. ⊠ *Piazza della Ragione*

☎ 049/8205006 🏛 *Salone €4, free with PadovaCard* ⊗ *Feb.–Oct., Tues.–Sun. 9–7; Nov.–Jan., Tues.–Sun. 9–6.*

Piazza dei Signori. Some fine examples of 15th- and 16th-century buildings line this square. On the west side, the **Palazzo del Capitanio** (facade constructed 1598–1605) has an impressive **Torre dell'Orologio,** with an astronomical clock dating from 1344 and a portal made by Falconetto in 1532 in the form of a Roman triumphal arch. The 12th-century **Battistero del Duomo** (Cathedral Baptistry), with frescoes by Giusto de Menabuoi (1374–78), is a few steps away. ⊠ *Piazza dei Signori* ☎ *049/656914* 🏛 *Battistero: €2.80, free with PadovaCard* ⊗ *Daily 10–6.*

FAMILY **Villa Pisani.** Extensive grounds with rare trees, ornamental fountains, and garden follies surround this extraordinary palace in Stra, 13 km (8 miles) southeast of Padua. Built in 1721 for the Venetian doge Alvise Pisani, it recalls Versailles more than a Veneto villa. This was one of the last and grandest of many stately residences constructed along the Brenta River from the 16th to 18th century by wealthy Venetians for their *villeggiatura*—vacation and escape from the midsummer humidity. Gianbattista Tiepolo's (1696–1770) spectacular frescoes on the ballroom ceiling alone are worth the visit. For a relaxing afternoon, explore the gorgeous park and maze. To get here from Venice, take Bus 53 from Piazzale Roma. The villa is a five-minute walk from the bus stop in Stra. ■TIP→ This is the place where Mussolini invited Hitler for their first meeting, but they only stayed one night because of the mosquitos. The mosquitoes remain: if you're visiting the park in the late afternoon in the summer, be sure to bring some mosquito repellant. ⊠ *Via Doge Pisani 7, Stra* ☎ *049/502074* ⊕ *www.villapisani.beniculturali.it* 🏛 *€7.50; park only, €4.50* ⊗ *Villa and park: Apr.–Sept., Tues.–Sun. 9–7; Oct., Tues.–Sun. 9–5; Nov.–Mar., Tues.–Sun. 9–4. Maze closed Nov.–Feb.*

WORTH NOTING

Chiesa degli Eremitani. This 13th-century church houses substantial fragments of Andrea Mantegna's frescoes (1448–50), damaged by Allied bombing in World War II. Despite their fragmentary condition, Mantegna's still beautiful and historically important depictions of the martyrdom of Saint James and Saint Christopher show the young artist's mastery of extremely complex problems of perspective. ⊠ *Piazza degli Eremitani* ☎ *049/8756410* ⊗ *Mon.–Sat. 8–6, Sun. 10–1 and 4–7.*

Musei Civici degli Eremitani (*Civic Museum*). A former monastery now houses works of Venetian masters, as well as fine collections of archaeological finds and ancient coins. Notable are the Giotto Crucifix, which once hung in the Scrovegni Chapel, and the *Portrait of a*

THE VENETIAN ARC, PAST AND PRESENT

Long before Venetians made their presence felt on the mainland in the 15th century, Ezzelino III da Romano (1194–1259) laid claim to Verona, Padua, and the surrounding lands and towns. He was the first of a series of brutal and aggressive rulers who dominated the cities of the region until the rise of Venetian rule. Because of Ezzelino's cruel and violent nature, Dante consigned his soul to Hell.

After Ezzelino was ousted, powerful families such as Padua's Carrara and Verona's della Scala (Scaligeri) vied throughout the 14th century to dominate these territories. With the rise of Venetian rule came a time of relative peace, when noble families from the lagoon and the mainland commissioned Palladio and other accomplished architects to design their palazzi and villas. This rich classical legacy, superimposed upon medieval castles and fortifications, is central to the identities of present-day Padua, Vicenza, and Verona.

The region remained under Venetian control until the Napoleonic invasion and the fall of the Venetian Republic in 1797. The Council of Vienna ceded it, along with Lombardy, to Austria in 1815. The region revolted against Austrian rule and joined the Italian Republic in 1866.

Friuli–Venezia Giulia has been marched through, fought over, hymned by patriots, and romanticized by writers that include James Joyce, Rainer Maria Rilke, Pier Paolo Passolini, and Jan Morris. The region has seen Fascists and Communists, Romans, Habsburgs, and Huns. It survived by forging sheltering alliances—Udine beneath the wings of San Marco (1420), Trieste choosing Duke Leopold of Austria (1382) over Venetian domination.

Some of World War I's fiercest fighting took place in Friuli–Venezia Giulia, where memorials and cemeteries commemorate hundreds of thousands who died before Italian troops arrived in 1918 and liberated Trieste from Austrian rule. Trieste, along with the whole of Venezia Giulia, was annexed to Italy in 1920. During World War II the Germans occupied the area and placed Trieste in an administrative zone along with parts of Slovenia. The only Nazi extermination camp on Italian soil, the Risiera di San Sabba, was in a suburb of Trieste. After the war, during a period of Cold War dispute, Trieste was governed by an allied military administration; it was officially reannexed to Italy in 1954, when Italy ceded the Istrian peninsula to the south to Yugoslavia. These arrangements were not finally ratified by Italy and Yugoslavia until 1975.

Young Senator by Giovanni Bellini (1430–1516). ⊠ *Piazza Eremitani 8* ☎ *049/82045450* 🖾 *€10, €13 with Scrovegni Chapel, free with Padova Card* ☉ *Tues.–Sun. 9–7.*

Orto Botanico (*Botanical Garden*). The Venetian Republic ordered the creation of Padua's botanical garden in 1545 to supply the university with medicinal plants, and it still maintains its original layout. You can stroll the arboretum—still part of the university—and wander through hothouses and beds of plants that were first introduced to Italy in this late-Renaissance garden. A St. Peter's palm, planted in 1585, inspired

The Giotto frescoes at Padua's Cappella degli Scrovegni are some of northern Italy's greatest art treasures.

Goethe to write his 1790 essay "The Metamorphosis of Plants." ✉ *Via Orto Botanico 15* ☎ *049/8272119* ⊕ *www.ortobotanico.unipd.it* 🎟 *€4, free with PadovaCard* ☉ *Apr.–Oct., daily 9–1 and 3–7; Nov.–Mar., Mon.–Sat. 9–1.*

Palazzo del Bo'. The University of Padua, founded in 1222, centers around this predominently16th-century palazzo with an 18th-century facade. It's named after the Osteria del Bo' (*bo'* means "ox"), an inn that once stood on the site. It's worth a visit to see the exquisite and perfectly proportioned anatomy theater (1594), the beautiful "Old Courtyard," and a hall with a lectern used by Galileo. You can enter only as part of a guided tour. Most guides speak English, but it is worth checking ahead by phone. ✉ *Via VIII Febbraio* ☎ *049/8275111 University switchboard* ⊕ *www.unipd.it* 🎟 *€5* ☉ *Nov.–Feb., Mon., Wed., and Fri. at 3:15 and 4:15, Tues., Thurs., and Sat. at 10:15 and 11:15; Mar.–Oct., Mon., Wed., and Fri. at 3:15, 4:15, and 5:15; Tues., Thurs., and Sat. at 9:15, 10:15, and 11:15.*

WHERE TO EAT

$ ✗ **Enoteca dei Tadi.** In this cozy and atmospheric cross between a wine
NORTHERN bar and a restaurant you can put together an inexpensive dinner from
ITALIAN the various classic dishes on offer. Portions are small, but so are the prices—just follow the local custom and order a selection. Dishes are made with first-rate ingredients and are coupled with a fine selection of wines. Start with fresh *burrata* (*mozzarella's* creamier, richer cousin) with tomatoes, or choose from a selection of *prosciutto crudo* or salamis. Don't pass up the house specialty, lasagna, with several kinds on

the menu. Main courses are limited, but include a savory Veneto stew with polenta. $ *Average main: €25* ✉ *Via dei Tadi 16* ☎ *049/8364099, 388/4083434 cell phone* ⊕ *www. enotecadeitadi.it* ⬧ *Reservations essential* ☾ *No lunch. Closed Mon.*

$$$
MODERN ITALIAN

✕ **La Finestra.** One of the trendier restaurants in Padua, La Finestra, is cozy yet elegant. The carefully prepared and creatively presented dishes may not always stick to tradition, but no one can claim that owners Carlo Vidali and Hélène Dao don't know what they're doing in the kitchen. Try their wonderful black bean soup with ginger, prawns and sour cream—not grandma's bean soup, but it's heavenly—followed by seared tuna with saffron and onions, or a more traditional beef tagliata with rosemary. The service is attentive and helpful. $ *Average main: €22* ✉ *Via dei Tadi 15* ☎ *049/650313* ⊕ *www.ristorantefinestra.it* ⬧ *Reservations essential* ☾ *Closed Mon., first wk in Feb. and 3 wks in Aug. No lunch Tues.–Thurs., no dinner Sun.*

$
WINE BAR

✕ **L'Anfora.** This mix between a traditional *bacaro* (wine bar) and an *osteria* (tavernlike restaurant) is a local institution. Stand at the bar shoulder to shoulder with a cross section of Padovano society, from construction workers to professors, and let the friendly and knowledgeable proprietors help you choose a wine. The reasonably priced menu offers simple *casalinga* (home-cooked dishes), plus salads and a selection of cheeses. Portions are ample, and no one will look askance if you don't order the full meal. The place is packed with loyal regulars at lunchtime, so come early or expect a wait. $ *Average main: €15* ✉ *Via Soncin 13* ☎ *049/656629* ☾ *Closed Sun. (except in Dec.), 1 wk in Jan., and 1 wk in Aug.*

$$$$
MODERN ITALIAN

✕ **Le Calandre.** If you are willing to shell out around €500 for a dinner for two and are gastronomically adventurous, include the quietly elegant place major critics consistently judge to be one of Italy's top three restaurants on your list. Traditional Veneto recipes are given a highly sophisticated and creative treatment—traditional squid in its ink comes as a "cappuccino," in a glass with a crust of potato foam—while dishes such as sole with a grapefruit and curry sauce leave the Veneto far behind. Owner-chef Massimiliano Alajmo's creative impulses, together with seasonal changes, augment the signature dishes, but Alajmo considers food to be an art form rather than nourishment, so be prepared for minuscule portions. Reserve well in advance. $ *Average main: €220* ✉ *Via Liguria 1, 7 km (4 miles) west of Padua, Sarmeola di*

Rubano ☎ *049/630303* ⊕ *www.calandre.com* ⬧ *Reservations essential* ⊗ *Closed Sun. and Mon., Jan. 1–17, and Aug. 14–31.*

$$
VENETIAN

✕ **Osteria Dal Capo.** A friendly trattoria in the heart of what used to be Padua's Jewish ghetto serves almost exclusively traditional Veneto dishes and does so with refinement and care. The liver and onions is extraordinarily tender. Even the accompanying polenta is grilled to perfection—slightly crisp on the outside and moist on the inside. The desserts are nothing to scoff at, either. Word is out among locals about this tiny place, and it fills up quickly, so reservations are a must. ⑤ *Average main: €20* ⊠ *Via degli Oblizzi 2* ☎ *049/663105* ⬧ *Reservations essential* ⊗ *Closed Sun., 2 wks in early Jan., and 3 wks in Aug. No lunch Mon.*

WHERE TO STAY

For expanded hotel reviews, visit Fodors.com.

$
HOTEL

⌂ **Al Fagiano.** The delightfully funky surroundings include sponge-painted walls, brush-painted chandeliers, and some views of the spires and cupolas of the Basilica di Sant'Antonio. **Pros:** large rooms; relaxed atmosphere; convenient location. **Cons:** no room service or help with baggage; some find the eccentric decoration a bit much. ⑤ *Rooms from: €75* ⊠ *Via Locatelli 45* ☎ *049/8750073* ⊕ *www.alfagiano.com* ↩ *40 rooms* ⦿ *No meals.*

$$
HOTEL

⌂ **Albergo Verdi.** One of the best-situated hotels in the city provides tastefully renovated rooms that tend toward the minimalist without being severe and have the rare virtue of being absolutely quiet. **Pros:** excellent location close to the Piazza dei Signori; attentive staff; pleasant and warm atmosphere. **Cons:** rooms, while ample, are not large; few views; charge for Wi-Fi; hefty parking fee. ⑤ *Rooms from: €150* ⊠ *Via Dondi dell'Orologio 7* ☎ *049/8364163* ⊕ *www.albergoverdipadova.it* ↩ *14 rooms* ⦿ *Breakfast.*

$
HOTEL

⌂ **Methis.** Four floors of sleekly designed guest rooms reflect the elements: gentle earth tones, fiery red, watery cool blue, and airy white in the top-floor suites. **Pros:** attractive rooms; helpful and attentive staff; pleasant little extras like umbrellas. **Cons:** a 15-minute walk from major sights and restaurants; public spaces are cold and uninviting. ⑤ *Rooms from: €120* ⊠ *Riviera Paleocapa 70* ☎ *049/8725555* ⊕ *www.methishotel.com* ↩ *52 rooms, 7 suites* ⦿ *Breakfast.*

NIGHTLIFE AND THE ARTS

CAFÉS AND WINE BARS

Fodor'sChoice ★

Caffè Pedrocchi. No visit to Padua is complete without taking time to sit in this massive café, as the French writer Stendahl did shortly after the café was established in 1831, and observe a good slice of Veneto life, especially, as he noted, the elegant ladies sipping their coffee. Built in a style reflecting the fashion set by Napoleon's expeditions in Egypt, Pedrocchi has long been central to the city's social life. Its restaurant also serves lunch (12:30 to 2:30) and is proud of its innovative menu. ⊠ *Piazzetta Pedrocchi* ☎ *049/8781231* ⊕ *www.caffepedrocchi.it.*

7

Hostaria Ai Do Archi. Padova's most popular *bacari* is famous for its impressive platters of sliced meats, its selections of wine, and as a meeting place for reggae fans. The music can be overwhelming, there are very few tables so you may have to stand all evening, and the service a bit casual, but if reggae is your passion or you want a good taste of Padua student nightlife, this is the place. ⊠ *Via Nazario Sauro 23* ☎ *049/652335.*

VICENZA

74 km (46 miles) west of Venice, 43 km (27 miles) west of Padua.

Vicenza bears the distinctive signature of the 16th-century architect Andrea Palladio, whose name has been given to the "Palladian" style of architecture. He emphasized the principles of order and harmony using the classical style of architecture established by Renaissance architects such as Brunelleschi, Alberti, and Sansovino. He used these principles and classical motifs not only for public buildings but also for private dwellings. His elegant villas and palaces were influential in propagating classical architecture in Europe, especially Britain, and later in America—most notably at Thomas Jefferson's Monticello.

In the mid-16th century Palladio was commissioned to rebuild much of Vicenza, which had been greatly damaged during wars waged against Venice by the League of Cambrai (1505), an alliance of the papacy, France, the Holy Roman Empire, and several neighboring city-states. He made his name with the renovation of the Basilica, begun in 1549 in the heart of Vicenza, and then embarked on a series of lordly buildings, all of which adhere to the same classicism and principles of harmony.

GETTING HERE AND AROUND

Vicenza is midway between Padua and Verona; several trains leave from Venice every hour. By car, take the Autostrada Brescia–Padova/Torino–Trieste A4/E70 to SP247 North directly into Vicenza.

VISITOR INFORMATION

Vicenza Tourism Office ⊠ *Piazza Giacomo Matteotti 12* ☎ *0444/320854* ⊕ *www.vicenzae.org.*

EXPLORING VICENZA

TOP ATTRACTIONS

Fodor'sChoice **Teatro Olimpico.** Palladio's last, and perhaps most spectacular work, was
★ begun in 1580 and completed in 1585, after his death, by Vincenzo Scamozzi (1552–1616). Based closely on the model of ancient Roman theaters, it represents an important development in theater and stage design and is noteworthy for its acoustics and the cunning use of perspective in Scamozzi's permanent backdrop. The anterooms are frescoed with images of important figures in Venetian history. One of the few Renaissance theaters still standing is used for concerts and other performances. ⊠ *Piazza Matteotti* ☎ *0444/222800* ⊕ *www.teatrolimpico.it* ☜ *€8.50, includes admission to Palazzo Chiericati; €10, includes admis-*

sion to Palazzo Chiericati and Palazzo Barbaran da Porto (Palladio Museum) ☉ *Tues.–Sun. 9–5.*

Fodor's Choice
★

Villa della Rotonda (Villa Almerico Capra). This beautiful Palladian villa, commissioned in 1556 as a suburban residence for Paolo Almerico, is undoubtedly the purest expression of Palladio's architectural theory and aesthetic. It's more a villa-temple than a residence, and in this respect it contradicts the rational utilitarianism of Renaissance architecture. Rather, it can be called a prime example of mannerist architecture, demonstrating the priority Palladio gave to architectural symbolism of celestial harmony over practical considerations. Although a visit to view the interior may be difficult to schedule—it's still privately owned—it is well worth the effort in order to get an idea of how the people who commissioned the villa actually lived. Even without a peek inside, viewing the exterior and the grounds is a must for any visit to Vicenza. The villa is a 20-minute walk from town or a short ride on bus 8 from Vicenza's Piazza Roma. ⊠ *Via della Rotonda* ☎ *0444/321793* ⊕ *www.villalarotonda.it* 🎟 *€10; grounds only, €5* ☉ *Villa interior Mar. 13–early Nov., Wed. 10–noon and 3–6. Grounds Mar. 13–early Nov., Tues.–Sun. 10–noon and 3–6; early Nov.–Mar. 12, Tues.–Sun. 10–noon and 2:30–5. Hours may be modified during inclement weather.*

Fodor's Choice
★

Villa Valmarana ai Nani. Inside this 17th- to 18th-century country house, named for the statues of dwarfs adorning the garden, is a series of frescoes executed in 1757 by Gianbattista Tiepolo depicting scenes from classical mythology, *The Illiad*, Tasso's *Gerusalemme Liberata*, and Ariosto's *Orlando Furioso*. They include his *Sacrifice of Iphigenia*, a major masterpiece of 18th-century painting. The neighboring *foresteria* (guest house) is also part of the museum; it contains frescoes showing 18th-century life at its most charming, and scenes of chinoiserie popular in the 18th century, by Tiepolo's son Giandomenico (1727–1804). The garden dwarves are probably taken from designs by Giandomenico. You can reach the villa on foot by following the same path that leads to Palladio's Villa della Rotonda. ⊠ *Via dei Nani 2/8* ☎ *0444/321803* ⊕ *www.villavalmarana.com* 🎟 *€9* ☉ *Early Mar.–early Nov., Tues.–Sun. 10–12:30 and 3–6. Visits at other times are possible at an additional price.*

WORTH NOTING

Palazzo Barbaran da Porto (Palladio Museum). Palladio executed this beautiful city palace for the Vicentine noble Montano Barbarano between 1570 and 1575. The noble patron, however, did not make things easy for Palladio; the plan had to incorporate at least two preexisting medieval houses, with irregularly shaped rooms, into his classical, harmonious plan, and to support the great hall of the *piano nobile* above the fragile walls of the original medieval structure. The wonder of it is that this palazzo is one of Palladio's most harmonious constructions; the viewer has little indication that this is actually a transformation of a medieval structure. The palazzo also contains a museum dedicated to Palladio and is the seat of a center for Palladian studies. ⊠ *Contra' Porti 11* ☎ *0444/323014* 🎟 *€6; €10, includes admission to Palazzo Chiericati and Teatro Olimpico (Palladio Museum)* ☉ *Tues.–Sun 10–6.*

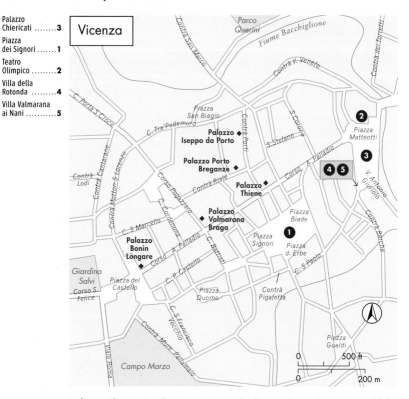

Palazzo Chiericati. This imposing Palladian palazzo (1550) would be worthy of a visit even if it didn't house Vicenza's **Museo Civico.** Because of the ample space surrounding the building, Palladio combined elements of an urban palazzo with those he used in his country villas. The museum's important Venetian collection includes significant paintings by Cima, Tiepolo, Piazzetta, and Tintoretto, but its main attraction is an extensive collection of highly interesting and rarely found painters from the Vicenza area, such as Jacopo Bassano (1515–92) and the eccentric and innovative Francesco Maffei (1605–60), whose work foreshadowed important currents of Venetian painting of subsequent generations. ⊠ *Piazza Matteotti* 🖾 *0444/325071* 🖃 *€8.50, includes admission to Teatro Olimpico; €10, includes admission to Teatro Olimpico and Palazzo Barbaran da Porto (Palladio Museum)* ⊘ *Tues.–Sun. 9–5.*

Piazza dei Signori. At the heart of Vicenza, this square contains the **Palazzo della Ragione** (1549), the project with which Palladio made his name by successfully modernizing a medieval building, grafting a graceful two-story exterior loggia onto the existing Gothic structure. Commonly known as Palladio's basilica, the palazzo served as a courthouse and public meeting hall (the original Roman meaning of the term "basilica") and is now open only when it houses exhibits, but the main point of interest, the loggia, is visible from the piazza. Take a look also at the **Loggia del Capitaniato,** opposite, which Palladio designed but never completed.

Santa Corona. An exceptionally fine *Baptism of Christ* (1502), a work of Giovanni Bellini's maturity, hangs over the altar on the left, just in front of the transept. The church also houses the elegantly simple Valmarana chapel, designed by Palladio. ✉ *Contrà S. Corona* ☎ *0444/222811* 🕑 *Tues.–Sun. 9–noon and 3–6.*

WHERE TO EAT

$$ ✕ **Antico Ristorante agli Schioppi.** When they want to eat well, Vicentini
NORTHERN generally head to the countryside, so it is telling that this is one of the
ITALIAN few restaurants in the city frequented by local families and the business
community. In Veneto country style, with enormous murals, it offers
simple, well-prepared regional cuisine with some modern touches. The
risotto, delicately flavored with wild mushrooms and zucchini flowers,
is creamy and beautifully textured—or try the Vicenza specialty *bac-
calà* (a cod dish). The "Menu Palladiana" presents 16th-century dishes
featuring spices common during that period, such as cinnamon and
cloves, and omitting items like tomatoes and potatoes, which were new
to Europe at that time. ⑤ *Average main: €18* ✉ *Contrà Piazza del Cas-
tello 26* ☎ *0444/543701* ⊕ *www.ristoranteaglischioppi.com* 🕑 *Closed
Sun. No lunch Mon.*

$ ✕ **Da Vittorio.** You'll find little in the way of atmosphere or style, but
PIZZA Vicentini flock to this small, casual place for what may be the best
pizza north of Naples. There's an incredible array of toppings, from the
traditional to the exotic (mangoes), but the pizzas are all so authentic
that they will make you think you are sitting by the Bay of Naples. The
service is friendly and efficient. This is a great place to stop for lunch if
you're walking to Palladio's Rotonda or the Villa Valmarana. ⑤ *Aver-
age main: €12* ✉ *Borgo Berga 52* ☎ *0444/525059* ▭ *No credit cards*
🕑 *Closed Tues. and 2 wks in July.*

$$ ✕ **Ponte delle Bele.** Vicenza lies at the foot of the Alps, and many wealth-
NORTHERN ier residents spend at least a part of summer in the mountains to escape
ITALIAN the heat. The Alpine cuisine that's been incorporated into the local culture can be enjoyed at this popular and friendly trattoria. The house
specialty, *stinco di maiale al forno* (roast port shank), is wonderfully
fragrant, with herbs and aromatic vegetables. Game dishes include venison with blueberries and guinea fowl roasted with white grapes. They're
also justly proud of their *baccalà alla vicentina* (cod in an onion, herb,
and Parmesan sauce, served with polenta). The rather kitschy interior
in no way detracts from the good, hearty food. ⑤ *Average main: €22*
✉ *Contrà Ponte delle Bele 5* ☎ *0444/320647* ⊕ *www.pontedellebele.it*
🕑 *Closed Sun. and 2 wks in mid-Aug.*

$ ✕ **Righetti.** For a city of its size, Vicenza has few outstanding restaurants.
ITALIAN That's why many people gravitate to this popular cafeteria, which serves
excellently prepared classic dishes without putting a dent in your wallet. There's frequently a hearty soup such as *orzo e fagioli* (barley and
bean) on the menu. The classic *baccalà alla vicentina*, a cod dish, is a
great reason to stop by on Tuesday or Friday. Righetti tends to be a

bit crowded at lunch, so be patient. It's open until 10 or so for dinner. $ *Average main: €12* ⊠ *Piazza Duomo 3* ☎ *0444/543135* ▭ *No credit cards* ⊘ *Closed weekends, 1st wk in Jan., and Aug.*

WHERE TO STAY

During annual gold fairs in January, May, and September, it may be quite difficult to find lodging. If you're coming then, be sure to reserve well in advance and expect to pay higher rates.

For expanded hotel reviews, visit Fodors.com.

$$
HOTEL

🖵 **Campo Marzio.** Rooms at this comfortable, full-service hotel, a five-minute walk from the train station and right in front of the city walls, are ample and furnished in various styles, from modern to traditional and romantic. **Pros:** central location; more amenities than its competitors; set back from the street, so it's quiet and bright. **Cons:** public spaces are uninspiring; incredibly expensive during fairs. $ *Rooms from: €140* ⊠ *Viale Roma 21* ☎☎ *0444/5457000* ⊕ *www.hotelcampomarzio.com* ⇆ *36 rooms* |◯| *Breakfast.*

$
HOTEL
Fodor'sChoice
★

🖵 **Due Mori.** Rooms at one of the oldest (1883) hotels in the city, just off the Piazza dei Signori, are filled with turn-of-the-20th-century antiques, and regulars favor the place because the high ceilings in the main building make it feel light and airy. **Pros:** comfortable, tastefully furnished rooms; friendly staff; central location; rate same year-round. **Cons:** no air-conditioning (although ceiling fans minimize the need for it); no one to help with baggage; no TV. $ *Rooms from: €90* ⊠ *Contrà Do Rode 24* ☎ *0444/321886* ⊕ *www.hotelduemori.com* ⇆ *53 rooms* ⊘ *Closed 1st 2 wks of Aug. and 2 wks in late Dec.* |◯| *No meals.*

VERONA

114 km (71 miles) west of Venice, 60 km (37 miles) west of Vicenza.

On the banks of the fast-flowing River Adige, enchanting Verona has timeless monuments, a picturesque town center, and a romantic reputation as the setting of Shakespeare's *Romeo and Juliet*. With its lively Venetian air and proximity to Lake Garda, it attracts hordes of tourists, especially Germans and Austrians. Tourism peaks during summer's renowned season of open-air opera in the arena and during spring's **Vinitaly** (⊕ *www.vinitaly.com*), one of the world's most important wine expos. For five days you can sample the wines of more than 3,000 wineries from dozens of countries.

Verona grew to power and prosperity within the Roman Empire as a result of its key commercial and military position in northern Italy. With its Roman arena, theater, and city gates, it has the most significant monuments of Roman antiquity north of Rome. After the fall of the empire, the city continued to flourish under the guidance of barbarian kings such as Theodoric, Alboin, Pepin, and Berenger I, reaching its cultural and artistic peak in the 13th and 14th centuries under the della Scala (Scaligero) dynasty. (Look for the *scala*, or ladder, emblem all over town.) In 1404 Verona traded its independence for security and placed

Continued on page 206

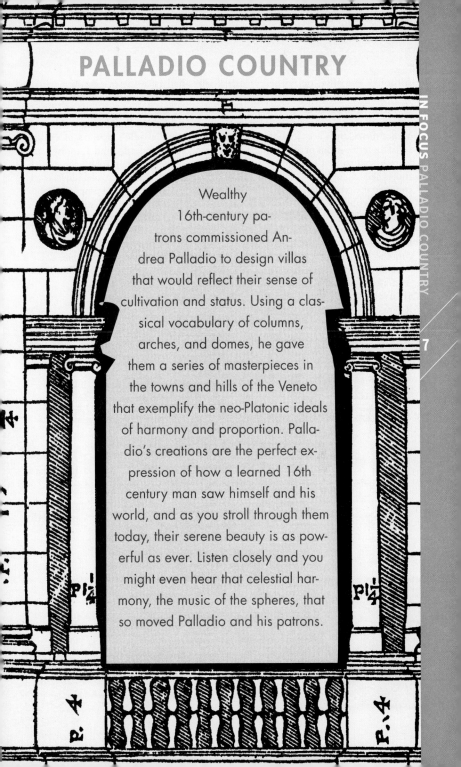

PALLADIO COUNTRY

Wealthy 16th-century patrons commissioned Andrea Palladio to design villas that would reflect their sense of cultivation and status. Using a classical vocabulary of columns, arches, and domes, he gave them a series of masterpieces in the towns and hills of the Veneto that exemplify the neo-Platonic ideals of harmony and proportion. Palladio's creations are the perfect expression of how a learned 16th century man saw himself and his world, and as you stroll through them today, their serene beauty is as powerful as ever. Listen closely and you might even hear that celestial harmony, the music of the spheres, that so moved Palladio and his patrons.

TOWN & COUNTRY

Although the villa, or "country residence," was still a relatively new phenomenon in the 16th century, it quickly became all the rage once the great lords of Venice turned their eyes from the sea toward the fertile plains of the Veneto. They were forced to do this once their trade routes had faltered when Ottoman Turks conquered Constantinople in 1456 and Columbus opened a path to the riches of America in 1492. In no time, canals were built, farms were laid out, and the fashion for *villeggiatura*—the attraction of idyllic country retreats for the nobility—became a favored lifestyle. As a means of escaping an overheated Rome,

villas had been the original brainchild of the ancient emperors and it was no accident that the Venetian lords wished to emulate this palatial style of country residence. Palladio's method of evaluating the standards, and standbys, of ancient Roman life through the eye of the Italian Renaissance, combined with Palladio's innate sense of proportion and symmetry, became the lasting foundation of his art. In turn, Palladio threw out the jambalaya of styles prevalent in Venetian architecture—Oriental, Gothic, and Renaissance—for the pure, noble lines found in the buildings of the Caesars.

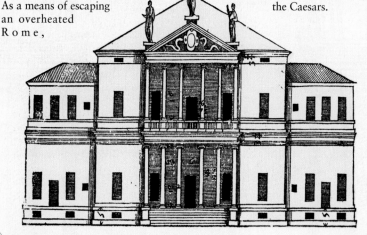

PALLADIO, STAR ARCHITECT

Andrea Palladio (1508–1580)

"Face dark, eyes fiery. Dress rich. His appearance that of a genius." So was Palladio described by his wealthy mentor, Count Trissino. Trissino encouraged the young student to trade in his birth name, Andrea di Pietro della Gondola,

for the elegant Palladio. He did, and it proved a wise move indeed. Born in Padua in 1508, Andrea moved to nearby Vicenza in 1524 and was quickly taken up by the city's power elite. He experienced a profound revelation on his first

THE OLD BECOMES NEW

La Malcontenta

Studying ancient Rome with the eyes of an explorer, Palladio employed a style that linked old with new—but often did so in unexpected ways. Just take a look at Villa Foscari, nicknamed **"La Malcontenta"** (Mira, 041/5470012, www.lamalcontenta.com €8. Open May–Oct., Tues. and Sat. 9–noon; from Venice, take an ACTV bus from Piazzale Roma to Mira or opt for a boat ride up on the Burchiello). Shaded by weeping willows and mirrored by the Brenta Canal, "The Sad Lady" was built for Nicolò and Alvise Foscari and is the quintessence of Palladian poetry. Inspired by the grandeur of Roman public buildings, Palladio applied the ancient motif of a temple facade to a domestic dwelling, topped off by a pediment, a construct most associated with religious structures. Inside, he used the technique of vaulting seen in ancient Roman baths, with giant windows and immense white walls ready-made for the colorful frescoes painted by Zelotti. No one knows for certain the origin of the villa's nickname—some say it came from a Venetian owner's wife who was exiled there due to her scandalous behavior. Regardless of the name, it's hard today to associate such a beautiful, graceful villa with anything but harmony and contentment.

trip, in 1541, to Rome, where he sensed the harmony of the ancient ruins and saw the elements of classicism that were working their way into contemporary architecture. This experience led to his spectacular conversion of the Vicenza's Palazzo della Ragione (1545) into a basilica recalling the great meeting halls of antiquity. In years to come, after relocating to Venice, he created some memorable churches, such as S. Giorgio Maggiore (1564). Despite these varied projects, Palladio's unassailable position as one of the world's greatest architects is tied to the countryside villas, which he spread across the Veneto plains like a firmament of stars. Nothing else in the Veneto illuminates more clearly the idyllic beauty of the region than these elegant residences, their stonework now nicely mellowed and suntanned after five centuries.

VICENZA, CITY OF PALLADIO

Palazzo della Ragione

La Rotonda

To see Palladio's pageant of palaces, head for Vicenza. His **Palazzo della Ragione**, or "Basilica," marks the city's heart, the Piazza dei Signori. This building rocketed young Palladio from an unknown to an architectural star. Across the way is his redbrick **Loggia dei Capitaniato**.

One block past the Loggia is Vicenza's main street, appropriately named Corso Andrea Palladio. Just off this street is the Contrà Porti, where you'll find the **Palazzo Barbaran da Porto** (1570) at No. 11, with its fabulously rich facade erupting with Ionic and Corinthian pillars. Today, this is the Centro Internazionale di Studi di Architettura Andrea Palladio (0444/323014, www.cisapalladio.org), a study center which mounts impressive temporary exhibitions. A few steps away, on the Contrà San Gaetano Thiene, is the Palazzo Thiene (1542-58), designed by Giulio Romano and completed by Palladio.

Doubling back to Contrà Porti 21, you find the **Palazzo Iseppo da Porto** (1544), the first palazzo where you can see the neoclassical effects of young Palladio's trip to Rome. Following the Contrà Reale, you come to Corso Fogazzaro 16 and the **Palazzo Valmarana Braga** (1565). Its gigantic pilasters were a first for domestic architecture.

Returning to the Corso Palladio, head left to the opposite end of the Corso, about five blocks, to the Piazza Mattoti and **Palazzo Chiericati** (1550). This was practically a suburban area in the 16th century, and for the palazzo Palladio combined elements of urban and rural design. The pedestal raising the building and the steps leading to the entrance—unknown in urban palaces—were to protect from floods and to keep cows from wandering in the front door. (For opening times and details, see the main text).

Across the Corso Palladio is Palladio's last and one of his most spectacular works, the **Teatro Olimpico** (1580). By careful study of ancient ruins and architectural texts, he reconstructed a Roman theater with archaeological precision. Palladio died before it was completed, but he left clear plans for the project. (For opening times and details, see the main text.)

Although it's on the outskirts of town, the **Villa Almerico Capra**, better known as **La Rotonda** (1566), is an indispensable part of any visit to Vicenza. It's the iconic Palladian building, the purest expression of his aesthetic. (For opening times, details, and a discussion of the villa, see the main text.)

A MAGNIFICENT COLLABORATION

Villa Barbaro

At the **Villa Barbaro** (1554) near the town of Maser in the province of Treviso, 48 km (30 miles) northeast of Vicenza, you can see the results of a one-time collaboration between two of the greatest artists of their age.

Palladio was the architect, and Paolo Veronese decorated the interior with an amazing cycle of trompe l'oeil frescoes—walls dissolve into landscapes, and illusions of courtiers and servants enter rooms and smile down from balustrades.

Legend has it a feud developed between Palladio and Veronese, with Palladio feeling the illusionistic frescoes detracted from his architecture; but there is prac-tically nothing to support the idea of such a rift.

It's also noteworthy that Palladio for the first time connected the two lateral granaries to the main villa. This was a working farm, and Palladio thus created an architectural unity by connecting with graceful arcades the working parts of the estate to the living quarters, bringing together the Renaissance dichotomy of the active and the contemplative life. *Via Cornuda 7, Maser, 0432/923004 www. villadimaser.it, €5 Open April–October Tues. and weekends 3-6; Nov.–March, weekends 2:30–5, or by reservation; Closed 24 Dec.–6 Jan.*

ALONG THE BRENTA CANAL

During the 16th century the Brenta was transformed into a landlocked version of Venice's Grand Canal with the building of nearly 50 waterside villas. Back then, boating parties viewed them in *"burchielli"*—beautiful boats. Today, the Burchiello excursion boat (Via Orlandini 3, Padua, 049/8206910, www.ilburchiello. it) makes full- and half-day tours along the Brenta, from March to November, departing from Padua on Wednesday, Friday, and Sunday and from Venice on Tuesday, Thursday, and Saturday; tickets are €40–€71 and can also be bought at American Express at Salizzada San Moisè in Venice. You visit three houses, including the Villas Pisani and Foscari, with a lunchtime break in Oriago. Another canal excursion is run by the Battelli del Brenta (www.battellidel brenta.it). Note that most houses are on the left side coming from Venice, or the right from Padua.

itself under the control of Venice. (The other recurring architectural motif is the lion of Saint Mark, a symbol of Venetian rule.)

If you're going to visit more than one or two sights, it's worth purchasing a VeronaCard, available at museums, churches, and tobacconists for €15 (two days) or €20 (five days). It buys a single admission to most of the city's significant museums and churches, plus you can ride free on city buses. If you're mostly interested in churches, a €6 Chiese Vive Card is sold at Verona's major houses of worship and gains you entry to the Duomo, San Fermo Maggiore, San Zeno Maggiore, and Sant'Anastasia. Note that Verona's churches strictly enforce their dress code: no sleeveless shirts, shorts, or short skirts.

GETTING HERE AND AROUND

Verona is midway between Venice and Milan. Several trains per hour depart from any point on the Milan–Venice line. By car, from Venice, take the Autostrada Trieste–Torino A4/E70 to the SS12 and follow it north into town.

VISITOR INFORMATION

Verona Tourism Office ✉ *Piazza Brà, Via Degli Alpini 9* ☎ *045/8068680* ⊕ *www.tourism.verona.it.*

EXPLORING VERONA

TOP ATTRACTIONS

FAMILY

Fodor's Choice

★

Arena di Verona. Only Rome's Colosseum and Capua's arena would dwarf this amphitheater, built for gymnastic competitions, choreographed sacrificial rites, and games involving hunts, fights, battles, and wild animals. Though four arches are all that remain of the arena's outer arcade, the main structure is complete and dates from AD 30. In summer, you can join up to 16,000 people packing the stands for spectacular opera productions. Even those who aren't crazy about opera can sit in the stands and enjoy Italians enjoying themselves—including, at times, singing along with their favorite hits. Note that the open hours are sometimes reduced in the late fall and winter. ■TIP→ **The main interest is to see an opera in the arena; when there is no opera performance, you can still enter the interior, but be aware that the arena is much less impressive inside than the Colosseum or other Roman ampitheaters.** ✉ *Piazza Brà 5* ☎ *045/596517* ⊕ *www.arena.it* 🎟 *€6, free with Chiese Vive and VeronaCard* ⊙ *Daily 8:30–7:30 (closes at 5 on days when operas are performed).*

Fodor's Choice

★

Castelvecchio. This crenellated, russet brick building with massive walls, towers, turrets, and a vast courtyard was built for Cangrande II della Scala in 1354 and presides over a street lined with attractive old buildings and palaces of the nobility. Only by going inside the **Museo di Castelvecchio** can you really appreciate this massive castle complex with its vaulted halls. You also get a look at a significant collection of Venetian art, medieval weapons, and jewelry. The interior of the castle was restored and redesigned as a museum between 1958 and 1975 by the notable architect Carlo Scarpa. Behind the castle is the Ponte Scaligero (1355), which spans the River Adige. ✉ *Corso Castelvecchio 2*

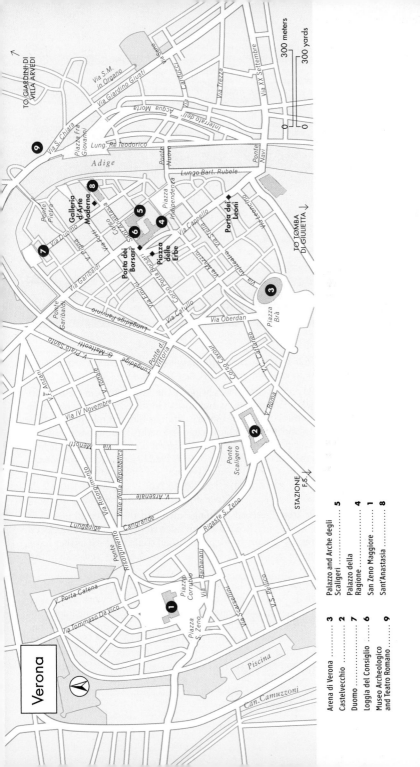

Verona

TO GIARDINI DI VILLA ARVEDI

Via S.M. in Organo
Via Giardino Giusti
Interrato dell'Acqua Morta
Via Carducci
Via Trezza
Via XX Settembre

300 meters
300 yards
0
0

Via S. Chiara
Piazza Fra Giovanni
Lung. Re Teodorico
Adige
Lungo Bart. Rubele
Ponte Navi
Ponte Nuovo
Piazza Independenza
Ponte Pietra
Galleria d'Arte Moderna
Ponte Pietra
Via Duomo
Via Garibaldi
Via Pigna
Via Emilei
Via S. Anastasia
Corso S. Anastasia
Porta dei Borsari
Piazza delle Erbe
Via Cappello
Via Mazzini
Via Stella
Via Leoni
Porta dei Leoni
TO TOMBA DI GIULIETTA
Corso Porta Borsari
Corso Cavour
Via Cattaneo
Via Catullo
Via Oberdan
Piazza Brà
Via Roma
Lungadige Panvinio
Ponte Garibaldi
Ponte di Vittoria
Ponte Scaligero
STAZIONE F.S.
V. Anzani
V. Prato Santo
Via IV Novembre
Via Toffalo
Via Menotti
V. Arsenale
Viale della Repubblica
Via Risorgimento
Lungadige Cangrande
Lungadige
Ponte Risorgimento
Porta Catena
V. Porta Catena
Via Tommaso Da Vico
Piazza S. Zeno
Piazza Corrubio
Via Barbarani
V. Scarsellini
V.S. Procolo
Rigaste S. Zeno
Piscina
Can. Camuzzoni

The skyline of central Verona.

☎ 045/8062611 🎟 €6, *free with Chiese Vive and VeronaCard* ⊗ *Mon. 1:30–7:30, Tues.–Sun. 8:30–7:30; last entry 6:45.*

Duomo. The present church was begun in the 12th century in the Romanesque style; its later additions are mostly Gothic. On pilasters guarding the main entrance are 12th-century carvings thought to represent Oliver and Roland, two of Charlemagne's knights and heroes of several medieval epic poems. Inside, Titian's *Assumption* (1532) graces the first chapel on the left. ⊠ *Via Duomo* ☎ *045/592813* ⊕ *www.chieseverona.it* 🎟 *€3, free with Chiese Vive and VeronaCard* ⊗ *Mar.–Oct., Mon.–Sat. 10–5:30, Sun. and holidays 1:30–5:30; Nov.–Feb., Mon.–Sat. 10–4, Sun. and holidays 1:30–4. Open at other times for religious purposes.*

Piazza delle Erbe. Frescoed buildings surround this beautiful medieval square, where a busy Roman forum once stood. During the week it's still bustling, as vendors hawk produce and trinkets, much as they have been doing for generations. Relax at one of the cafés and take in the lively scene.

Sant'Anastasia. Verona's largest church, begun in 1290 but only consecrated in 1471, is a fine example of Gothic brickwork and has a grand doorway with elaborately carved biblical scenes. The main reason for visiting this church, however, is *St. George and the Princess* (dated 1434, but perhaps earlier) by Pisanello (1377–1455) above the Pellegrini Chapel off the main altar. As you come in, look also for the *gobbi* (hunchbacks) supporting holy-water stoups. ⊠ *Vicolo Sotto Riva 4* ☎ *045/592813* 🎟 *€2.50, free with Chiese Vive and VeronaCard* ⊗ *Nov.–Feb., Mon.–Sat. 10–1 and 1:30–5, Sun. 12:30–5; Mar.–Oct., Mon.–Sat. 9–6, Sun. 1–6.*

Fodor'sChoice **San Zeno Maggiore.** One of Italy's finest Romanesque churches is filled
★ with treasures. A rose window by the 13th-century sculptor Brioloto
represents a wheel of fortune, with six of the spokes formed by statues
depicting the rising and falling fortunes of mankind. The 12th-century
porch is the work of Maestro Niccolò and flanked by 12th-century
marble reliefs by Niccolò and Maestro Guglielmo depict scenes from
the Old and New Testaments and scenes from the legend of Theodoric.
The bronze doors are from the 11th and 12th centuries; some were
probably imported from Saxony and some are from Veronese workshops. They combine allegorical representations with scenes from the
lives of saints. Inside, look for the 12th-century statue of San Zeno
to the left of the main altar. In modern times it has been dubbed the
"Laughing San Zeno" because of a misinterpretation of its conventional Romanesque grin. A justly famous *Madonna and Saints* triptych
by Andrea Mantegna (1431–1506) hangs over the main altar, and a
peaceful cloister (1120–38) lies to the left of the nave. The detached
bell tower was begun in 1045, before the construction of much of the
present church, and finished in 1173. ⊠ *Piazza San Zeno* ☎ *045/592813*
⊕ *www.chieseverona.it* 🎫 *€3, free with Chiese Vive and VeronaCard*
🕙 *Nov.–Feb., Mon.–Sat. 10–1 and 1:30–5, Sun. 12:30–5; Mar.–Oct.,*
Mon.–Sat. 8:30–6, Sun. 12:30–6.

WORTH NOTING

Arche Scaligere. On a little square off the Piazza dei Signori are the fantastically sculpted Gothic tombs of the della Scalas, who ruled Verona
during the late Middle Ages. The 19th-century English traveler and
critic John Ruskin described the tombs as graceful places where people
who have fallen asleep live. The tomb of Cangrande I (1291–1329)
hangs over the portal of the adjacent church and is the work of the
Maestro di Sant'Anastasia. The tomb of Mastino II, begun in 1345,
has an elaborate baldachin, originally painted and gilded, and is surrounded by an iron grillwork fence and topped by an equestrian statue.
The latest and most elaborate tomb is that of Cansignorio (1375), the
work principally of Bonino di Campione. The major tombs are all visible from the street. ⊠ *Via Arche Scaligere.*

Fodor'sChoice **Arco dei Gavi.** This stunning structure is simpler and less imposing, but
★ also more graceful, than the triumphal arches in Rome. Built in the 1st
century AD by the architect Lucius Vitruvius Cerdo to celebrate the
accomplishments of the patrician Gavia family, it was highly esteemed
by several Renaissance architects, including Palladio. ⊠ *Corso Cavour.*

Loggia del Consiglio. This graceful structure on the north flank of the
Piazza dei Signori was finished in 1492 and built to house city council
meetings. Although the city was already under Venetian rule, Verona
still had a certain degree of autonomy, which was expressed by the
splendor of the loggia. Very strangely for a Renaissance building of
this quality, its architect remains unknown, but it is undoubtedly the
finest surviving example of late-15th-century architecture in Verona.
The building is not open to the public, but the exterior is worth a visit.
⊠ *Piazza dei Signori.*

Museo Archeologico and Teatro Romano. Housed in a 15th-century former monastery, the museum's archeological collections were amassed largely out of the donated collections of Veronese citizens proud of their city's classical past. Though there are few blockbusters here, there are some very noteworthy pieces (especially among the bronzes), and it is interesting to see what was collected by cultured Veronese during the 17th to 19th

centuries. The museum complex includes the Teatro Romano, ancient Verona's theater, dating from the 1st century AD, which is open to visitors. ⊠ *Rigaste del Redentore 2* ☎ *045/8000360* 💰 *€4.50, free with VeronaCard* ⊙ *Mon. 1:30–7:30, Tues.–Sun. 8:30–7:30. Last entry 6:45.*

Palazzo degli Scaligeri (Palazzo di Cangrande). The della Scalas ruled Verona from this stronghold, built at the end of the 13th century by Cangrande I. At that time Verona controlled the mainland Veneto from Treviso and Lombardy to Mantua and Brescia. The portal facing the Piazza dei Signori was added in 1533 by the accomplished Renaissance architect Michele Sanmicheli. You have to admire the palazzo from the outside, as it's not open to the public. ⊠ *Piazza dei Signori.*

Palazzo della Ragione. An elegant 15th-century pink marble staircase leads up from the *mercato vecchio* (old market) courtyard to the magistrates' chambers in this 12th-century palace, built at the intersection of the main streets of the ancient Roman city. The renovated interior is now used for occasional exhibitions of art from the Galleria dell'Arte Moderna, which was recently moved to this location. You can get the highest view in town from atop the attached 270-foot-high, Romanesque Torre dei Lamberti. About 50 years after a lightning strike in 1403 knocked its top off, it was rebuilt and extended to its current height. ⊠ *Piazza dei Signori* ☎ *045/8032726* 💰 *Free; Tower €6 or free with VeronaCard* ⊙ *Tower: Daily 8:30–7:30 (open until 8:30 pm in summer). Palazzo open only for exhibitions.*

Fodor's Choice **Porta dei Borsari.** As its elegant decoration suggests, this is the main
★ entrance to ancient Verona, and, in its present state, dates from the 1st century AD. It's at the beginning of Corso Porta Borsari, just a few steps from Piazza della Erbe. ⊠ *Corso Porta Borsari.*

Porta dei Leoni. The oldest of Verona's elegant and graceful Roman portals, the Porta dei Leoni (on Via Leoni, just a few steps from Piazza delle Erbe), dates from the 1st century BC, but its original earth-and-brick structure was sheathed in local marble during early Imperial times. Like the city's other Roman structures, the gate gives us an idea of the high aesthetic standards of the time. ⊠ *Via Leoni.*

OFF THE BEATEN PATH	**Tomba di Giulietta.** If you want to believe that Juliet is buried in this old chapel near the river, you'll have to put aside the fact that the structure is a former orphanage and Franciscan monastery. In the crypt there's an open sarcophagus labeled as Juliet's tomb that was fashioned in 1937 for touristic purposes; by conducting civil weddings in the chapel, the city of Verona perpetuates the fantasy that Romeo and Juliet existed and were married here. ⊠ *Via del Pontiere 35* ☎ *045/8000361* 🎟 *€3, free with VeronaCard* 🕓 *Mon. 1:30–7:30, Tues.–Sun. 8:30–7:30; last entry 6:45.*

WHERE TO EAT

$
NORTHERN
ITALIAN

✕ **Antica Osteria al Duomo.** This friendly side-street eatery, lined with old wood paneling and decked out with musical instruments, serves Veronese food to a Veronese crowd; they come for the local wine (€1 to €3 per glass) and to savor excellent versions of local dishes like *bigoli con sugo di asino* (thick whole-wheat spaghetti with sauce made from donkey meat) and *pastissada con polenta* (horse-meat stew with polenta). Don't be deterred by the unconventional meats—they're tender and delicious, and this is probably the best place in town to sample them. This first-rate home cooking is reasonably priced and served by helpful, efficient staff. It's popular, so arrive early. Reservations are not possible on weekends. ⑤ *Average main: €15* ⊠ *Via Duomo 7/A* ☎ *045/8007333* 🕓 *Closed Sun. (except in Dec. and during wine fair).*

$$$$
NORTHERN
ITALIAN

✕ **Dodici Apostoli.** In a city where many high-end restaurants tend toward nouvelle cuisine, this is an exceptional place to enjoy classic dishes made with elegant variations on traditional recipes. Near Piazza delle Erbe, it stands on the foundations of a Roman temple. Specialties include gnocchi *di zucca e ricotta* (with squash and ricotta cheese), *vitello alla Lessinia* (veal with mushrooms, cheese, and truffles), and a signature *pasta e fagioli* (pasta and bean soup). ⑤ *Average main: €30* ⊠ *Vicolo Corticella San Marco 3* ☎ *045/596999* ⊕ *www.12apostoli.it* 🍴 *Reservations essential* 🕓 *Closed Mon., two wks in Jan. and two wks in June. No dinner Sun.*

$$$$
MODERN ITALIAN

✕ **Il Desco.** *Cucina dell'anima*—food of the soul—is how Chef Elia Rizzo describes his cuisine. True to Italian culinary traditions, he preserves natural flavors through quick cooking and selective ingredients, but tradition gives way to invention, even daring, in the combination of ingredients in dishes such as duck breast with grappa, grapes, and eggplant puree, or beef cheeks with goose liver and caramelized pears. Some find his creative combinations, such as adding truffles to a fish filet, difficult to understand. For a spendy gastronomic adventure, there's a multi-course tasting menu. The interior is elegant, if overdone, with tapestries, paintings, and an impressive 16th-century lacunar ceiling. Service, while efficient, is not exactly friendly. ⑤ *Average main: €45* ⊠ *Via Dietro San Sebastiano 7* ☎ *045/595358* 🍴 *Reservations essential* 🕓 *Closed Sun. and Mon. (but open for dinner Mon. in July, Aug., and Dec.), 2 wks in June and during Christmas.*

$$$
MODERN ITALIAN

✕ **Ostaria La Fontanina.** Veronese come here to enjoy a sumptuous meal under vine-covered balconies on a quiet street in one of the oldest sections of town. The Tapparini family takes great pride in the kitchen's

7

modern versions of traditional dishes. There are such standards as *risotto al Amarone* made with Verona's treasured red wine, and an excellent version of *baccalà* (cod), or for the more adventurous, a luscious wild boar confit with a savory fruit sauce laced with *ricioto,* Verona's famous sweet wine. There are several reasonably priced set menus. $ *Average main: €25* ⊠ *Portichiette fontanelle S. Stefano 3* ☎ *045/913305* ⊕ *www.ristorantelafontanina.com* ⌒ *Reservations essential* ⊘ *Closed Sun., 1 wk in Jan., and 2 wks in Aug. No lunch Mon.*

WHERE TO STAY

Book hotels months in advance for spring's Vinitaly, usually the second week in April, and for opera season. Verona hotels are also very busy during the January, May, and September gold fairs in neighboring Vicenza. Hotels jack up prices considerably at all these times.

For expanded hotel reviews, visit Fodors.com.

$$ 🛏 **Armando.** In a residential area a few minutes' walk from the Arena,
HOTEL this contemporary Best Western hotel offers respite from the busy city as well as easier parking. **Pros:** large rooms for Italy; central location; helpful staff; good breakfast. **Cons:** no valet to help with parking; simple rather than luxurious rooms. $ *Rooms from: €125* ⊠ *Via Dietro Pallone 1* ☎ *045/8000206* ⊕ *www.hotelarmando.it* ⟿ *19 rooms* ⊘ *Closed 2 wks late Dec.–early Jan.* ⋈*Breakfast.*

$$$$ 🛏 **Gabbia d'Oro.** Occupying a historic building off Piazza delle Erbe
HOTEL in the ancient heart of Verona, this hotel is a romantic fantasia of ornamentation, rich fabrics, and period style furniture. **Pros:** central location; great breakfast; romantic atmosphere. **Cons:** Some very small rooms; small bathrooms; what's romantic to some may seem overly ornate and stuffy to others. $ *Rooms from: €350* ⊠ *Corso Porta Borsari 4/a* ☎ *045/8003060* ⊕ *www.hotelgabbiadoro.it* ⟿ *8 rooms, 19 suites* ⋈*Breakfast.*

$$$ 🛏 **Hotel Accademia.** The columns and arches of the stately facade of this
HOTEL hotel in the center old Verona are a good indication of what you can discover inside: elegance, gracious service, and comfy, traditional furnishings. **Pros:** central location; old-world charm; up-to-date services. **Cons:** expensive parking; prices go way up during the summer opera season and trade fairs. $ *Rooms from: €225* ⊠ *Via Scala 12* ☎ *045/596222* ⊕ *www.accademiavr.it* ⟿ *93 rooms* ⋈*Breakfast.*

$$$$ 🛏 **Hotel Victoria.** Busy business executives and tourists enjoy a bit of
HOTEL pampering in these traditionally decorated, comfortable rooms—standard rooms are attractive and well proportioned, and the "superior" rooms and suites are really quite lavish (some have hydromassage showers). **Pros:** quiet and tasteful rooms; central location near the Piazza delle Erbe; good business center. **Cons:** no views; expensive parking (and rates); staff not particularly helpful. $ *Rooms from: €306* ⊠ *Via Adua 8* ☎ *045/5905664* ⊕ *www.palazzovictoria.com* ⟿ *58 rooms, 13 suites* ⋈*No meals.*

$ 🛏 **Torcolo.** In addition to a central location close to the arena and Piazza
HOTEL Brà, you can count on this budget choice for a warm welcome, helpful service, and pleasant rooms with late-19th-century furniture. **Pros:**

Opera productions at the Arena di Verona often include larger-than-life sets.

nice rooms; staff gives reliable advice. **Cons:** some street noise; showers but no tubs; pricey parking. $ *Rooms from: €95* ⊠ *Vicolo Listone 3* ☎ *045/8007512* ⊕ *www.hoteltorcolo.it/* ↙ *19 rooms* ☉ *Closed Christmas and 2 wks in Jan. and Feb.* ⏀ *Breakfast.*

NIGHTLIFE AND THE ARTS

OPERA

Fodor's Choice
★
Arena di Verona. Milan's La Scala or Parma's Teatro Regio offer performances more likely to satisfy serious opera fans, but none offers a greater spectacle than the Arena di Verona. Many Italian opera lovers claim their enthusiasm was initiated when they were taken as children to a production at the arena. During its summer season (July–September) audiences of as many as 16,000 sit on the original stone terraces or in modern cushioned stalls. Most of the operas presented are the big, splashy ones, like *Aïda* or *Turandot,* which demand huge choruses, lots of color and movement, and, if possible, camels, horses, or elephants. Order tickets by phone or online through the Arena website: if you book a spot on the cheaper terraces, be sure to take or rent a cushion—four hours on a 2,000-year-old stone bench can be an ordeal. ⊠ *Box office, Via Dietro Anfiteatro 6/b* ☎ *045/8005151* ⊕ *www.arena.it* ✉ *Tickets for most performances start at €21* ☉ *Box office Sept.–June 20, weekdays 9–noon and 3:15–5:45, Sat. 9–noon; June–Aug. (during the opera festival), performance days 10–9, non-performance days 10–5:45.*

SHOPPING

FOOD AND WINE

Istituto Enologico Italiano. Verona is the epicenter of wine culture in northern Italy, and the shop run by the Istituto Enologico is undoubtedly the best place to sample and buy choice wines, not only from the Veneto, but from all over northern Italy. The atmospheric, historic wine cellar pairs a suberb shopping opportunity with a pleasant and informative cultural experience. ⊠ *Via Sottoriva 7* ☎ *045/590366* ⊕ *www. istitutoenologico.it.*

FRIULI–VENEZIA GIULIA

The peripheral location of the Friuli–Venezia Giulia region in Italy's northeastern corner makes it easy to overlook, but with its mix of Italian, Slavic, and Central European cultures, along with a legendary wine tradition, it's a fascinating area to explore. Venetian culture spread northward until it merged with Northern European style evident in places like the medieval city of Udine. The old Austrian port of Trieste was, in the late 19th and early 20th centuries, an important center of Italian literature.

UDINE

127 km (79 miles) northeast of Venice.

Udine, the largest city on the Friuli side of the region, has a provincial, genteel atmosphere and lots of charm. The city sometimes seems completely unaffected by tourism, and things are still done the way they were decades ago. In the medieval and Renaissance historical center of town, you'll find unevenly spaced streets with appealing wine bars and open-air cafés. Friulani are proud of their culture, with many restaurants featuring local cuisine, and street signs and announcements written in both Italian and Friulano (Furlan), which, although it is classified as a dialect, is really a separate language from Italian. A compelling reason for devoting some time to Udine is to see works by the last of the great Italian painters, Giambattista Tiepolo (1696–1770). Distributed in several palaces and churches around town, this is the greatest assembly of his art outside Venice. Udine calls itself, in fact, *la città di Tiepolo.*

Commanding a view from the Alpine foothills to the Adriatic Sea, Udine stands on a mound that, according to legend, was erected so Attila the Hun could watch the burning of Aquileia, an important Roman center to the south. Although the legend is unlikely (Attila burned Aquileia about 500 years before the first historical mention of Udine), the view from Udine's castle across the alluvial plane down to the sea is impressive. In the Middle Ages Udine flourished, thanks to its favorable trade location and the right granted by the local patriarch to hold regular markets.

GETTING HERE AND AROUND

There's frequent train service from both Venice and Trieste; the trip takes about two hours from Venice, and a little over an hour from Trieste. By car from Venice, take the SR11 to the E55 and head east. Take the E55 (it eventually becomes the Autostrada Alpe Adria) to SS13 (Viale Venezia) east into Udine. Driving from Trieste, take the SS202 to the E70, which becomes the A4. Turn onto the E55 north, which is the same road you would take coming from Venice. Driving times are 1½ to 2 hours from Venice and 1 hour from Trieste.

VISITOR INFORMATION

Udine Tourism Office ✉ *Piazza I Maggio 7* ☎ *0432/295972* ⊕ *www. turismo.fvg.it* ⊗ *Mon.–Sat. 9–7 (closes at 6 Oct.–Apr.), Sun. and holidays 9–1.*

EXPLORING

Castello. From its hilltop site, the castle (construction began 1517) has panoramic views extending to Monte Nero (7,360 feet) in neighboring Slovenia. Here Udine's civic museums of art and archaeology are centralized under one roof. Particularly worth seeing is the national and regional art collection in the **Galleria d'Arte Antica,** which has canvases by Venetians Vittore Carpaccio (circa 1460–1525) and Giambattista Tiepolo, an excellent Caravaggio, and a carefully selected collection of works by lesser known but still interesting Veneto and Friuli artists. The museum also has a small but wonderful collection of drawings, containing several by Tiepolo; some find his drawings even more moving than his paintings. ⊠ *Via Lionello 1* ☎ *0432/271591* 🖃*€3, or free with Card Udine Museale (€6), which allows admission to most museums in Udine and the Chiesa della Purità* ⊙ *Tues.–Sat. 9:30–12:30 and 3–6, Sun. 9:30–noon.*

Duomo. A few steps from the Piazza della Libertà is Udine's 1335 Duomo. Its Cappella del Santissimo has important early frescoes by Tiepolo, and the Cappella della Trinità sports a Tiepolo altarpiece. There is also a beautiful late Tiepolo *Resurrection* (1751) in an altar by the sculptor Giuseppi Toretti. Ask the Duomo's attendant to let you into the adjacent **Chiesa della Purità** to see more important late paintings by Tiepolo. ⊠ *Piazza del Duomo 1* ☎ *0432/506830* 🖃 *Free* ⊙ *Daily, 7–noon and 4–7.*

Fodor'sChoice **Palazzo Arcivescovile.** The Palazzo Arcivescovile (also known as Pala-
★ zzo Patriarcale) contains several rooms of frescoes by the young Gianbattista Tiepolo, painted from 1726 to 1732, that comprise the most important collection of early works by Italy's most brilliant 18th-century painter. The Galleria del Tiepolo (1727) contains superlative Tiepolo frescoes depicting the stories of Abraham, Isaac, and Jacob. The *Judgment of Solomon* (1729) graces the Pink Room. There are also beautiful and important Tiepolo frescoes in the staircase, throne room, and palatine chapel of this palazzo. Even in these early works we can see the Venetian master's skill in creating an illusion of depth, not only through linear perspective, but also through subtle gradations in the intensity of the colors, with the stronger colors coming forward and the paler ones receding into space. Tiepolo was one of the first artists to use this method of representing space and depth, which reflected the scientific discoveries of perception and optics in the 17th century. In the same building, the **Museo Diocesano** features a collection of sculptures from Friuli churches from the 13th through the 18th century. ⊠ *Piazza Patriarcato 1* ☎ *0432/25003* ⊕ *www.musdioc-tiepolo.it* 🖃 *€5, includes Museo Diocesano* ⊙ *Wed.–Sun. 10–1 and 3–6.*

Piazza della Libertà. Udine was conquered by the Venetians in 1420, so there is a distinctly Venetian stamp on the architecture of the historic center, most noticeably here, in the large main square. The Loggia del Leonello, begun in 1428, dominates the square and houses the municipal government. Its similarity to the facade of Venice's Palazzo Ducale (finished in 1424) is clear, but there is no evidence that it is an imitation of that palace. It's more likely a product of the same architectural fashion. Opposite stands the Renaissance Porticato di San Giovanni (1533–35) and the Torre dell'Orologio, a 1527 clock tower with naked *mori* (Moors, who strike the hours) on the top.

WHERE TO EAT

$$ ✕**Hostaria alla Tavernetta.** One of Udine's most trusted food addresses
FRIULIAN since 1954 is steps from the Piazza Duomo. It has rustic fireside din-
Fodor'sChoice ing downstairs and smaller, more elegantly decorated rooms upstairs,
★ where there's also a small terrace. On the menu are regional specialties

such as *orzotto* (barley prepared like risotto), delicious *cjalzòns* (ravioli stuffed with ricotta, apples, raisins, and spices and topped with smoked ricotta, butter, and cinnamon), and perhaps the most tender suckling pig you have ever eaten. The restaurant offers a reasonably priced prix-fixe menu. The service is pleasant and attentive, and there's a fine selection of Friuli's celebrated wines and grappas. $ *Average main: €18* ⊠ *Via di Prampero 2* ☎ *0432/501066* ☉ *Closed Sun. and Mon., 2nd wk in Jan. 1 wk in June, 2 wks in mid-Aug.*

$

FRIULIAN

✗ **Osteria Al Vecchio Stallo.** This former stable bursts with character, its beautiful courtyard shaded by grape arbors. The menu includes a wide choice of traditional Friuli home cooking prepared simply, without much elaboration. As an appetizer, try the prized prosciutto from the neighboring village of San Daniele, which some regard even more highly than the famous Parma version. Start with *cjalzòns* (the region's answer to ravioli), or the *mignàculis con luagne* (pasta with local sausage), followed by Friuli classics such as *frico con patate* (hash-brown potatoes with Montasio cheese) or goulash with polenta. On Friday there are also fish dishes. There's a great selection of wines by the glass. $ *Average main: €18* ⊠ *Via Viola 7* ☎ *0432/21296* ▭ *No credit cards* ☉ *Closed Wed. Sept.–June, Sun. in July and Aug., 3 wks in Aug., and Dec. 25–Jan. 7.*

WHERE TO STAY

For expanded hotel reviews, visit Fodors.com.

$$

HOTEL

🏨 **Hostaria Hotel Allegria.** Comfortable lounges and guest rooms in this 15th-century building are done with plenty of wood, polished into finely crafted furnishings and wall features, and lighting is designed to dramatic effect. **Pros:** well-appointed rooms; great staff; discounted weekend rates; within easy walking distance to the center. **Cons:** rooms may be too minimalist for some; restaurant is closed Sunday and for Monday lunch; fee for parking. $ *Rooms from: €140* ⊠ *Via Grazzano 18* ☎ *0432/201116* ⊕ *www.hotelallegria.it* ⤳ *21 rooms* ⦿ *Breakfast.*

$

HOTEL

🏨 **Hotel Clocchiatti.** You have two choices here: in the 19th-century villa, canopy beds and Alpine-style wood ceilings and paneling, and in the "Next Wing," rich colors and spare furnishings in starkly angular rooms. **Pros:** individually decorated rooms; quiet surroundings; swimming pool; excellent breakfast. **Cons:** 10-minute drive from town center; small bathrooms; no restaurant. $ *Rooms from: €90* ⊠ *Via Cividale 29* ☎🖨 *0432/505047* ⊕ *www.hotelclocchiatti.it* ⤳ *27 rooms* ⦿ *Breakfast.*

AQUILEIA

123 km (77 miles) east of Venice, 42 km (25 miles) south of Udine.

This sleepy little town is refreshingly free of the tourists that you might expect at such a culturally historic place. In the time of Emperor Augustus, it was Italy's fourth most important city (after Rome, Milan, and Capua), as well as the principal northern Adriatic port of Italy and the beginning of Roman routes north. Aquileia's Roman and early Christian remains offer an image of the transition from pagan to Christian Rome.

GETTING HERE AND AROUND

Getting to Aquileia by public transportation is difficult but not impossible. There's frequent train service from Venice and Trieste to Cervignano di Friuli, which is 8 km (5 miles) away from Aquileia by taxi (about €20) or infrequent bus service. (Ask the newsstand attendant or the railroad ticket teller for assistance.) By car from Venice or Trieste, take Autostrada A4 (Venezia–Trieste) to the Palmanova exit and continue 17 km (11 miles) to Aquileia. From Udine, take Autostrada A23 to the Palmanova exit.

VISITOR INFORMATION

Aquileia Tourism Office ⊠ *Bus Terminal, Via Iulia Augusta, Aquileia* ☎ *0431/919491.*

EXPLORING

Archaeological Site. Unfortunately, many of the excavations of Roman Aquileia could not be left exposed because of the extremely high water table under the site and had to be reburied after archaeological studies had been conducted; nevertheless, what remains aboveground, along with the monuments in the archaeological museum, gives an idea of the grandeur of this ancient city. Roman remains of the forum, houses, cemetery, and port are surrounded by cypresses. The little stream was once an important waterway extending to Grado. ⊠ *Near basilica, Aquileia* ⊕ *www.museoarcheo-aquileia.it* ⊠ *Free* ☉ *Daily 8:15–7.*

Fodor'sChoice ★ **Basilica.** The highlight of this monument is the spectacular 3rd- to 4th-century mosaic covering the entire floor of the basilica and the adjacent crypt, comprising one of the most beautiful and important of early-Christian monuments. Theodore, the basilica's first bishop, built two parallel basilicas, now the north and the south halls, on the site of a Gnostic chapel in the 4th century. These were joined by a third hall, forming a U, with the baptismal font in the middle. The complex was rebuilt between 1021 and 1031, and later accumulated the Romanesque portico and the Gothic bell tower, producing the church you see today. The mosaic floor of the present-day basilica is essentially the remains of the floor of Theodore's south hall, while those of the Cripta degli Scavi are those of his north hall, along with the remains of the mosaic floor of a pre-Christian Roman house and warehouse.

The mosaics of the basilica are important not only because of their beauty, but also because they provide a window into Gnostic symbolism and the conflict between Gnosticism and the early-Christian church. In his north hall, Theodore retained much of the floor of the earlier Gnostic chapel, whose mosaics, done largely in the 3rd century, represent the ascent of the soul, through the realm of the planets and constellations, to God, who is represented as a ram. (The ram, at the head of the zodiac, is the Gnostic generative force.) Libra is not the scales, but rather a battle between good (the rooster) and evil (the tortoise); the constellation Cancer is represented as a shrimp on a tree. The basis for the representation in Aquileia is the Pistis Sophia, a 2nd-century Gnostic tract written in Alexandria.

This integration of Gnosticism into a Christian church is particularly interesting, since Gnosticism had already been branded a heresy by influential early Church fathers. In retaining these mosaics, Theodore may have been publicly expressing a leaning toward Gnosticism. Alternatively, the area of the north hall may have been Theodore's private residence, where the retention of Gnostic symbolism may have been more acceptable.

The 4th-century mosaics of the south hall (the present-day nave of the basilica) are somewhat more doctrinally conventional, and represent the story of Jonah as prefiguring the salvation offered by the Church.

Down a flight of steps, the **Cripta degli Affreschi** contains beautiful 12th-century frescoes, among them Saint Peter sending Saint Mark to Aquileia and the beheading of Saints Hermagoras and Fortunatus, to whom the basilica is dedicated. ⊠ *Aquileia* ☎ *0431/91067* ⊕ *www. aquileia.net* ✉ *Basilica free, both crypts €3, campanile €1.20* ☾ *Basilica: Apr.–Sept., daily 9–7; Mar. and Oct., daily 9–6; Nov.–Mar., weekdays 9–4:30, weekends 9–5. Campanile: Apr.–Sept., daily 9:30–1:30 and 3:30–6:30; Oct., weekends only; closed Nov.–Mar. Note: The Basilica sometimes has shorter hours or is even closed for a day. Phone ahead or check the website.*

TRIESTE

163 km (101 miles) east of Venice, 77 miles (48 km) east of Aquileia.

Trieste is built along a fringe of coastline where a rugged *karst* plateau tumbles abruptly into the beautiful Adriatic. It was the only port of the Austro-Hungarian Empire and, therefore, a major industrial and financial center. In the early years of the 20th century, Trieste and its surroundings also became famous by their association with some of the most important names of Italian literature, such as Italo Svevo, and Irish and German writers. James Joyce drew inspiration from the city's multiethnic population, and Rainer Maria Rilke was inspired by the seacoast west of the city.

The city has lost its importance as a port and a center of finance, but perhaps because of its multicultural nature, at the juncture of Latin, Slavic, and Germanic Europe, it's never fully lost its role as an intellectual center. In recent years the city has become a center for science and technology. The streets hold a mix of monumental, neoclassical, and art nouveau architecture built by the Austrians during Trieste's days of glory, granting an air of melancholy stateliness to a city that lives as much in the past as the present.

Italian revolutionaries of the 1800s rallied their battle cry around Trieste, because of what they believed was foreign occupation of their motherland. After World War II the sliver of land including Trieste and a small part of Istria became an independent, neutral state that was officially recognized in a 1947 peace treaty. Although it was actually occupied by British and American troops for its nine years of existence, the Free Territory of Trieste issued its own currency and stamps. In 1954 a Memorandum of Understanding was signed in London, giving civil administration of Trieste to Italy.

Trieste's Canal Grande

GETTING HERE AND AROUND

Trains to Trieste depart regularly from Venice, Udine, and other major Italian cities. By car, it's the eastern terminus of the Autostrada Torino–Trieste (E70).

VISITOR INFORMATION

Trieste Tourism Office ⊠ *Via dell'Orologio 1, corner of Piazza dell'Unità d'Italia* ☎ *040/3478312* ⊕ *www.triesteturismo.com* ⊗ *Mon.–Sat. 9–6; Sun. 9–1.*

EXPLORING

Castello di San Giusto. This hilltop castle, built between 1470 and 1630, was constructed on the ruins of the Roman town of Tergeste. Given the excellent view, it's no surprise that 15th-century Venetians turned the castle into a shipping observation point; the structure was further enlarged by Trieste's subsequent rulers, the Habsburgs. The castle also contains the Civic Museum, which has a small collection of furnishings, tapestries, and weaponry. ⊠ *Piazza della Cattedrale 3* ☎ *040/309362* ⊠ *€4* ⊗ *Daily 9–5.*

Cattedrale di San Giusto. Dating from the 14th century and occupying the site of an ancient Roman forum, the cathedral contains remnants of at least three previous buildings, the earliest a hall dating from the 5th century. A section of the original floor mosaic still remains, incorporated into the floor of the present church. In the 9th and 11th centuries two adjacent churches were built—the Church of the Assumption and the Church of San Giusto. The beautiful apse mosaics of these churches, done in the 12th and 13th centuries by a Venetian artist, still remain in the apses of the side aisles of the present church. The mosaics in the main apse date from 1932. In the 14th century the two churches were joined and a Romanesque-Gothic facade was attached, ornamented with fragments of Roman monuments taken from the forum. The jambs of the main doorway are the most conspicuous Roman element. ⊠ *Piazza della Cattedrale 3* ☎ *040/309666* ⊗ *Daily 8:30–noon and 4–7.*

Civico Museo Revoltella e Galleria d'Arte Moderna. Founded in 1872, when the city inherited the palazzo, library, and art collection of shipping magnate Baron Pasquale Revoltella, the collection holds almost exclusively 19th- and 20th-century Italian art, much of which was collected by Revoltella himself. Along with the palace, the museum presents a good picture of the tastes of a Triestino captain of industry during the city's days of glory. The museum's rooftop café, where the view rivals the artwork, is open some evenings in summer. ⊠ *Via Armando Diaz 27* ☎ *040/6754350* ⊠ *€6.50* ⊗ *Wed.–Mon. 10–7. Call for hours during special exhibits.*

Piazza della Borsa. A statue of Habsburg emperor Leopold I looks out over this square, which contains Trieste's original stock exchange, the **Borsa Vecchia** (1805), an attractive neoclassical building now serving as the chamber of commerce. It sits at the end of the Canal Grande, dug in the 18th century by the Austrian empress Maria Theresa as a first step in the expansion of what was then a small fishing village of 7,000 into the port of her empire.

Piazza dell'Unità d'Italia. The imposing square, ringed by grandiose facades, was set out as a plaza open to the sea, like Venice's Piazza San Marco, in the late Middle Ages. It underwent countless changes through the centuries and its present size and architecture are essentially products of late-19th- and early-20th-century Austria. Named and renamed, according to the political fortunes of the city, it was given its current name in 1955, when Trieste was finally given to Italy. On the inland side of the piazza note the facade of the **Palazzo Comunale** (Town Hall), designed by the Triestino architect Giuseppi Bruni in 1875. It was from this building's balcony in 1938 that Mussolini proclaimed the infamous racial laws, depriving Italian Jews of most of their rights. The sidewalk cafés on this vast seaside piazza are popular meeting places in the summer months.

Risiera di San Sabba. In September 1943 the Nazi occupation established Italy's only concentration camp in this rice-processing factory outside of Trieste. In April 1944 a crematorium was put into operation. The Nazis destroyed much of the evidence of their atrocities before their retreat, but a good deal of the horror of the place is still perceivable in the reconstructed museum (1975). It has been an Italian national monument since 1965, and now receives more than 100,000 visitors per year. It can be reached easily by municipal bus 8 or 10; by car it is off the Autostrada A4, exit Valmaura/Stadio/Cimitero. ⊠ *Via Giovanni Palatucci 5* ☎ *040/826202* ⊠ *Free, guided tour €3* ⊗ *Daily 9–7.*

San Silvestro. This beautiful, small Romanesque gem, dating from the 9th to 12th centuries, is the oldest church in Trieste that's still in use and in approximately its original form. Its interior walls still have some fragmentary remains of Romanesque frescoes. The church was deconsecrated under the secularizing reforms of the Austrian emperor Josef II in 1785 and was later sold to the Swiss Evangelical community; it then became, and is still, the Reformed Evangelical and Waldesian Church of Trieste. ⊠ *Piazza San Silvestro 1* ☎ *040/363952* ⊘ *Thurs. and Sat. 10–noon.*

OFF THE BEATEN PATH

Castello Di Duino. This 14th-century castle, where in 1912 Rainer Maria Rilke wrote his masterpiece, the *Duino Elegies*, is just 12 km (7½ miles) from Trieste. Take Bus 44 or 51 from the Trieste train station. The easy path along the seacoast from the castle toward Trieste has gorgeous views that rival the Amalfi Coast and the Cinque Terre. The castle itself, still the property of the Princes of Thurn and Taxis, contains a fine collection of antique furnishings and an amazing Palladian circular staircase, but the main attractions are the surrounding gardens and the spectacular views. ⊠ *Frazione Duino 32, Duino-Ausina* ☎ *040/208120* ⊕ *www.castellodiduino.it* 🎫 *€7* ⊘ *Apr.–Oct., Wed.–Mon. 9:30–5:30; Nov.–Mar. weekends 9:30–4; open sporadically at other times.*

WHERE TO EAT

$$$
SEAFOOD

✕ **Al Bagatto.** At this warm little seafood place near the Piazza Unità, chef-owner Roberto Marussi personally shepherds your meal from start to finish. The menu includes both traditional dishes, such as *baccalà mantecato* (creamed cod with olive oil), and more inventive creations, such as a tartare of sea bass with fresh ricotta. Roberto's dishes often integrate nouvelle ingredients without overshadowing the freshness of whatever local fish he bought in the market that morning. $ *Average main: €28* ⊠ *Via L. Cadorna 7* ☎ *040/301771* 🍴 *Reservations essential* ⊘ *Closed Sun.*

$
SEAFOOD

✕ **Antipastoteca di Mare.** Hidden halfway up the hill to the Castello di San Giusto, in what the Triestini call the old city, this informal little restaurant specializes in traditional preparations from the *cucina povera*—literally the "cooking of the poor," though nowadays it's a culinary movement in which creative flair transforms the humblest ingredients. The inexpensive fish—bluefish, sardines, mackerel, mussels, and squid—are accompanied by salad, potatoes, polenta, and house wine. The consistently tasty and fresh dishes, especially the fish soup and the *sardoni in savor* (large sardines with raisins, pine nuts, and caramelized onions—"savor" is the Triestino-dialect equivalent of the Venetian "saor"), show what a talented chef can do on a limited budget. $ *Average main: €12* ⊠ *Via della Fornace 1* ☎ *040/309606* 🍴 *Reservations essential* ⊜ *No credit cards* ⊘ *Closed Mon. No dinner Sun.*

$
NORTHERN ITALIAN FAMILY

✕ **Buffet da Siora Rosa.** Serving delicious and generous portions of traditional Triestino buffet fare—think boiled pork and sausages, with savory sauerkraut—Siora Rosa is a bit more comfortable than many buffets. In addition to ample seating in its simple but cozy dining room, it has tables outside for when the weather is good. It is frequented mainly by Triestini, including students and faculty from the nearby university. You may be the only tourist in the place, but the helpful waitresses generally speak English. $ *Average main: €20* ⊠ *Piazza Hortis 3* ☎ *040/301460* ⊜ *No credit cards* ⊘ *Closed weekends and holidays.*

$ **× Da Pepi.** A Triestino institution, this is the oldest and most esteemed
NORTHERN of the many "buffet" restaurants serving pork and sausages around
ITALIAN town. It and similar holes-in-the-wall (few tables, simple interior) are
as much a part of the Triestino scene as the cafés. It specializes in *bol-
lito di maiale*, a dish of boiled pork and pork sausages accompanied by
delicately flavored sauerkraut, mustard, and grated horseradish. Unlike
other Italian restaurants, buffets don't close between lunch and dinner,
and tap beer is the drink of choice. ⑤ *Average main: €12* ⊠ *Via Cassa
di Risparmio 3* ☎ *040/366858* ⊘ *Closed Sun. and last 2 wks in July.*

$$$ **× Suban.** An easy trip just outside town, this landmark trattoria oper-
NORTHERN ated by the hospitable Suban family has been in business since 1865.
ITALIAN Sit by the dining room fire or relax on a huge terrace and watch the
sunset. This is Triestino food with a Slovene, Hungarian, and Austrian
accent. Start with *jota carsolina* (a rich soup of cabbage, potatoes, and
beans), and then you might order a roast joint of veal fragrant with
rosemary and thyme, or a tender pork filet with red and yellow peppers,
sausage, and sweet paprika. ■TIP→ **Although the kitchen has central
European roots, portions tend to be small, so if you're hungry, be sure
to order both a first and second course, as well as an antipasto. To get
here you can take Bus 35 from Piazza Oberdan.** ⑤ *Average main: €22*
⊠ *Via Comici 2* ☎ *040/54368* ⊛ *Reservations essential* ⊘ *Closed Tues.,
2 wks in early Jan., and 1st 3 wks in Aug. No lunch.*

WHERE TO STAY
For expanded hotel reviews, visit Fodors.com.

$$ ▦ **Duchi d'Aosta.** Each of these rooms on the spacious Piazza Unità
HOTEL d'Italia is beautifully furnished in Venetian-Renaissance style, with
Fodor'sChoice dark-wood antiques, rich carpets, and plush fabrics. **Pros:** lots of charm
★ paired with modern convenience; great location; attentive staff; sumptuous breakfast. **Cons:** rooms overlooking the piazza can be very expensive, depending on the season; restaurant overpriced; late check-in (3
pm), although rooms are frequently ready sooner; expensive parking.
⑤ *Rooms from: €189* ⊠ *Piazza Unità d'Italia 2/1* ☎ *040/7600011*
⊕ *www.grandhotelduchidaosta.com* ⇥ *55 rooms* ⑩ *Breakfast.*

$$ ▦ **Filoxenia.** Simple, fresh rooms at reasonable prices and a waterfront
HOTEL location make this a good budget choice. **Pros:** central; friendly staff;
great price given the location; discounts for longer stays. **Cons:** some
very small, spartan rooms; some street noise; showers are cramped.
⑤ *Rooms from: €150* ⊠ *Via Mazzini 3* ☎ *040/3481644* ⊕ *www.
filoxenia.it* ⇥ *20 rooms* ⑩ *Breakfast.*

$$ ▦ **L'Albero Nascosto Hotel Residence.** Rooms on a busy, narrow street
B&B/INN in the historic center contain paintings by local artists and antique
furniture, and most have kitchenettes; they don't have phones, but the
kindly owners offer loaner cell phones. **Pros:** very central; spacious and
simple but tasteful rooms; excellent value. **Cons:** no elevator; no staff
on-site after 8 pm (though late arrivals can be arranged); street noise
can be a problem—if you are noise sensitive, ask for a room in the back.
⑤ *Rooms from: €165* ⊠ *Via Felice Venezian 18* ☎ *040/300188* ⊕ *www.
alberonascosto.it* ⇥ *10 rooms* ⑩ *Breakfast.*

$$$ ▦ **Riviera & Maximilian's.** Guest rooms come in different styles and
HOTEL sizes, but they all share the glorious vista across the Golfo di Trieste,

and an elevator whisks guests down to a private bathing quay and children's play area. **Pros:** great views; gorgeous grounds. **Cons:** far from town; some rooms are cramped. ⑤ *Rooms from: €205* ⊠ *Strada Costiera 22, 7 km (4½ miles) north of Trieste* ☎ *040/224551* ⊕ *www. hotelrivieraemaximilian.com* ➵ *56 rooms, 2 suites, 9 apartments* ⃝❘ *Breakfast.*

NIGHTLIFE AND THE ARTS

OPERA

Teatro Verdi. This is Trieste's main opera house, built under Austrian rule in 1801. It is of interest not only for music lovers, but also for its architecture—the interior was designed by the architect of Venice's La Fenice, Gian Antonio Selva, and the facade was designed by the architect of Milan's La Scala, Matteo Pertsch. You'll have to go to a performance to see the interior, since guided tours are not given to individuals.

The opera season here runs from October through May, with a brief operetta festival in July and August. ⊠ *Piazza Verdi 1* ☎ *040/9869883* ⊕ *www.teatroverdi-trieste.com.*

CAFÉS

Trieste is justly famous for its coffee. The elegant civility of Trieste plays out beautifully in a caffè culture combining the refinement of Vienna with the passion of Italy. In Trieste, as elsewhere in Italy, ask for a caffè and you'll get a thimbleful of high-octane espresso. Your cappuccino here will come in the Viennese fashion, with a dollop of whipped cream. Many cafés are part of a *torrefazione* (roasting shop), so you can sample a cup and then buy beans to take with you.

Antico Caffè San Marco. Few cafés in Italy can rival Antico Caffè San Marco for its bohemian atmosphere. First founded in 1914, it was largely destroyed in World War I and rebuilt in the 1920s, then restored several more times, but some of the original art nouveau interior remains. It became a meeting place for local intellectuals and was the haunt of the Triestino writers Italo Svevo and Umberto Saba. It remains open until midnight. ⊠ *Via Battisti 18* ☎ *040/363538.*

Caffè Degli Specchi. For a great view of the great piazza, you couldn't do better than Caffè Degli Specchi, where the many mirrors heighten the opportunities for people-watching. Originally opened in 1839, it was taken over by the British Navy after World War II, and Triestini were not allowed in unless accompanied by an Englishman. Because of its location, it's the café most frequented by tourists, and it's open from 8 am to 9 pm. ⊠ *Piazza dell'Unità d'Italia 7* ☎ *040/365777.*

Caffè Tommaseo. Founded in 1830, this classic cafè is a comfortable place to linger, especially on weekend evenings and Sunday lunchtime (11–1:30), when there's live music. While you can still have just a coffee, Tommaseo has evolved into a pastry shop and restaurant, with an extensive menu. It's open daily from 8 am until 12:30 am. ⊠ *Piazza Tommaseo 4/C* ☎ *040/362666.*

TRAVEL SMART
VENICE

GETTING HERE AND AROUND

▌ AIR TRAVEL

Most nonstop flights between North America and Italy serve Rome and Milan, where connections to Venice are available, though the airport in Venice also now accommodates some nonstop flights from the U.S. International flights land at Milan's Malpensa airport, so make sure a connecting flight to Venice also leaves from there rather than Linate, Milan's other airport. It's also easy, and often more convenient, to connect to Venice via other European hubs, such as Paris or Amsterdam.

Flying time to Milan, Rome, or Venice is approximately 8–8½ hours from New York, 10–11 hours from Chicago, and 11½ hours from Los Angeles. Flight time from Rome or Milan to Venice is about an hour.

Labor strikes are not as frequent in Italy as they were some years ago, but when they do occur they can affect not only air travel, but also local public transit that serves airports. Your airline will have usually have details about strikes affecting its flight schedules.

Airline Security Issues Transportation Security Administration (TSA). The agency has answers for almost every security question that might come up. ⊕ www.tsa.gov.

Contact A helpful website for information (location, phone numbers, local transportation, etc.) about all of the airports in Italy is ⊕ *www.italianairportguide.com.*

AIRPORTS

Venice is served by Aeroporto di Venezia Marco Polo (VCE). The airport is small but well equipped with restaurants, snack bars, shopping, and Wi-Fi access.

Airport Information Aeroporto di Venezia (VCE, also called Marco Polo). ⊠ 6 km (4 miles) north of Venice ☎ 041/2609260 ⊕ www. veniceairport.com.

Airline Contacts Alitalia ☎ 800/223–5730 in U.S., 892/010 in Italy, 06/65640 Rome office ⊕ www.alitalia.it. **British Airways** ☎ 800/247–9297 in U.S., 02/69633602 in Italy ⊕ www.britishairways.com. **Delta Air Lines** ☎ 800/241–4141 for international reservations, 02/38591451 in Italy ⊕ www.delta.com. **EasyJet** ☎ +44843/1045454 from outside U.K., 199/201840 in Italy, 0843/1045000 from inside U.K. ⊕ www.easyjet.com. **Ryanair** ☎ 0871/2460002 in U.K., 899/552589 in Italy— toll number ⊕ www.ryanair.com.

Domestic Carriers Air One ☎ 091/2551047 outside Italy, 892/444 in Italy ⊕ www.flyair one.it.

AIRPORT TRANSFERS

WATER TRANSFER

From Marco Polo terminal it's a mostly covered seven-minute walk to the dock where ferries depart for Venice's historic center. It's quite possible, though, that your hotel will be nowhere near one of the ferry stops, so check in advance. Another option is a *motoscafo* (water taxi), which carries up to four people and four bags to the city center in a powerboat—with a base cost of €95 for the 25-minute trip. Each additional person over five people costs €10 extra.

Alilaguna. This company has regular, scheduled ferry service from predawn until nearly midnight. During most of the day there are two departures from the airport to Venice every hour, at 15 and 45 minutes after the hour. Early morning and evening departures are less frequent, but there is at least one per hour. The charge is €15, including bags, and it takes about 1½ hours to reach the landing near Piazza San Marco; some ferries also stop at Fondamente Nove, Murano, Lido, the Cannaregio Canal, and the Rialto. Slight reductions are possible if you book a round trip on line. ☎ 041/2401701 ⊕ *www.alilaguna.it.*

LAND TRANSFER

Depending on your hotel's location, the most convenient way to reach it may be by bus from the airport to Piazzale Roma and vaporetto from there.

ATVO. Buses run by ATVO make a quick (20 minute) and cheap (€6) trip from the airport to Piazzale Roma, from where you can get a vaporetto to the stop nearest your hotel. Tickets are sold from machines and at the airport ground transportation booth (open daily 9–7:30), and on the bus when tickets are otherwise unavailable. The public ACTV Bus #5 also runs to the Piazzale Roma in about the same time. Tickets (€6) are available at the airport ground transportation booth. A taxi to Piazzale Roma costs about €35. ☎ 0421/383672 ⊕ www.atvo.it.

CAR TRAVEL

There are no cars in Venice, so plan to arrive by train or plane, or if you do drive, return your rental on the outskirts of the city as soon as you arrive. Several rental agencies have outlets in Piazzale Roma, the terminus of road access to Venice.

Venice is at the end of SR11, just off the east-west A4 autostrada. If for some reason you choose to keep a car while visiting Venice, you will have to park in one of the garages on the outskirts of the city around Piazzale Roma or on the island of Tronchetto.

PARKING IN VENICE

A warning: don't be waylaid by illegal touts, often wearing fake uniforms, who try to flag you down and offer to arrange parking and hotels; use one of the established garages. Consider reserving a space in advance. The **Autorimessa Comunale** (☎ 041/2727211 ⊕ www.asmvenezia.it) costs €24 for 24 hours. The **Garage San Marco** (☎ 041/5232213 ⊕ www.garagesan marco.it) costs €24 for up to 12 hours and €30 for 12 to 24 hours with online reservations. On its own island, **Isola del Tronchetto** (☎ 041/5207555) charges €21 for 6 to 24 hours. Watch for signs coming over the bridge—you turn right just before Piazzale Roma. Many hotels and the casino have guest discounts with San Marco or Tronchetto garages. A cheaper, and perfectly convenient, alternative is to park in Mestre, on the mainland, and take a train (10 minutes, €1) or bus into Venice. The garage across from the station and the Bus 2 stop costs €8–€10 for 24 hours.

GONDOLA TRAVEL

Hiring a gondola is fun but not a practical way to get around. The price of a 40-minute ride is €80 for up to six passengers, increasing to €100 between 7:30 pm and 8 am. Agree on cost and duration of the ride beforehand.

TRAGHETTO TRAVEL

Traghettos are gondolas that cross the Grand Canal at strategic points along the waterway. A one-stop traghetto crossing takes just a few minutes—it's customary to stand—and can be a lot more convenient than using one of the few bridges over the waterway. It's €2 for tourists, and cheaper for Venice residents.

TRAIN TRAVEL

FROM–TO	TIME	COST
Venice to Padova	25–30 minutes, up to 1 hour on a local train	€9 (express-Freccia) €3.55 (local or regionale)
Venice to Vicenza	45 minutes, up to 1 hour 30 minutes on a local train	€9 (express-Freccia) €5.20 (local or regionale)
Venice to Verona	1 hour 10 minutes, up to 2 hours, 20 minutes on a local train	€19 (express-Freccia) €7.50 (local or regionale)

Venice has rail connections with many major cities in Italy and Europe. Note that Venice's train station is **Venezia Santa Lucia,** not to be confused with Venezia-Mestre, which is the mainland stop prior to arriving in the city. Some trains do not continue beyond the Mestre station; in such cases you can catch the next Venice-bound train. Get a €1 ticket from the newsstand on the platform and validate it (in the yellow time-stamp machine) to avoid a fine.

Traveling by train in Italy is simple and efficient. Service between major cities is frequent, and trains usually arrive on schedule. The fastest trains on the Trenitalia Ferrovie dello Stato (FS)—the Italian State Railways—are Freccie Rosse Alta Velocità. Ferrari mogul Montezemolo launched the competing Italo high-speed service in 2012. Bullet trains on both services run between all major cities from Venice, Milan, and Turin down through Florence and Rome to Naples and Salerno. Seat reservations are mandatory, and you'll be assigned a specific seat; to avoid having to squeeze through narrow aisles, board only at your designated coach (the number on your ticket matches the one near the door of each coach). Reservations are also required for Eurostar and the slower Intercity (IC) trains; tickets for the latter are about half the price of the faster trains. If you miss your reserved train, go to the ticket counter within the hour and you may be able to move your reservation to a later one (this depends on the type of reservation, so check rules when booking). Note that you'll still need to reserve seats in advance if you're using a rail pass.

There are often significant discounts when you book well in advance. On the websites, you'll be presented with available promotional fares, such a Trenitalia's "Mini" (up to 60% off), "Famiglia" (a 20% discount for one adult and at least one child), and "A/R" (a round-trip in a day). Italo offers "Low Cost" and "Economy." The caveat is that the discounts come with restrictions on changes and cancellations; make sure you understand them before booking.

Many cities have more than one train station, **so be sure you get off at the right station.** In Venice, it is important to note that the Venezia-Mestre station is not in Venice itself but is the stop for the mainland industrial city across the lagoon. You can purchase train tickets and review schedules online, at travel agencies, at train station ticket counters, and at automatic ticketing machines located in all but the smallest stations. If you'd like to board a train and don't have a ticket, seek out the conductor prior to getting on; he or she will tell you whether you may buy a ticket onboard and what the surcharge will be (usually €8). Fines for attempting to ride a train without a ticket are €50 plus the price of the ticket.

For trains without a reservation **you must validate your ticket before boarding** by punching it at wall- or pillar-mounted yellow or green boxes in train stations or at the track entrances of larger stations. If you forget, find a conductor immediately to avoid a hefty fine.

Train strikes of various kinds are not uncommon, so it's wise to ensure that your train is actually running. During a strike minimum service is guaranteed (especially for distance trains); ask at the station or search online to find out about your particular reservation.

Traveling by night can be a good deal—and somewhat of an adventure—because you'll pass a night without having to have a hotel room. Comfortable trains run on the longer routes (Sicily–Rome, Sicily–Milan, Rome–Turin, Lecce–Milan); request the good-value T3 (three single beds), Intercity Notte, and Carrozza Comfort. The Vagone Letto has private bathrooms and single-, double-, or twin-bed suites. Overnight trains also travel to international destinations like Paris, Vienna, Munich, and other cities.

Information FS–Trenitalia ☎ 06/68475475 *from outside Italy (English), 892021 inside Italy* ⊕ *www.trenitalia.com.*

TRAIN PASSES

Rail passes promise savings on train travel. Italy is one of 24 countries that accept the Eurail Pass, which provides unlimited first- and second-class travel. If you plan to rack up miles across the Continent, get a Global Eurail Pass (covering all participating nations). The Eurail Select Pass allows for travel in three to five contiguous countries. Other options are the Eurail Youth Pass (for those under 26), the Eurail Flexipass (valid for a certain number of travel days within a set period), and the Eurail Saver (aimed at two to five people traveling together).

The Eurail Italy Pass, available for non-European residents, allows a certain number of travel days within the country over the course of two months. Three to 10 days of travel cost from $295 to $539 (1st class) or $240 to $439 (2nd class). If you're in a group of more than three, consider the **Eurail Italy Pass Saver**: good for 3 to 10 travel days, the price per person is $251 to $459 (1st class) or $205 to $374 (2nd class); family passes offer further discounts for children under 12; kids under 4 travel free. **Eurail Italy Youth** (for those under 26) is second-class only and costs from $195 to $357 for one to 10 days of travel. All passes must be purchased before you leave for Europe. Keep in mind that even with a rail pass you still need to reserve seats on the trains that require them.

Attractive as a pass may seem, compare prices with actual fares to determine whether it will actually pay off; you may have to do a great deal of train traveling to make a pass worthwhile. Generally, the more often you plan to travel long distances on high-speed trains, the more sense a rail pass makes. You can calculate how much you will be spending on individual tickets by using the Trenitalia website.

Contacts Italia Rail ☎ 877/375–7245 *in U.S.* ⊕ *www.italiarail.com.* **Rail Europe** ☎ 800/622–8600 *in U.S.* ⊕ *www.raileurope. com.* **RailPass** ⊕ *www.railpass.com.*

▌VAPORETTO TRAVEL

Venice's primary public transportation is the vaporetto (water bus). The ACTV operates *vaporetti* (water buses) on routes throughout the city. Departures are quite frequent; during the day, for example, Line 1 from Piazzale Roma along the Grand Canal to the Lido, departs every 10 minutes. The trip from Ferrovia to San Marco takes about 35 minutes. Most other lines depart frequently as well, at least every 20 minutes. During times of heavy traffic, ACTV sometimes puts on extra vaporetti, so that departures are even more frequent. Beginning at about 11:30 pm there's limited, but fairly frequent, night service. Although most landings are well marked, the system takes some getting used to; check before boarding to make sure the boat is going in your desired direction.

Individual tickets are €7 and are good for 60 minutes one way. Considerable savings are possible if you buy a pass: €18 for 12 hours, €20 for 24 hours, €35 for 72 hours, and €50 for a week of unlimited travel. Travelers ages 14–29 can opt for the €4 Rolling Venice card (available from the HelloVenezia booth at principal vaporetto stops), which allows 72 hours of travel for €18. A ticket to take the vaporetto one stop across the Grand Canal is €4. Tickets are available at the airport, from tobacco shops, and from machines or booths at some, but not all, vaporetto stops. Tickets are checked frequently, and fines for using the vaporetto without a ticket are substantial.

Contacts ACTV ☎ 041/2424 ⊕ *www. hellovenezia.com.*

ESSENTIALS

▮ ACCOMMODATIONS

The lodgings we list are the cream of the crop in each price category. Properties are assigned price categories based on the rate for two people sharing a standard double room in high season, including tax and service.

APARTMENT AND HOUSE RENTALS

Renting a vacation property can be economical depending on your budget and the number of people in your group. Most are owned by individuals and managed by rental agents who advertise online. In some cases rental agents handle only the online reservation and financial arrangements; in others, the agent and/or owner may meet you at the property for the initial check-in. Issues to keep in mind when renting an apartment in Venice are the location (street noise, ambience, and accessibility to public transport), the availability of an elevator or number of stairs, air-conditioning and ventilation, hot water, the furnishings (including pots and linens), what's supplied on arrival (dishwashing liquid, coffee or tea), and the cost of utilities (are all covered by the rental rate?).

Contacts Airbnb ✉ *Venice* ⊕ *www.airbnb. com.* **At Home Abroad** ☎ *212/421–9165* ⊕ *www.athomeabroadinc.com.* **Barclay International Group** ☎ *800/845–6636, 516/364–0064* ⊕ *www.barclayweb.com.* **Drawbridge to Europe** ☎ *541/482–7778* ⊕ *www.drawbridgetoeurope.com.* **Italy Rents** ☎ *202/821–4273, 06/39728556 in Italy* ⊕ *www.italyrents.com.* **Vacation Rentals by Owner** ☎ *877/228–0710* ⊕ *www.vrbo.com.*

HOME EXCHANGES

With a direct home exchange you stay in someone else's home while they stay in yours. Some outfits also deal with vacation homes, so you're not really occupying someone's full-time residence, just their vacant weekend place.

Venetians have historically not been as enthusiastic about home exchanges as others; however, there are some apartments in Venice owned by foreigners (Americans, English, etc.) who use the home-exchange services.

Exchange Clubs Home Exchange.com. Membership is $7.95 monthly. ☎ *800/877–8723, 310/798–3864* ⊕ *www.homeexchange. com.*

▮ COMMUNICATIONS

INTERNET

Getting online in Venice: Wi-Fi is widely available in hotels and restaurants, and there are still a few Internet cafés in operation. Many business-oriented hotels also offer in-room broadband, though some (ironically, often the more expensive ones) charge for broadband and Wi-Fi access. Note that chargers and power supplies may need plug adapters to fit European-style electric sockets (a converter probably won't be necessary).

Venice is continuing to develop citywide Internet and expand services at a daily or weekly rate for temporary access. However, coverage is still quite limited and progress in extending coverage has been quite slow.

Paid and free Wi-Fi hot spots can be found in major airports and train stations and shopping centers; they will most likely be free in bars or cafés that want your business.

PHONES

CALLING ITALY FROM ABROAD

When telephoning Italy from North America, dial 011 (to get an international line), followed by Italy's country code, 39, and the phone number, including any leading 0. Note that Italian cell numbers have 10 digits and always begin with a 3; Italian landline numbers will contain from 4 to 10 digits and always begin with

LOCAL DO'S AND TABOOS

GREETINGS

Upon meeting and leave-taking, both friends and strangers wish each other good day or good evening (*buongiorno, buona sera*); *ciao* isn't used between people who are not on very familiar terms with each other, or where there is a very great age or status difference. Venetians who are friends greet each other with a kiss, usually first on the left cheek, then on the right. When you meet a new person, shake hands and give your name.

SIGHTSEEING

Shorts, tank tops, and sleeveless garments are taboo in most churches throughout the country. To avoid being denied entrance, carry a shawl or other item of clothing to cover bare shoulders.

You should never bring food into a church, and don't sip from your water bottle inside. If you have a cell phone, turn it off before entering. Ask whether photographs are allowed—and *never use a flash*. Most churches in Venice will allow visits for touristic purposes even when a service is being conducted, but you are expected to be respectful of the worshippers and not disturb the mass by talking or seeking access to parts of the church involved in the service.

OUT ON THE TOWN

When you've finished your meal and are ready to go, ask for the check (*il conto*); a waiter will not put a bill on your table until you've requested it.

In Venice a cocktail or a glass of aperitif wine is usually taken at a bar before the meal, but in elegant restaurants you may be offered an aperitif. It is customary, especially if you have ordered a complete meal with all the courses, for the restaurant owner to treat you to a grappa or other digestif after a meal. Public drunkenness is abhorred, and smoking has been banned in all public establishments.

It is considered uncivilized to eat or drink while walking—except when eating gelato—and especially rude while seated on the steps of a building or bridge. You may see some Italian tourists or students breaking such rules, but you can be sure that they are not from Venice.

It is illegal to appear in public without shoes or a shirt.

LANGUAGE

One of the best ways to connect with Italians is to learn a little of the local language. You need not strive for fluency; just mastering a few basic words and terms is bound to make interactions more rewarding.

"Please" is *per favore*, "thank you" is *grazie*, "you're welcome" is *prego*, and "excuse me" is *scusi (or "permesso" when you need to move past someone, as on a bus)*.

Most hotels have English speakers at their reception desks. You may have trouble communicating in the countryside, but expressive gestures and a good phrase book—like *Fodor's Italian for Travelers* (available at bookstores everywhere)—will go a long way. Need audio assistance? Click ⊕ *www.fodors. com/language/italian* to hear more than 150 essential phrases.

a 0. So, for example, when calling Venice, where local numbers start with 041, dial 011 + 39 + 041 + phone number; for a cell phone, dial 011 + 39 + cell number.

CALLING WITHIN ITALY

For all calls within Italy, whether local or long-distance, you'll dial the entire phone number that starts with 0, or 3 for cell phone numbers. Calling a cell phone may cost significantly more than calling a landline, depending on the calling plan. Italy uses the prefix "800" for toll-free or *numero verde* (green) numbers.

MAKING INTERNATIONAL CALLS

The country code for the U.S. and Canada is 1 (dial 00 + 1 + area code and number).

Because of the high rates charged by most hotels for long-distance and international calls, you're better off making such calls from your mobile phone and/or using an international calling card (⇨ *Calling Cards*).

With the advent of mobile phones, public pay phones are becoming increasingly scarce in Venice. You can use your U.S. mobile phone in Italy, but to avoid exorbitant roaming costs, even if you are doing only a moderate amount of calling, it is best to purchase a prepaid Italian SIM card from any tobacconist or mobile phone service provider shop. You will pay only for outgoing calls.

Make sure, however, that your phone uses the GSM system (not all U.S. phones do) and is unlocked (that you can use it with SIM cards from any service provider). If your phone is not GSM, or permanently locked, consider buying an inexpensive mobile phone outfitted with a prepaid SIM card.

■TIP➜ **If you're carrying a laptop, tablet, or smartphone, investigate apps and services such as Skype, Viber, and Whatsapp, which offer free or low-cost calling and texting services.**

Access Codes AT&T Direct ☎ *800/172–444* ⊕ *www.att.com.* **MCI WorldPhone** ☎ *800/90–5825.* **Sprint International Access** ☎ *800/172-405.*

CALLING CARDS

If you will be making frequent calls to North America or other overseas locations from Venice, you may want to consider getting an international calling card; you call a toll-free number from any phone, including your cell phone, entering the access code found on the back of the card followed by the destination number. A reliable prepaid card for calling North America and elsewhere in Europe is the TIM Welcome card, which comes in two denominations, €5 and €10, and is available at tobacco shops and newsstands. When purchasing, specify your calling destination (the United States, or the country you prefer).

■TIP➜ **If you're a frequent international traveler, save your old mobile phone (ask your cell phone company to unlock it for you) or buy an unlocked, multiband phone online. Use it as a travel phone, buying a new SIM card with pay-as-you-go service in each destination.**

Contacts Cellular Abroad. This is a good source for SIM cards that work in many countries; travel-friendly phones can also be purchased or rented. ☎ *800/287–5072* ⊕ *www.cellularabroad.com.* **Mobal.** GSM phones that will operate in 190 countries are available for purchase (starting at $29) and rent. Per-call rates in Italy are $1.25 per minute; sending a text costs 80¢. ☎ *888/888–9162, 212/785–5800 Support* ⊕ *www.mobal.com.* **Planet Fone.** Rental cell phones, with per-minute rates costing 99¢–$1.98, are available. ☎ *888/988–4777* ⊕ *www.planetfone.com.*

▮ CUSTOMS AND DUTIES

Travelers from the United States should experience little difficulty clearing customs at any Italian airport. It may be more difficult to clear customs when returning to the United States, where residents are normally entitled to a duty-free exemption of $800 on items accompanying them. You'll have to pay a tax (most often a flat percentage) on the value of everything beyond that limit. When you shop in Italy, keep all your receipts handy, as customs inspectors may ask to see them as well as the items you purchased.

Fresh mushrooms, truffles, and fresh fruits and vegetables are forbidden. There are restrictions on the amount of alcohol allowed in duty-free, too. Generally, you can bring in one liter of wine, beer, or other alcohol without paying a customs duty; visit the travel area of the Customs and Border Patrol Travel website for complete information.

Italy requires documentation regarding the background of many antiques and antiquities before these items are taken out of the country. Under Italian law, some antiquities found on Italian soil are considered state property, and there are other restrictions on antique artwork. Even if purchased from a business in Italy, legal ownership of artifacts may be in question if brought into the United States. Therefore, although they don't necessarily confer ownership, documents such as export permits and receipts are required when importing such items into the United States.

Information in Italy Dogana Sezione Viaggiatori ☎ 06/50241 ⊕ www.agenziadogane.it.

U.S. Information U.S. Customs and Border Protection ☎ 877/227–5511 ⊕ www.cbp.gov.

▌EATING OUT

MEALS AND MEALTIMES
What's the difference between a *ristorante* and a *trattoria*? Can you order food at an *enoteca* (wine bar)? Can you go to a restaurant just for a snack or order only salad at a pizzeria? The following definitions should help.

Not long ago, *ristoranti* tended to be more elegant and expensive than *trattorie* (which serve traditional, home-style fare in an atmosphere to match) or *osterie* (which serve local wines and simple, regional dishes). But the distinction has blurred considerably, and an osteria in the center of town might now be far fancier

(and pricier) than a ristorante across the street. In any sit-down establishment, however, you're generally expected to order at least a two-course meal, such as a *primo* (first course) and a *secondo* (main course) or a *contorno* (vegetable side dish); an *antipasto* (starter) followed by either a primo or secondo; or a secondo and a *dolce* (dessert).

If you'd prefer to eat less, best head to an enoteca or pizzeria, where it's more common to order a single dish. An enoteca menu is often limited to a selection of cheese, cured meats, salads, and desserts, but if there's a kitchen you can also find soups, pastas, and main courses. The typical pizzeria serves *affettati misti* (a selection of cured pork), simple salads, various kinds of bruschetta, *crostini* (similar to bruschetta, with a variety of toppings).

The most convenient and least expensive places for a quick snack between sights are probably bars, cafés, and pizza *al taglio* (by the slice) spots. Pizza al taglio shops are easy to negotiate, but few have seats. They sell pizza by the slice: just point out which kind you want and how much. Since good pizza requires a wood-burning oven, which are not permitted in Venice because of fire hazard, and since Venetians considered pizza to be a "foreign" food imported from Naples, pizza in Venice is in general not very good. In many cafés and in all of the al taglio places, it is heated up in a microwave.

Much better options for fast food are the kebab shops, which have flourished throughout the city. The kebabs are generally fresh and served with Middle Eastern bread made with pizza dough—a rather delicious product of gastronomic fusion.

Bars in Italy resemble what we think of as cafés, and are primarily places to get a coffee and a bite to eat, rather than drinking establishments. Expect a selection of panini warmed up on the griddle (*piastra*) and *tramezzini* (sandwiches made of untoasted white bread triangles). Some bars also serve vegetable and fruit salads, cold pasta dishes, and gelato. Most offer beer and a variety of alcohol, as well as wines by the glass. A café is like a bar but typically has more tables. Pizza at a café should be especially avoided—it's usually heated in a microwave.

Most places charge for table use, even if you bring the food from the counter to the table yourself. In self-service bars and cafés it's good manners to clean your table before you leave. Menus are posted outside most restaurants (in English in tourist areas). If not, you might step inside and ask to take a look at the menu, but don't ask for a table unless you intend to stay.

If you have special dietary needs, make them known; they can usually be accommodated. Although mineral water makes its way to almost every table, you can order a carafe of tap water (*acqua di rubinetto* or *acqua semplice*) instead—which in Venice is quite good—but be prepared for an unenthusiastic reaction from your waiter.

A Venetian would seldom ask for olive oil and salt to dip bread in, but the culturally tolerant Venetians won't scoff if you do. They may even express mild curiosity. But don't be surprised if there's no butter to spread on bread, unless you're eating it with anchovies, a favorite north Italian snack. Wiping your bowl clean with a (small) piece of bread is usually considered a sign of appreciation, not bad manners. Spaghetti should be eaten with a fork only, although a little help from a spoon—a southern Italian custom—won't horrify locals the way cutting spaghetti into little pieces will. Order your caffè (Italians drink cappuccino only in the morning) after dessert, not with it. Since an Italian meal generally consists of several courses, portions tend to be small.

Breakfast (*la colazione*) is usually served from 7 to 10:30, lunch (*il pranzo*) from 12:30 to 2:30, and dinner (*la cena*) from 7:30 to 10; outside those hours best head for a bar. Peak times are usually 1:30 for lunch and 9 for dinner. Enoteche and Venetian *bacari* (wine bars) are also open in the morning and late afternoon for *cicchetti* (finger foods) at the counter. Most pizzerias open at 8 pm and close around midnight—later in summer and on weekends. Bars and cafés are open from 7 am until 8 or 9 pm; a few stay open until midnight.

Unless otherwise noted, the restaurants listed here are open for lunch and dinner, closing one or two days a week.

PAYING

Most restaurants have a cover charge per person, usually listed at the top of the check as *coperto* or *pane e coperto*. It should be a modest (€1–€3 per person) except at the most expensive restaurants. Whenever in doubt, ask before you order to avoid unpleasant discussions later. In Venice, as in many cities in Northern Italy, no tip is expected, even if the service is excellent. The price of fish dishes is often given by weight (before cooking), so the price quoted on the menu is for 100 grams of fish, not for the whole dish. (An average fish portion is about 350 grams.

Major credit cards are widely accepted in Venice; more restaurants take Visa and MasterCard than American Express or Diners Club. If you become a regular customer, you may find that the restaurant owner will give you a discount, without your asking for one. If that is the case, cash payment is preferred.

RESERVATIONS AND DRESS

Although we only mention reservations specifically when they're essential (there's no other way you'll ever get a table) or when they're not accepted, it's always safest to make one for dinner. Large parties should always call ahead to check the reservations policy. If you change your mind, be sure to cancel, even at the last minute.

We mention dress only when men are required to wear a jacket or a jacket and tie. In Venice, even the most elegant restaurants tend to be very casual about dress. Only very few restaurants will turn away patrons because they are wearing shorts.

WINES, BEER, AND SPIRITS

The grape has been cultivated in Italy since the time of the Etruscans, and Italians justifiably take pride in their local varieties, which are numerous. The Veneto and the neighboring regions of Friuli and Alto Adige are some of the prime wine-growing regions of Italy. Wine in Italy is less expensive than almost anywhere else, so it's often affordable to order a bottle of wine at a restaurant rather than sticking with the house wine (which is usually good but quite simple). Many bars have their own *aperitivo della casa* (house aperitif); Italians are imaginative with their mixed drinks, so you may want to try one.

You can purchase beer, wine, and spirits in any bar, grocery store, or enoteca, any day of the week, any time of the day. Italian and German beer is readily available, but it can be more expensive than wine.

There's no minimum drinking age in Italy. Italian children begin drinking wine mixed with water at mealtimes when they're teens (or thereabouts). Italians are rarely seen drunk in public, and public drinking, except in a bar or eating establishment, isn't considered acceptable behavior. Bars usually close by 11 pm; hotel and restaurant bars stay open until midnight. Brew-pubs and discos serve until about 2 am.

▮ ELECTRICITY

The electrical current in Italy is 220 volts, 50 cycles alternating current (AC); wall outlets accept continental-type plugs, with two or three round prongs.

You may purchase a universal adapter, which has several types of plugs in one lightweight, compact unit, at travel specialty stores, electronics stores, and online. You can also pick up plug adapters in Italy in any electric supply store for about €2 each. You'll likely not need a voltage converter, though. Most portable devices are dual voltage (i.e., they operate equally well on 110 and 220 volts);

just check label specifications and manufacturer instructions to be sure. Don't use 110-volt outlets marked "for shavers only" for high-wattage appliances such as hair dryers.

Contacts Global Electric and Phone Directory. This site has information on electrical and telephone plugs around the world as well as details on international telephone calls. ⊕ *www.kropla.com.*

▮ EMERGENCIES

No matter where you are in Italy, you can dial 113 in case of emergency: the call will be directed to the local police. Not all 113 operators speak English, so you may want to ask a local person to place the call. Asking the operator for *"pronto soccorso"* (first aid and also the emergency room of a hospital) should get you an *ambulanza* (ambulance). If you just need a doctor, ask for *"un medico."*

Italy has the *carabinieri* (national police force, their emergency number is *112* from anywhere in Italy) as well as the *polizia* (local police force). Both are armed and have the power to arrest and investigate crimes. Always report the loss of your passport to the caribinieri as well as to your embassy. When reporting a crime, you'll be asked to fill out *una denuncia* (official report); keep a copy for your insurance company.

Pharmacies are generally open weekdays 8:30–1 and 4–8, and Saturday 9–1. Local pharmacies rotate covering the off-hours in shifts: on the door of every pharmacy is a list of which pharmacies in the vicinity will be open late.

Foreign Embassies U.S. Consulate Florence ⊠ *Via Lungarno Vespucci 38, Florence* ☎ *055/266951* ⊕ *florence.usconsulate.gov.* **U.S. Consulate Milan** ⊠ *Via Principe Amedeo 2/10, Milan* ☎ *02/290351* ⊕ *milan.usconsulate. gov.* **U.S. Consulate Naples** ⊠ *Piazza della Repubblica, Naples* ☎ *081/5838111* ⊕ *naples. usconsulate.gov.*

General Emergency Contacts Emergencies
🖃 *115 Fire, 118 Ambulance.* **National and State Police** 🖃 *112 Polizia (National Police), 113 Carabinieri (State Police).*

▮ HOURS OF OPERATION

Religious and civic holidays are frequent in Italy. Depending on the holiday's local importance, businesses may close for the day. Businesses don't close Friday or Monday when the holiday falls on the weekend, though the Monday following Easter is a holiday.

Banks are open weekdays 8:30–1:30 and for one or two hours in the afternoon, depending on the bank. Most post offices are open Monday–Saturday 9–1:30, some until 2; central post offices are open 9–6:30 weekdays, 9–12:30 or 9–6:30 on Saturday.

Most churches are open from early morning until noon or 12:30, when they close for three hours or more; they open again in the afternoon, closing at about 6. San Marco, remains open all day. Many museums are closed one day a week, often Monday or Tuesday. During low season museums often close early; during high season many stay open until late at night.

Most shops are open Monday–Saturday 9–1 and 3:30 or 4–7:30. Barbers and hairdressers, with certain exceptions, are closed Sunday and Monday. Some bookstores and fashion- or tourist-oriented shops in Venice are open all day, as well as Sunday. Many branches of large chain supermarkets, such as Billa and COOP, don't close for lunch and are usually open Sunday; smaller *alimentari* (delicatessens) and other food shops are usually closed one evening during the week and are almost always closed Sunday.

HOLIDAYS

The national holidays in 2014 include January 1 (New Year's Day); January 6 (Epiphany); April 20 and 21 (Easter Sunday and Monday); April 25 (Liberation Day); May 1 (Labor Day or May Day); June 2 (Festival of the Republic); August 15 (Ferragosto); November 1 (All Saints' Day); December 8 (Immaculate Conception); and December 25 and 26 (Christmas Day and the Feast of Saint Stephen). Venice's feast of Saint Mark is April 25, the same as Liberation Day, so the Madonna della Salute on November 21 makes up for the lost holiday.

▮ MAIL

The Italian mail system has a bad reputation but has become noticeably more efficient in recent times with some privatization. Allow from 7 to 15 days for mail to get to the United States. Receiving mail in Italy, especially packages, can take weeks, usually due to customs (not postal) delays.

Most post offices are open Monday–Saturday 9–1:30; central post offices are open weekdays 9–6:30, Saturday 9–12:30 (some until 6:30). You can buy stamps at tobacco shops as well as post offices.

Posta Prioritaria (for regular letters and packages) is the name for standard postage. It guarantees delivery within Italy in three to five business days and abroad in five to six working days. The more expensive express delivery, *Postacelere* (for larger letters and packages), guarantees one-day delivery to most places in Italy and three- to five-day delivery abroad. Note that the postal service has no control over customs, however, which makes international delivery estimates meaningless. Mail sent as Posta Prioritaria Internazionale to the United States costs €2 for up to 20 grams, €3.50 for 21–50 grams, and €4.50 for 51–100 grams. Mail sent as Postacelere to the United States costs €46.57 for up to 500 grams.

Reliable two-day international mail is generally available during the week in all major cities and at popular resorts via UPS and Federal Express—but again, customs delays can slow down "express" service.

SHIPPING SERVICES

Sending a letter or small package to the United States via Federal Express takes at least two days and costs about €45. Other package services to check are Quick Pack Europe (for delivery within Europe) and Express Mail Service (a global three- to five-day service for letters and packages). Compare prices with those of Postacelere to determine the cheapest option.

If you've purchased antiques, ceramics, or other fragile objects, ask if the vendor will do the shipping for you. In most cases this is possible, and preferable, because many merchants have experience with these kinds of shipments. If so, ask whether the article will be insured against breakage.

■ MONEY

Prices in Venice are high, but no higher than in Milan or in other European cities and resorts. Within Venice, there is a substantial difference between prices in the Piazza San Marco area and those in residential districts such as Cannaregio, Santa Croce, or in the working-class neighborhood of Castello. Bars and cafés must, by law, post their charges, both for consumption standing at the bar and for consumption at a table (regardless if there is table service or not). If you are in a bar or café patronized largely by tourists, you may want to consult the price list before you order or sit down. The cafés in the Piazza San Marco put on a hefty supplementary charge for music.

ATMS AND BANKS

An ATM (*bancomat* in Italian) is the easiest way to get euros in Italy. There are numerous ATMs around Venice, and since there are ATMs at Marco Polo Airport, there is no need to buy euros before you depart the U.S. Be sure to **memorize your PIN in numbers,** as ATM keypads in Italy won't always display letters. Check with your bank to confirm that you have an international PIN (*codice segreto*) that will be recognized in the countries you're visiting; to raise your maximum daily withdrawal allowance; and to learn what your bank's fee is for withdrawing money (Italian banks don't charge withdrawal fees). ■ TIP➔ **Be aware that PINs beginning with a 0 (zero) tend to be rejected in Italy.**

Your own bank may charge a fee for using ATMs abroad and/or for the cost of conversion from euros to dollars. Nevertheless, you can usually get a better rate of exchange at an ATM than you will at a currency-exchange office or even when changing money inside a bank with a teller, the next-best option. Whatever the method, extracting funds as you need them is safer than carrying around a large amount of cash. Finally, it's advisable to carry more than one card that can be used for cash withdrawal, in case something happens to your main one.

CREDIT CARDS

It's a good idea to **inform your credit-card company before you travel,** especially if you're going abroad and don't travel internationally often. Otherwise, the credit-card company might put a hold on your card owing to unusual activity—not a welcome occurrence halfway through your trip. Record all your credit-card numbers—as well as the phone numbers to call if your cards are lost or stolen. Keep these in a safe place, so you're prepared should something go wrong. American Express, MasterCard, and Visa have general numbers you can call (collect if you're abroad) if your card is lost.

■ TIP➔ **North American toll-free numbers aren't available from abroad, so be sure to obtain a local number with area code for any business you may need to contact.**

Although it's usually cheaper (and safer) to use a credit card abroad for large purchases (so you can cancel payments or be reimbursed if there's a problem), note that some credit-card companies *and* the banks that issue them add substantial percentages to all foreign transactions, whether they're in a foreign currency or not. Check on these fees before leaving home, so there won't be any surprises when you get the bill. Because of these fees, avoid using your credit card for ATM withdrawals or cash advances (use a debit or cash card instead).

Venetian merchants prefer MasterCard and Visa, but American Express is usually accepted in popular tourist destinations. Credit cards aren't accepted everywhere, though; if you want to pay with a credit card in a small shop, hotel, or restaurant, it's a good idea to make your intentions known early on.

Reporting Lost Cards American Express
☎ 800/528–4800 in U.S., 905/474–0870 collect from abroad ⊕ www.americanexpress. com. **Diners Club** ☎ 800/234–6377 in U.S., 514/881–3735 collect from abroad, 800/393939 in Italy ⊕ www.dinersclub. com. **MasterCard** ☎ 800/627–8372 in U.S., 636/722–7111 collect from abroad, 800/151616 in Italy ⊕ www.mastercard.us. **Visa** ☎ 800/847–2911 in U.S., 303/967–1096 from abroad, 800/819014 in Italy ⊕ usa.visa. com.

CURRENCY AND EXCHANGE

The euro is the main unit of currency in Italy. Under the euro system there are 100 *centesimi* (cents) to the euro. There are coins valued at 1, 2, 5, 10, 20, and 50 centesimi as well as 1 and 2 euros. There are seven notes: 5, 10, 20, 50, 100, 200, and 500 euros. At this writing, 1 euro was worth about 1.35 U.S. dollars.

Post offices exchange currency at good rates, but employees speak limited English, so be prepared. (Writing your request can help in these cases.)

■TIP➔ Even if a currency-exchange booth has a sign promising no commission, rest assured that there's some kind of huge, hidden fee. You're almost always better off getting foreign currency at an ATM or exchanging money at a bank or post office.

▮ PASSPORTS AND VISAS

U.S. citizens need only a valid passport to enter Italy for stays of up to 90 days.

PASSPORTS

Although somewhat costly, a U.S. passport is relatively simple to obtain and is valid for 10 years. You must apply in person if you're getting a passport for the first time; if your previous passport was lost, stolen, or damaged; or if it has expired and was issued more than 15 years ago or when you were under 16. All children under 18 must appear in person to apply for or renew a passport. Both parents must accompany any child under 14 (or send a notarized statement with their permission) and provide proof of their relationship to the child.

There are 25 regional passport offices as well as 7,000 passport acceptance facilities in post offices, public libraries, and other governmental offices. If you're renewing a passport, you may do so by mail; forms are available at passport acceptance facilities and online, where you trace the application's progress.

The cost of a new passport is $135 for adults, $105 for children under 16; renewals are $110 for adults, $105 for children under 16 plus. Allow four to six weeks for processing, both for first-time passports and renewals. For an expediting fee of $60 you can reduce this time to two to three weeks. If your trip is less than two weeks away, you can get a passport even more rapidly by going to a passport office with the necessary documentation. Private expediters can get things done in as little as 48 hours, but charge hefty fees for their services.

■TIP➔ Before your trip, make two copies of your passport's data page (one for someone at home and another for you to carry separately). Or scan the page and email it to someone at home and/or yourself.

GENERAL REQUIREMENTS FOR ITALY	
Passport	Must be valid for 6 months after date of arrival.
Visa	Tourist visas aren't needed for stays of 90 days or less by U.S. citizens.
Vaccinations	None
Driving	International driver's license required. CDW is compulsory on car rentals and will be included in the quoted price.

VISAS

When staying for 90 days or less, U.S. citizens aren't required to obtain a visa prior to traveling to Italy. A recent law requires that you fill in a declaration of presence within eight days of your arrival—the stamp on your passport at airport arrivals substitutes for this.

U.S. Passport Information U.S. Department of State ☎ 877/487–2778 ⊕ *www.travel.state.gov/passport.*

U.S. Passport Expediters A. Briggs Passport & Visa Expeditors ☎ 800/806–0581 toll-free, 202/338–0111 ⊕ www.abriggs.com. **American Passport Express** ☎ 800/455–5166 ⊕ www.americanpassport.com. **Passport Express** ☎ 800/362–8196 ⊕ www.passportexpress.com. **Travel Document Systems** ☎ 800/874–5100 ⊕ www.traveldocs.com. **Travel the World Visas** ☎ 866/886–8472, 202/223–8822 ⊕ www.world-visa.com.

▍ TAXES

A 10% V.A.T. (value-added tax) is included in the rate at all hotels. No tax is added to the bill in restaurants. A service charge of approximately 10%–15% is usually added to your check.

The V.A.T. is 22% on clothing, wine, and luxury goods. On consumer goods it's already included in the amount shown on the price tag (look for the phrase "IVA inclusa"), whereas on services it may not be. If you're not a European citizen and if your purchases in a single day total more than €154.94, you may be entitled to a refund of the V.A.T.

When making a purchase, ask whether the merchant gives refunds—not all do, nor are they required to. If they do, they'll help you fill out the V.A.T. refund form, which you then submit to a company that will issue you the refund in the form of cash, check, or credit-card adjustment.

Alternatively, as you leave the country (or, if you're visiting several European Union countries, on leaving the EU), present your merchandise and the form to customs officials, who will stamp it. Once through passport control, take the stamped form to a refund-service counter for an on-the-spot refund (the quickest and easiest option). You may also mail it to the address on the form (or on the envelope with it) after you arrive home, but processing time can be long, especially if you request a credit-card adjustment. Note that in larger cities the cash refund can be obtained at in-town offices prior to departure; just ask the merchant or check the envelope for local office addresses.

Global Blue is the largest V.A.T.-refund service with 225,000 affiliated stores and more than 700 refund counters at major airports and border crossings. Its refund form, called a Tax Free Check, is the most common across the European continent. Premier Tax Free is another company that represents more than 70,000 merchants worldwide; look for their logos in store windows.

V.A.T. Refunds Global Blue ☎ 866/706–6090 in North America, 421 232/111111 from abroad, 00800/32111111 from Italy ⊕ www.global-blue.com. **Premier Tax Free** ☎ 905/542–1710 from U.S., 06/699–23383 from Italy ⊕ www.premiertaxfree.com.

▍ TIME

Italy is in the Central European Time Zone (CET). From March to October it institutes daylight saving time (*ora legale*). Italy is 6 hours ahead of U.S. Eastern

Standard Time, 1 hour ahead of Great Britain, 10 hours behind Sydney, and 12 hours behind Auckland. Like the rest of Europe, Italy uses the 24-hour (or "military") clock, which means that after noon you continue counting forward: 13:00 is 1 pm, 23:30 is 11:30 pm.

▌ TIPPING

In Venice, is in most of northern Italy, tipping is not expected in restaurants, bars, taxis, or for other services, even for excellent service. The only exception is to tip a bellhop €2–€2.50 per bag for carrying your bags to your room.

▌ TOURS

Venice has tour guides licensed by the government. Some are eminently qualified in relevant fields such as architecture and art history and are a pleasure to spend time with. Lots of private guides have websites, and you can check the travel forums at fodors.com for recommendations (it's best to book before you leave home, as popular guides and tours are in demand). Once in Venice, tourist offices and hotel concierges can also provide the names of knowledgeable local guides and the rates for certain services.

Recommended Generalists **Abercrombie & Kent** ☎ 800/554–7016 ⊕ www. abercrombiekent.com. **Maupin Tour** ☎ 800/255–4266, 954/653–3820 ⊕ www. maupintour.com. **Perillo Tours** ☎ 800/431–1515 ⊕ www.perillotours.com. **Travcoa** ☎ 800/992–2003, 310/649–7104 ⊕ www. travcoa.com.

Culinary Tour Contact **Epiculinary** ☎ 707/815–1415 ⊕ www.epiculinary.com.

▌ TRIP INSURANCE

Comprehensive policies typically cover trip cancellation and interruption, letting you cancel or cut your trip short because of illness (yours or that of someone back home), or, in some cases, acts of terrorism in your destination. Such policies usually also cover evacuation and medical care. (For trips abroad you should have at least medical and medical evacuation coverage. With a few exceptions, Medicare doesn't provide coverage abroad, nor does regular health insurance.) Some also cover you for trip delays because of bad weather or mechanical problems as well as for lost or delayed luggage.

Another type of coverage to consider is financial default—that is, when your trip is disrupted because a tour operator, airline, or cruise line goes out of business. Generally you must buy this when you book your trip or shortly thereafter, and it's available to you only if your operator isn't on a list of excluded companies.

Many travel insurance policies have exclusions for preexisting conditions as a cause for cancellation. Most companies waive those exclusions, however, if you take out your policy within a short period (which varies by company) after the first payment toward your trip.

Always read the fine print of your policy to make sure that you're covered for the risks that most concern you. Compare several policies to be sure you're getting the best price and range of coverage available.

Comprehensive Insurers **Allianz** ☎ 866/884–3556 ⊕ www. allianztravelinsurance.com. **CSA Travel Protection** ☎ 877/243–4135, 240/330–1529 collect ⊕ www.csatravelprotection.com. **HTH Worldwide** ☎ 610/254–8700 ⊕ www. hthworldwide.com. **Travel Guard** ☎ 800/826–1300, 800/345–0505 toll free from Italy ⊕ www.travelguard.com. **Travel Insured International** ☎ 800/243–3174, 603/328–1707 collect ⊕ www.travelinsured.com. **Travelex Insurance** ☎ 800/228–9792, 603/328–1739 collect ⊕ www.travelexinsurance.com.

Insurance Comparison Info **Insure My Trip** ☎ 800/487–4722, 401/773–9300 ⊕ www. insuremytrip.com. **Square Mouth** ☎ 800/240–0369, 727/564–9203 ⊕ www.squaremouth. com.

INDEX

PHOTO CREDITS

NOTES

NOTES

NOTES

NOTES

NOTES

NOTES

NOTES

NOTES

NOTES

ABOUT OUR WRITERS

Bruce Leimsidor studied Renaissance literature and art history at Swarthmore College and Princeton University, and in addition to his scholarly works, he has published articles on political and social issues in the *International Herald Tribune* and the *Frankfurter Allgemeine Zeitung*. He lives in Venice, where he teaches at the university, collects 17th- and 18th-century drawings, and is rumored to make the best *pasta e fagioli* in town. He worked on the Experience, Exploring, Side Trips, and Travel Smart chapters for this edition.

Nan McElroy traveled throughout Italy before relocating to Venice in 2004. She is the author of the palm-size, purely practical *Italy: Instructions for Use*, produces the Vap Map downloadable vaporetto guide, and the apps Venice Eats and Venice Shops. Nan is also an AIS sommelier who conducts wine tastings and she is an avid practitioner of the *voga alla venetam,* traditional Venetian rowing. She updated the Where to Eat, Where to Stay, Nightlife and the Arts, and Shopping chapters.